Praise for *The Leader in Me*

What Education Influencers Are Saying

"*The Leader in Me* is one of the most inspired efforts taking hold today in our schools. The authors beautifully tell the story and elegantly explain the process's principles and promise. If you care about education, you need to read this book."

— *Daniel Pink, author of* To Sell Is Human *and* Drive

"Education is meant to develop children's individual abilities and help them make their way in the world. The more standardized it becomes, the more it overlooks their real talents and stifles their creativity, curiosity, and appetite for learning. If we're to help children flourish, we must think very differently about what they are capable of achieving and the schools they really need. *The Leader in Me* is full of uplifting examples of how this can be done. It sets out a transformative process that is rooted in inspiring ideas about children's—and teachers'—real capabilities, and it's supported by the practical experiences of schools around the world, which have used it to effect radical and positive change. *The Leader in Me* shows that the leadership we need to transform education is not outside our schools but within them, and especially in the children themselves."

— *Sir Ken Robinson, International Advisor on Education and* New York Times *bestselling author of* The Element: How Finding Your Passion Changes Everything

"As schools go so goes our future. Educated, self-disciplined, civil adults are first educated, self-disciplined, and civil students. Like the sand that polished the stone, school experiences bring forth the brilliance hidden within each child.

"*The Leader in Me* is based on a mindset of a better world and comprehensive set of proven principles to get us there. I strongly recommend this framework to all educational leaders striving to advance the 'learning for all' mission."

—*Lawrence W. Lezotte, Effective Schools Consultant*

"If America is going to reverse the decline of its schools, we need to rethink how we can guarantee that all of our kids get a great education. This terrific book shows educators what is possible, demonstrating how schools can foster the critical character traits students need to reach their potential and achieve the American dream."

—*Geoffrey Canada, President and CEO, Harlem Children's Zone*

"The Freedom Writers and I created the Freedom Writers Foundation with a simple goal—to change the world one student, one teacher, one class, and one school at a time. *The Leader in Me* is the ideal blueprint for every school to change the world through education. I have had the distinct privilege of meeting the passionate teachers and innovative administrators who have implemented the process. I've been inspired by the students who boldly walk up to me, look me in the eye, shake my hand, and assert that they 'are being proactive!' I've seen them implement the 7 Habits in real time and have witnessed remarkable results. Most important, I use this tried and true process and the 7 Habits with my own colleagues and staff to help us reach our goal."

—*Erin Gruwell, Teacher and Founder of the Freedom Writers*

"External efforts to perk up schools have failed. They miss the secret of success. A cohesive culture, developed within a local school, unites teachers, students, parents, and the community in a common quest of making learning meaningful and joyful. *The Leader in Me* demonstrates vividly through stories and testimony how schools can reclaim soul and spirit."

—*Terrence Deal, coauthor of* Shaping School Culture: Pitfalls, Paradoxes, and Promises *and the upcoming book* How Great Leaders Think

"*The Leader in Me* book tells how the process is transforming schools, one school at a time, and is changing the lives of students around the world. Every child has the individual potential and worth to succeed in life and to accomplish any goal they set. If they have teachers who inspire them and believe in them, they will come to see in themselves that they are leaders, not just today, but for the rest of their lives. Truly, a remarkable book and process."

—*Ron Clark, Founder and Teacher at the Ron Clark Academy*

"I recommend *The Leader in Me* to anyone and everyone who is willing to go through a rigorous process to really improve the entire system. In schools that are implementing correctly, children are driving the work, there is an increased level of self-esteem, and discipline issues become nonexistent or a lot lower than they would be."

—*Jean-Claude Brizard, Senior Advisor, College Board, Washington, D.C.*

"I believe the children of today will become our leaders tomorrow. I believe we need to prepare our children to be the kind of leaders that will create a brighter and better future. I believe in *The Leader in Me*. It's the book, process, and pathway to develop leaders that will positively transform our schools, communities, and future."

—*Jon Gordon, bestselling author of* The Energy Bus *and* The Energy Bus for Kids

"The principles taught and modeled in *The Leader in Me* are the very elements we want the leaders of today to possess. To have our children practicing and developing these traits in their youth can translate to men and women who understand what truly matters in measuring success."

—*Professor Clayton Christensen, Professor, Harvard Business School, and author of* The Innovator's Dilemma, Disrupting Class: How Disruptive Innovation Will Change the Way the World Learns, *and* How Will You Measure Your Life?

"Far more often than not, young people live up to high expectations—when those expectations have personal meaning. In a time when the endgame in schools can be little more than a standardized test score, *The Leader in Me* helps young learners see their potential to develop a vision for who they can become, take charge of their lives, work with peers to solve problems, and make positive decisions about their well-being. The process reminds them that learning can and should be magical, and that pursuit of quality extends both learning and the learner. The process's habits of success, which on some level are affective and environmental aspects of learning success, integrate seamlessly into academic content as well, endowing that content with extended purpose and meaning—for students and teachers alike."

—Carol Ann Tomlinson, Ed.D., William Clay Parrish Jr.
Professor and Chair, Educational Leadership, Foundations,
and Policy, Curry School of Education, University of Virginia

"I have witnessed firsthand in schools how *The Leader in Me* has transformed the culture of the school from one of resignation to one of hope and belief that every child has the potential to get a successful learning experience in school."

—Jacob Kragh, President, LEGO Education, Denmark

"Educators are doing their very best to meet the challenges that accompany our schools today. They are passionate about education and are deeply committed to their students' success. But, they cannot do it alone. *The Leader in Me* process offers schools and educators the opportunity to build a strong culture of student empowerment and self-discipline, so that students are taking responsibility for their own education and success. It is so inspiring to see the success in numerous schools throughout the world that have employed the process and in which students are becoming twenty-first century leaders in their own right."

—Dr. Daniel Domenech, Executive Director,
American Association of School Administrators,
The School Superintendents Association

"*The Leader in Me* has the ability to interrupt generational cycles of truancy and marginalization by engaging students with a most effective tool: their own self-worth. These schools are empowering children to become a living difference, both in their own lives and within the world."

—Lisa Fenn, Journalist, Boston, Massachusetts

"The *Leader in Me* is a wonderful book—relevant, thoughtful, and enormously useful. The core ideas are presented through an engaging array of stories, narratives, examples, and photographs of real schools. This book should be on the shelf of every school that wants to be successful, caring, and serving every child in their community."

—Dr. Kent D. Peterson, Professor Emeritus,
University of Wisconsin–Madison, and coauthor of
Shaping School Culture: Pitfalls, Paradoxes, and Promises

"*The Leader in Me,* the culmination of something exciting in our schools, began at a school in North Carolina where they dreamed of what was possible for students. Muriel Summers and Sean Covey together created a new nexus we hadn't seen in schools. They have challenged us to reflect on our core values and nurture those of the young people we serve. As educators, and especially educators in magnet schools, we are acutely aware of the limitless possibilities in every student. *The Leader in Me* shows a path to engage and support students in ways that will lead to extraordinary opportunities. All students need to understand how to not only harness their potential but simultaneously serve in capacities that will force them to know who they are and what they stand for. Our country will depend on these leaders, and educators can devote themselves to inspiring and training the leaders we need for tomorrow. *The Leader in Me* has applications that go far beyond the classroom and have given me, as a parent, incredible insight and ways to guide the development of my own children."

—Scott Thomas, Executive Director, Magnet Schools of America

"I have personally visited A.B. Combs Elementary and was blown away by the mature student body that greeted and interviewed me. This school is a phenomenal example of how an institution can take *The Leader in Me*, build upon the *7 Habits*, and prepare students for their undefined futures. This book proves that there truly is greatness in every student and in every staff member, and that through this process greatness can be realized."

—Jeff Jones, CEO, Solution Tree

"Working with thousands of students over the years opened my eyes to the 'untaught lessons' of contemporary education: do what you're told, look good on paper, and seek external validation. I spent years watching brilliant young people feel they were anything but brilliant because their particular approach to adding value to the world couldn't be adequately measured or rewarded through essays and written tests. *The Leader in Me* creates a different culture in schools. It asks students and staff to assess and do what they think is right, to empower themselves and others, and to recognize and foster the existing capacities for greatness within themselves. Perhaps most important, it creates rewards that are accessible to each and every student. Ultimately, the greatest endorsement for *The Leader in Me* is to meet the students who have been impacted by its approach. They are, quite simply, different. Nowhere else in the world have I met students with the confidence and passion of those I've met from *Leader in Me* schools. I once asked a young man from a *Leader in Me* school, 'What do you hope the future will bring?' With a smile he confidently replied, 'Big things.' Consider making *The Leader in Me* a part of your school's culture. You too can expect big things."

—*Drew Dudley, Founder and Chief Catalyst, Nuance Leadership Inc.*

"*The Leader in Me* is at the core of my formula for changing the culture of the toughest schools in America! One small part of Dr. Covey's huge legacy will be his inspirational message on leadership to children, teachers, and administrators around the world. Sean Covey has continued to carry the torch of leadership for young people in a powerful way! You want true school reform, read *The Leader in Me*!"

—*Salome Thomas-EL (Principal EL), Award-Winning Educator and author of* The Immortality of Influence *and* I Choose to Stay

"When I walked into A.B. Combs in 2007, I knew immediately that something was different. In my years of serving the education community, I have walked into countless schools on behalf of LEGO Education solutions. However, this was the first time I was greeted by a second grade student who introduced herself, welcomed me to the school, inquired my purpose for visiting, and offered to take me to see the principal, Ms. Muriel Summers. I was enthralled. As I came to know more of the school, the remarkable work of Muriel and her team, and, more important, the outcomes achieved by the students repeatedly and reliably, I learned about the unique implementation of Stephen R. Covey's 7 Habits. I was well versed in these habits, having added them to my leadership toolset, skillset, and mindset early on in my career. Seeing them implemented in such a school-wide setting encompassing the entire range of the child's experience confirmed what I already knew. If the culture is right, the results will be right. If your goals are to prepare students for the twenty-first century workforce, you know that deep content, twenty-first century skills, hands-on learning, and a culture of respect and leadership are the keys to success. *The Leader in Me* process is a crown jewel in the transformation of school culture, freeing children to imagine, learn, and succeed."

—Stephan Turnipseed, President Emeritus and
Executive Director Strategic Partnerships, LEGO Education US

What Administrators and Teachers Are Saying

"*The Leader in Me* fits well into our district's belief in educating the whole child. We want to graduate well-rounded students who are compassionate, competitive, critical thinkers, and life-long learners. *The Leader in Me* is helping us to make it a reality."

—Pat Sanford, Leadership Development Specialist,
North East Independent School District, San Antonio, Texas

"*The Leader in Me* empowers students to be in charge of their daily actions and learning. It has been one of the most profound processes I have experienced as an educator. It has completely transformed our school's culture, decreased discipline referrals, increased staff, student, and parent involvement, and elevated our academic achievement."

—Jan McCartan, Principal,
Beaumont Elementary, Waterford, Michigan

"Students as young as age five know what it means to Be Proactive, Think Win-Win, and use leadership tools to solve problems. Discipline issues on the bus have dropped dramatically. Our students set personal and academic goals and make a plan to achieve those goals. The intrinsic satisfaction of achieving one's goals is immeasurable, and students continue to raise the bar both personally and academically each time they meet their goal. We no longer are presented with bully-type behaviors by students. Teacher, parent, community, and student engagement is at an all-time high!"

—Deborah Pennell, Principal,
Ardena Elementary, Farmingdale, New Jersey

"Since Winchester implemented *The Leader in Me*, students have shown improvement in reading benchmark tests, and homework responsibilities, but more importantly in self-confidence. Students show more initiative and willingness to be risk takers where before they were reluctant learners. I have witnessed life-changing events for members of my staff. Parents are implementing the habits within the family structure. I truly believe this process can be the educational reform that is needed for all who want to make a difference in the life of a child and all who want to create greatness in themselves."

—*Kathy Brachmann, Principal,*
Winchester Elementary, West Seneca, New York

"It is saving lives."

—*Angie Taillon, Principal, Neil Armstrong Elementary,*
Port Charlotte, Florida

"We have implemented *The Leader in Me* from day one of opening the doors of our school. The formal training of our staff and incorporation of the 7 Habits into subject lessons has worked in tandem to create a culture of trust, accountability, and leadership among our staff and student body. This led directly to our school's designation as the number one school in New York City Public Schools, as measured by the Department of Education's Progress Report."

—*Rose Kerr, Founding Principal, Staten Island School of*
Civic Leadership, Staten Island, New York

"Our aim was to move a good school forward to something better. Previous initiatives had been effective in the short term but did not have long-term impact on students' ability to develop self-responsibility or on their learning. Since implementing *The Leader in Me*, parents have been very supportive and see how everything fits together to help their child. Staff members see it as a positive way to help students be the best they can be and do the best they can do."

—*Jennie Werakso, Principal, St. Brigid's, Gwynneville, NSW, Australia*

"Every student in our school is a leader in some capacity. This is not me. This is a team of teachers working hard and doing the organizing with the students."

—*Lisa VanLeeuwen, Principal,*
Ryerson Heights Elementary, Brantford, Ontario, Canada

"I received *The Leader in Me* from a friend on my way to a winter holiday. Its message touched me so deeply that I couldn't go relax before I had read the entire book! It has truly enabled greatness in all aspects of my life, in my family, and in my schools."

—*Lise K. Furuseth, Founder and Director,*
Hoppensprett Schools and Day Care Centres, Norway

"Our ultimate goal is to prepare students for life, not to guide every moment of every day of their existence. What better way to do that than through teaching the timeless principles of the 7 Habits?"

—*Dr. Beth Sharpe, Executive Director of Elementary Education,*
Seminole County Public Schools, Florida

"In only two weeks we saw dramatic changes, from both staff and parent perspectives. After five months of implementing *The Leader in Me* with students, we have seen an 85 percent decrease of behavior referrals."

—*Deirdre Brady, Principal, Heritage Elementary, Highland, Michigan*

"*The Leader in Me* is a blueprint for whole school change."

—*Eileen Cronin, Literacy Coach, Boston Public Schools, Massachusetts*

"*The Leader in Me* has many leadership tools that help students to solve problems. If we introduce these principles from the beginning, we can help them in the future to be great problem solvers."

—*Sri Wahyuni, Teacher, An-Nisaa' School, Jakarta, Indonesia*

"Sachem Central School District is one of the largest suburban districts in the United States. *The Leader in Me* has positively impacted our students, our staff members, and our families. It is not a curriculum. It is an ongoing process of sharing, modeling, and personal growth. Many of our principals have reported that discipline referrals have dropped significantly. Parents have told countless stories of the positive impact on their children and families."

—*James J. Nolan, Superintendent,*
Sachem Central School District, Long Island, New York

"*The Leader in Me* is all about relationships. As a result of it, our students have increased confidence and achievement, particularly through the goal-setting process. Teachers are highly engaged. Our common language has increased, as has parent involvement and communication. This is truly the most rewarding work I have engaged in."

—Matt Miller, Principal,
Wren Hollow Elementary, Manchester, Missouri

"As a director and as a parent of a student at the school, every day I hear the common language and witness the application of the 7 Habits. Instead of telling my son, 'Go to bed early!' or 'Study before you play video games!' I hear, 'Mom, don't forget to put first things first!' or 'Grandpa, try to think win-win, don't fight with grandma!' The 7 Habits and *The Leader in Me* are amazingly magical!"

—Juno Ding Hong, Director and Parent,
Lih-Jen School, Taipei, Taiwan

"As the new principal of Saxe Gotha Elementary, I was charged with developing a restructuring plan because the school had not made adequate progress for five years. After months of researching possibilities, it became clear that the 7 Habits and *The Leader in Me* would help create the lasting change for which our students, staff, and families yearned. During our third year of implementation, we were recognized as one of three finalists for the South Carolina Title One Reward School of the Year for Progress. Being part of that transformation has been the most rewarding experience of my career."

—Beth A. Houck, Principal,
Saxe Gotha Elementary, Lexington, South Carolina

"From the start, children and staff have been encouraged to identify their strengths—though in a non-boastful way. Teachers are now more familiar with each other's talents, and with the talents of their students. Parents have welcomed the focus on the positive attributes, and it has contributed to the students' development."

—Carla Luycx, Principal, Atlantis, Amersfoort, Netherlands

"Teaching leadership skills and the 7 Habits has changed me as a teacher, as a parent, and as a wife. It has helped me to organize my life better. It has helped me to prioritize and to put my attention on the things that are most important."

—*Pam Almond, first-grade Teacher,*
A.B. Combs Elementary, Raleigh, North Carolina

"I just wish we had this thirty-five years ago."

—*Sharon Terwelp, fifth-grade Teacher,*
Blessed Sacrament K–8, Quincy, Illinois

"When I observe children these days, sometimes I feel they lack certain skills, like interpersonal skills or teamwork skills. Their parents are busy, their families tend to be small, and they have tons of homework. As a result, they do not have the chance to interact with other children or to develop these skills through play. So as a teacher, I feel privileged to teach skills like 'think win-win' and 'synergy.' They help students to be more effective as students and better able to handle life's challenges."

—*Mrs. Limmengkwang,*
Teacher, Chua Chu Kang Primary, Singapore

"Creating our common goal and having a common language has made a great difference in our daily work. A positive culture has been created where staff and children care for each other. Difficult conversations with students and parents have dropped dramatically. Teachers and staff have found their work joy and enthusiasm again. Cooperation between departments has improved. We are seeing academic improvement in all three of our schools."

—*Helen Solin, Head Principal,*
Jämjöskolor, Karlskrona, Sweden

"*The Leader in Me* has been instrumental in creating a cohesive, collaborative climate for students and staff. It has provided a quality foundation for establishing the change that we desired in our schools. The professional learning component changes the way teachers view themselves, their students, and the learning environment. It has been phenomenal what has happened."

—*Dr. Karen Woodward, Superintendent,*
Lexington School District 1, Lexington, South Carolina

"With a 'risk taker hat' and a desire to innovate and bring positive change, we implemented *The Leader in Me*. The process adds value to the school's 'end in mind' of strengthening children's character and provides them with the right environment for personal and academic growth. The emphasis on each child's worth strengthens them as unique individuals, and reinforces their self-confidence and their desire to 'synergize' and to build a better world."

—*Martha Rincón, Director, Buckingham School, Bogotá, Colombia*

What Parents Are Saying

"The first time I heard my second-grade son recite Dr. Covey's 7 Habits, my jaw almost dropped! Then I realized that he not only could recite, he could also explain to me the meaning of the 7 Habits. I am so thankful that my son has the opportunity to apply the 7 Habits at such a young age."

—*Liu Ju Chen Jen, Parent,*
Lih-Jen School, Taipei, Taiwan

"I have watched my children evolve before my very eyes largely due to *The Leader in Me*. My eighth grader has always possessed incredible self-confidence and is a natural-born leader, yet working in teams has never been her strength. Through exposure to the 7 Habits and taking on leadership responsibilities, she has truly evolved into an interdependent individual. My fourth grader has gained the confidence to go safely outside of his comfort zone, risk being a leader, and accomplish personal success in areas where he previously thought it impossible."

—*Jen Thomas, Parent,*
Crestview Middle School, Ellisville, Missouri

"My children have benefited tremendously from a broad range of leadership opportunities that are a part of the A.B. Combs experience. From opportunities to perform music, give speeches, speak on panels, lead tours, participate in family events like science nights and art shows, to assisting staff in coordinating events, my two very different daughters have developed confidence, drive, and high standards of personal performance that would not have been possible at other schools."

—*Hardin Engelhardt, Parent,*
A.B. Combs Elementary, Raleigh, North Carolina

"We have brought the principles into our home and feel the benefit in our family life. The emphasis is on encouraging accountability rather than placing blame, and on embracing the best within one's self as well as others."

—Jennifer Edwards, Parent,
Wards Creek Elementary, St. Augustine, Florida

"The leadership process is exactly what my son needed to get back on track. He started developing a proactive attitude toward his school work. Assignments were completed and turned in on time. Putting First Things First, he completed his math work almost always at school. Each week we could see his confidence growing and he went from being fearful and unsure of himself to being confident and empowered. Socially and athletically he is very competitive, but has developed a Win-Win approach and is able to synergize through class problems and group projects. When given the opportunity to take responsibility for his own actions, he did just that. We are forever grateful."

—Lori Helmy, Parent,
Mukilteo Elementary, Mukilteo, Washington

"When my ninth grader asks to play a video game before his homework is done, I enjoy hearing my kindergartner pipe up and say 'Put first things first, do your homework!'"

—Ericka Porrazza, Parent, Lehua Elementary School, Pearl City, Hawaii

"The 7 Habits have helped my son grow up in the past two years. Ever since the school started *The Leader in Me* he has become more responsible and confident in himself. He has learned how to take initiative in making plans, and pays more attention to other people's needs. As a parent, I am happy to see these changes, and very appreciative to the school."

—Hwei Lin Liu, Parent, Lih-Jen School, Taipei, Taiwan

"The 7 Habits have been a positive influence in my children's lives and in my own life. Once I was trying to tell my son, 'You're not listening, you're not being proactive.' But then he said to me, 'Mom, you are not listening to me. You are being reactive.' And I had a huge paradigm shift, a moment of, 'Oh my goodness, it is me.' So it is a two-way street. It has been really good for us, really good."

—Megan May, Parent, Crestwood Elementary,
Medicine Hat, Alberta, Canada

"Our children are learning and using the terminology to express their feelings in a healthy way as they communicate in our family setting. We are all learning to pause and seek to understand one another before we vent frustrations, resulting in more solid communication between us. Our family is becoming a more cohesive unit by following these strategies from school in our home."

—*Sharon Olson, Parent, Carey School, Carey, Idaho*

"Since the implementation of the 7 Habits, I have seen a marked difference in my children. The areas in which I have seen the most progress include their eagerness to prioritize their activities to ensure that their responsibilities are met. Their habits regarding homework, schoolwork, and chores have all dramatically improved."

—*Christopher W. Adamec, Parent,*
Wards Creek Elementary, St. Augustine, Florida

"We cannot begin to describe the difference employing the characteristics of strong leadership have made with our two daughters. They are learning traits and habits that will not only help them at the school setting, but will carry with them throughout their lives. We wholeheartedly believe in this approach to education and see it as a critical component that bridges the gap between home and school."

—*Ryan and Juley Sexton, Parents,*
A.B. Combs Elementary, Raleigh, North Carolina

What Business and Community Leaders Are Saying

"Starting from elementary school, students are allowed to be leaders, and truly come to believe they can be leaders in the future. So when I tell my friends about the schools we are sponsoring, I tell them we are supporting the future. In this way, we are able to pay back to a community that has really been so kind to us."

—*Peggy Cherng, Cofounder,*
Panda Express and Panda Cares, Rosemead, California

"Starting with kindergartners, in thirteen years, we've got the opportunity to change the mindset of an entire community. In only thirteen years!"

—*Donnie Lane, CEO, Enersolv, Decatur, Alabama*

"Our vision of introducing TLIM to PSKD Mandiri and Indonesia was to offer all stakeholders in the school, including staff, students, and parents, a common framework and language that would support all individuals in realizing their leadership abilities. After three years of implementing the process, PSKD Mandiri has reached Lighthouse School status and, by all measures, is achieving a degree of success that our vision had previously only imagined."

—*Laurel Tahija, Chairman, Dharma Bermakna Foundation, Indonesia*

"When I went to school we stuck only to academics. So when I see children learning about ethics, involvement in the community, and leadership, I find it very impressive, very worthwhile."

—*Kathleen Cresswell, Member, Rotary International, Florida*

"Instead of stealing cars, these kids are going to be buying cars."

—*Cliff Raynolds, Police Chief, Victorville, California*

"Some of our employees had taken the 7 Habits, so when one of them heard Crestwood Elementary was teaching the habits, we saw a real win-win between what the school was trying to do and what we were trying to do at our plant. The life skills they are learning in the 7 Habits are so critical to their future success."

—*Rick Redmond, Vice President,*
Criterion Catalysts and Technologies, Medicine Hat, Canada

"The best thing about *The Leader in Me* is that it is not just for the elite kids or the troubled kids. It is for every single student. It does not matter what their economic background is or what their social history is, it is for everybody."

—*Peggy Crim, United Way Board Member,*
City Treasurer, Quincy, Illinois

"Facing the twenty-first century, our school realized that people need strong character, so we prepared our students to learn and practise leadership skills in daily activities. Pillars of our school are 10 An-Nisaa' Core Values and The 7 Habits of Highly Effective People. We hope that our children become a true leader in their future, always concerned for the people around them."

—*Hj. Rosfia Rasyid, Chairman of the Foundation,*
An-Nisaa' School, Jakarta, Indonesia

"We work every day to building a better future for our country. We believe that by strengthening the quality of education we will close the social gap and develop a new generation of leaders. We see *The Leader in Me* as helping us to convert Colombian public schools into models of excellence and leadership, and thousands of Colombian children to become leaders in their personal and professional lives."

—*Silvia Madriñan, Director, Terpel Foundation, Colombia*

"The 7 Habits provide a simple, principle-based framework to help individuals successfully face their private and public challenges. As CEO of a large K–12 education company, we are now offering the 7 Habits to thousands of elementary and middle school students. Watching the academic and behavioral improvements among the students is one of the most rewarding professional experiences I have ever had."

—*Manoel Amorim, Chairman & CEO, Abril Educação, Brazil*

The
Leader
in Me

How Schools Around the World Are Inspiring
Greatness, One Child at a Time

Stephen R. Covey

Sean Covey,

Muriel Summers,

David K. Hatch

Simon & Schuster Paperbacks
New York   London   Toronto   Sydney   New Delhi

Simon & Schuster Paperbacks
A Division of Simon & Schuster, Inc.
1230 Avenue of the Americas
New York, NY 10020

First Simon & Schuster trade paperback edition August 2014

SIMON & SCHUSTER PAPERBACKS and colophon
are registered trademarks of Simon & Schuster, Inc.

For information about special discounts for bulk purchases,
please contact Simon & Schuster Special Sales at
1-866-506-1949 or business@simonandschuster.com.

The Simon & Schuster Speakers Bureau can bring authors to your live event. For
more information or to book an event, contact the Simon & Schuster Speakers
Bureau at 1-866-248-3049 or visit our website at www.simonspeakers.com.

Manufactured in the United States of America

10

Library of Congress Cataloging-in-Publication Data is available.

ISBN 978-1-4767-7218-9
ISBN 978-1-4767-7219-6 (ebook)

Every now and then,
life invites us to pause and seek a higher vantage point—
a place where we can scan the horizon
and reevaluate our courses and destinations.
May this book provide such a moment for you.

Contents

In Tribute   xxv

1. **Too Good to Be True?**   1
2. **How It Started—and *Why***   16
3. **Teaching the 7 Habits**   41
4. **Creating a Leadership Culture**   63
5. **Achieving School Goals**   96
6. **Bringing It Home**   128
7. **Engaging the Community**   155
8. **Shifting to Secondary and Beyond**   177
9. **Keeping It Alive**   208
10. **Ending with the Beginning in Mind**   235

Notes and References   251
About the Authors   261
Acknowledgments   265
FranklinCovey Education   267
The Leader in Me *You Can Leave a Legacy*   268
The Leader in Me *You Can Be the Difference*   269
Index   271

In Tribute

It was during final preparations for this second edition of *The Leader in Me* that Dr. Stephen R. Covey passed away. He was in his eightieth year.

It is hard to imagine how Stephen could have lived a more vibrant, meaning-filled life. He literally spanned the globe teaching timeless principles of personal and organizational effectiveness. Millions of people credit his influence for having bettered their lives.

When Stephen graduated from Harvard University's MBA program, it was assumed he would take a lead in his family's prospering business. Instead, he told his father he wanted to become a teacher. And he did. He spent the first twenty-five years of his career teaching university students. He loved seeing students' eyes light up when catching a new glimpse of their potential. His classes became so popular they had to be moved to an arena.

With time came numerous requests from corporate and government entities for Stephen to teach employees the same principles he was teaching students. Regardless of where he went, he captured people's minds and hearts and inspired them to greater heights. Those opportunities eventually led Stephen to leave the university to help build the FranklinCovey Company, which grew into one of the most influential leadership companies in the world, one that still thrives today. All the while, Stephen always considered himself first and foremost a teacher.

As the sun began to set on Stephen's professional career, many assumed he would slow down and spend more time with his family, which he did. Nevertheless, he never stopped pursuing his motto: "Live Life in Crescendo." He always believed and worked as if his greatest contribution was yet ahead. But what could such a "greater" contribution possibly be, considering the professional legacy he had already accumulated?

In his final years, Stephen's passion returned to the classroom. In the time since his landmark classic *The 7 Habits of Highly Effective People* had been published in 1989, more than a half million educators and over three million students had been taught the 7 Habits, mostly teens and university students. That thrilled Stephen. But what captured his energy even more was the excitement that was starting to bud at elementary schools. It began in 1999 at A.B. Combs Elementary in Raleigh, North Carolina, where some very creative teachers started teaching the 7 Habits to elementary school children—even to four-year-olds. What made their approach unique was that they were not just teaching the 7 Habits as a curriculum. Rather, they were using the 7 Habits as a framework for transforming their school's culture. In very little time, A.B. Combs went from being a school in dire need of improvement to being the number-one magnet school in America. Discipline referrals dropped dramatically. Students' self-confidence rose. Staff and parent satisfaction soared. And test scores went up.

Soon other schools were implementing the same process with similar eye-catching results. As word spread, people literally started approaching Stephen to insist he had a "moral obligation" to write about what was happening. In response, Stephen released the first edition of *The Leader in Me* at the end of 2008. It hit a nerve that started a wave of its own. Today, 200,000 copies of that edition have been sold, and more than 2,000 schools have begun implementing *The Leader in Me* process.

In getting these schools under way, much has been learned. Many best practices and tips for how to launch and sustain the process have emerged. So the decision was made to pursue this second edition of

The Leader in Me to capture at least a slice of the new stories, the new clarity, and the new vision. Sadly, Stephen passed away before the project could come to full fruition.

Therefore, it has been with much humility that three of us have united to finish this manuscript. As an introduction, Sean Covey, Stephen's son, is Executive Vice President of FranklinCovey, and leads FranklinCovey's Education team. Much of his career has been devoted to bringing the 7 Habits to students via his bestselling books *The 7 Habits of Highly Effective Teens* (more than 4 million copies sold), *The 6 Most Important Decisions You Will Ever Make,* and *The 7 Habits of Happy Kids,* which is tailored for younger audiences. All were *New York Times* bestsellers.

Muriel Summers you will come to know throughout this book. She helped pioneer *The Leader in Me* as principal of A.B. Combs Elementary. In addition to her daily responsibilities at the school, she is an outstanding keynote speaker and a proud mother. Dr. David K. Hatch brings a depth of experience in leading transformational change in corporate, government, and education settings. He was the lead researcher for the first edition, and has since consulted with hundreds of schools across the globe in implementing *The Leader in Me* process, while also filling the lead research role for this second edition.

Stephen would be the first to insist that credit for what is happening at the schools go not to him or to us but to an expanding community of committed, creative, and caring educators who have synergistically joined forces with parents, business leaders, and civic administrators to bring a measure of new hope to the field of education. Literally hundreds of teachers, superintendents, principals, parents, professors, and school board members have contributed wise input and rigorous review of this work. We honor them.

Additionally, Stephen would extend heartfelt gratitude to his long-standing partner, Boyd Craig, who from the beginning provided visionary direction to the overall scope of this work. He, along with FranklinCovey Education's team of consultants, client partners, client service coordinators, and headquarters' team, has offered significant insights. Their talents are exceeded only by their passion to help students and their professional service to educators.

In presenting this work, we are keenly aware that today's educators have been the targets of much negative press in recent years. Such is not the aim of this book. Rather than being critics, we prefer to promote the good that is happening in education. Indeed, it is rare to visit any school these days without leaving in absolute reverence of some incredible teachers who sacrifice much to make daily differences in young lives. We honor the greatness in them.

So welcome to the second edition of *The Leader in Me*. We hope you find what you are about to read inspiring. If in your reading you become impressed by what these educators are doing, we invite you to deeply consider how you might use your strengths to bring such an opportunity to a school or child near you. We hope you will join us in helping today's students to live more effective, fulfilling lives, both today and in the years ahead.

Sean Covey
Muriel Summers
David K. Hatch, Ph.D.
www.theleaderinmebook.com

The
Leader
in Me

1

Too Good to Be True?

When I first started telling people about this leadership model, there were several naysayers who thought it all a bunch of "fluff." But now they are believers.

—*Leslie Reilly, Seminole County Public Schools, Florida*

When the first edition of *The Leader in Me* was published toward the end of 2008, it began with the story of Drs. Rig and Sejjal Patel. They had just moved their family to Raleigh, North Carolina, and begun the task of looking for a school where their children could learn in a safe and mind-stimulating environment. As they talked to neighbors and colleagues, the name of one school kept popping up: A.B. Combs Elementary.

On paper, A.B. Combs was quite ordinary. It was a public school in a suburban neighborhood. There were nearly nine hundred students, of whom 18 percent spoke English as a second language, 40 percent qualified for free or reduced lunches, and 21 percent were placed in special programs. The building that housed them was fifty years old. Some teachers had been there for years.

But while on paper A.B. Combs appeared nothing too unusual, the stories the Patels kept hearing exceeded their loftiest expectations. They heard about confident and respectful students, an engaged staff, strong test scores, and a "Principal of the Year." Discipline problems were minimal, and students who had struggled at other schools were progressing well at this one. It all sounded pretty good. In fact, to the Patels, it sounded a bit "too good to be true."

The Patels decided to see the school firsthand. What they discovered was that just entering the front doors was an engaging experience. There was a feeling not felt in many schools. The walls were cheery and even motivational. Diversity was celebrated. They found that all students and staff learned *The 7 Habits of Highly Effective People,* the same leadership principles that top leaders around the world have been trained in for years. They observed that all students were assigned leadership roles, and that many decisions were made by students, not teachers. They saw students setting academic and personal goals and tracking progress in personalized notebooks. All this they found remarkable, enough so that they left the visit sensing that what they had been hearing about A.B. Combs was true after all.

The Patels ended up enrolling their children. Those children have now graduated and moved on, having had a memorable experience. Many other parents have since visited A.B. Combs to see for themselves if the school is too good to be true. Most are not only pleased

A.B. Combs Elementary is a public school located in Raleigh, North Carolina.

with what they see, they are delighted to discover that more than two thousand schools have now embarked on the same process, spanning over thirty countries.

What About for You?

The reason why the Patels, others, and perhaps even you have questioned the reports about A.B. Combs as being too good to be true is that they are in such stark contrast to what we have become accustomed to hearing in recent years. We are so inundated with stories of bullying, rude manners, low test scores, disrespect, lack of discipline, violence, poor graduation rates, mediocre teachers, and so forth, that many people are fully skeptical that anything so positive can come from schools. Either they find it too hard to believe, or they question its sustainability.

Such skepticism has value. It cautions us against latching on to every flashy fad or flimsy program that comes along, only to see it fade with no lasting impact. Yet while skepticism has its benefits, it is a sour source to draw upon for vision and passion. Skepticism is a critic, not a model. Skepticism does not think out of the box; it shrinks the box. Skepticism designs weak school-improvement strategies and anemic lesson plans. That is why skepticism and its peers—pessimism, cynicism, apathy, and despair—should never be hired to run a school, a classroom, a counseling office, a library, or a playground.

A far better source of inspiration for making decisions and leading in a school is hope. Hope informs us of better ways of doing things. Hope keeps students and staff members progressing. Hope shines light beyond the darkness of school tragedies. Hope sees potential in people—all people.

What the Patels and now many more parents are witnessing at A.B. Combs and these schools is hope. They see hope in the form of teachers engaged in their work. They see hope in the form of students learning skills that will help them throughout life. They see hope in the form of involved and satisfied parents. All this is bringing a new level of hope to the field of education under the banner of *The Leader in Me.*

As you come to the conclusion of this book, we hope you will have enough insight into *The Leader in Me* to determine whether or not you feel it is too good to be true.

Matching Today's Realities

A comment we hear regularly is that what the schools highlighted in this book are doing is "perfectly matched to today's realities." Let us explain.

Not that long ago, we lived in the information age. In that age, the individuals with the most "facts" in their heads scored highest on fact-based exams, which got them into the best fact-based universities, which accelerated their climb up the best fact-based career ladders. In those days, about all schools needed to worry about was inserting as many academic facts into students' brain cells as possible.

Well, that era is over. It has given way to the age of the knowledge worker. What happened is that the same facts that we formerly tried to cram into students' heads, and were once available only from top experts and top universities, are now accessible to most every nook on the planet. Whether sitting on a plane, waiting for a bus, working at a desk, or living in a thatched hut, people can now access more facts in a matter of seconds from pocket-sized devices than they could from spending an entire month in a university library only a short time ago. As a result, many of the elite jobs that previously required extensive factual knowledge are being handed off to computers or individuals with far fewer credentials. Factual knowledge alone, therefore, is no longer the great differentiator between those who succeed in the new reality and those who do not.

So if factual knowledge is no longer king, what then is the great differentiator between those who succeed in the new reality and those who do not? According to Daniel Pink and others, those who are succeeding are those who possess above-average creativity, strong problem-solving skills, and a knack for foresight. They are the inventors, designers, big-picture thinkers, meaning makers, and pattern recognizers. They are those who know how to analyze, optimize, synthesize, present, and do worthwhile things with facts. That is why they are called knowledge workers.

But there is more.

With the shift to the age of the knowledge worker has come simultaneous shifts in societal norms. Among them is the reality that more and more students are heading home after school to sit behind locked doors and play video games by themselves until mom or dad arrives home at night. Many of the games entail seek-to-destroy activities with no need to communicate or work out amenable solutions with others, and no real consequences. Other students are opting to get together with friends after school digitally rather than meeting face-to-face. One school we work with reports that 90 percent of its students come from single-mother homes, with most of those students having never met their fathers. Another is in a drug-infested area and its exterior walls are pocked with bullet holes.

> The last few decades have belonged to a certain kind of person with a certain kind of mind—computer programmers who could crank code, lawyers who could craft contracts, MBAs who could crunch numbers. But the keys to the kingdom are changing hands.
> —*Daniel Pink,* A Whole New Mind

Meanwhile, advances in technology and transportation have turned the world into a global playing field and more students are thinking in terms of being global citizens. Others feel they are entitled to certain privileges. And the list of societal shifts goes on, many of which are causing adults to wonder how today's students will ever learn to communicate properly, to resolve conflicts in a civil fashion, to work with people of diverse backgrounds, or to effectively lead their lives in a competitive world that is in commotion.

So yes, we know it is an old line but "Times have changed." In fact, they have changed so much that the age of the knowledge worker is no longer sufficient to describe our age. That is why Daniel Pink has observed that, in addition to possessing the traits of knowledge workers, the people who are truly thriving in today's reality are those who are also good listeners and team builders. They are able to "understand the subtleties of human interaction, to find joy in one's self and to elicit it in others." They may not know all the facts themselves but do know how to bring the right people together to assemble the facts and derive solutions. They are those who have empathy skills and can leverage people's opinions and talents. In other words, they not only have the ability to work with knowledge, they also have—surprise, surprise!—good people skills.

Pink is by no means singing solo. As we will see in Chapter 2, other experts have been signaling the same new reality for some time. They are not referring to a futuristic world, they are speaking of now! What they are calling for is for educators to take a hard, fresh look at how they approach three rapidly evolving challenges in the new reality:

Academics. In today's world, students must learn how to not just memorize and regurgitate academic facts but also apply them to authentic situations. They must have stronger analytical, critical-thinking, problem-solving, and creativity skills to succeed in the years ahead. For this to happen, educators must reexamine and adjust their teaching styles and curriculums to accommodate this way of learning and applying.

School culture. What school in today's reality is not scrambling to deal with disengaged students, bullying, discipline issues, low attendance, or student loneliness? What school does not face pockets of poor staff collaboration, low teacher engagement, a lack of common vision, resistance to change, poisonous gossip, or apathetic parents? Whereas in the past, schools could allow their culture to grow naturally, today's schools cannot afford to make culture building a passive endeavor. A more proactive approach is needed.

Life skills. There is an increasingly urgent call for more personal and interpersonal skills to be taught in schools. Sometimes they are called workforce-, career-, or college-readiness skills, or social-emotional learning skills, or simply life skills. Regardless of name, many students are showing up to college, work, parenthood, and life without them.

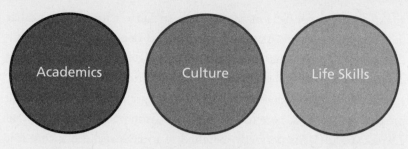

Three Evolving Challenges.

This deficit explains in part why more than 30 percent of students are dropping out of college in the first year. They lack skills for leading their lives, being on their own, or interfacing with others. It used to be assumed that they would learn such skills at home, but that no longer is a sound assumption.

Of course, none of these three challenges is entirely new. Schools have been dealing with all three for years. What is new is the seismic pressure being heaved upon educators to raise the bar in all three areas. It is all part of the new reality.

So how are today's schools responding to the new reality? According to the legendary Howard Gardner the answer is, not well. In his book *Five Minds for the Future* he asserts that "current formal education still prepares students primarily for the world of the past, rather than for the possible worlds of the future." Similarly, in *How Children Succeed*, Paul Tough insists that "the conventional wisdom about child development over the past few decades has been misguided. We have been focusing on the wrong skills and abilities in our children, and we have been using the wrong strategies to help nurture and teach these skills."

But one does not need to be a guru to make such observations. How often do we hear today's business leaders groan about the new employee they hired who is very bright yet has no clue how to work in teams, to prioritize time, or to present ideas clearly? How many parents complain that their newly crowned high school graduate excelled on all the college entrance exams but does not know how to pursue a goal, to resolve conflicts maturely, or to socialize with anything other than a digital screen? Ask these leaders and parents if they feel students are being adequately prepared for today's world, and chances are their responses will be a united and anguished "NO!"

More will be said about the three evolving challenges as the book progresses. Suffice it here to say that one reason people comment that *The Leader in Me* is perfectly matched to today's realities is that it is helping many schools to more effectively address all three challenges. And perhaps the best news is that many educators are saying, "This is not one more thing we have to do, but a better way of doing what we are already doing."

The new reality demands a new way of educating students the world over.

A New Level of Thinking?

A question always on our minds is if the field of education as a whole is approaching the three challenges at the right levels of thinking. Albert Einstein warned, "We cannot solve our problems with the same level of thinking that created those problems." In other words, before attempting to address the three challenges, we may need to step back and challenge our ways of thinking—to reexamine our paradigms.

For years, Dr. Martin Seligman has been one of the world's foremost psychologists. More recently he has become known as the father of positive psychology, a relatively new branch of study. It came about while he was president of the American Psychological Association (APA), but more specifically while he was in his garden. In his insightful book *Authentic Happiness,* he describes how he was tidying his garden one day while his five-year-old daughter, Nikki, was nearby and engaged in happy mischief. At some point Nikki's bouncing and ramblings became too much and he yelled at her, causing her to go away.

Before long, however, Nikki was back, saying, "Daddy, I want to talk to you." She said, "Daddy, do you remember before my fifth birthday? From when I was three until when I was five, I was a whiner. I whined every day. On my fifth birthday, I decided I wasn't going to whine anymore. That was the hardest thing I have ever done. And if I can stop whining you can stop being such a grouch."

To Seligman's credit, he listened. And after some soul-searching and marveling at his daughter's positive nature, he declared, "In that moment, I resolved to change."

That brief exchange not only inspired Dr. Seligman to change his disposition at home; it redirected his career. He realized that the field of psychology had for the better part of a century been focused on "fixing people." It was centered on identifying what was wrong and on relieving suffering. He began to wonder if there could be a field of psychology that focused instead on what makes people happy. In the process, he concluded that "[r]aising children . . . was far more than just fixing what was wrong with them. It was about identifying and amplifying their strengths and virtues, and helping them find the niche where they can live these positive traits to the fullest." It represented a new way of thinking for him.

The new way of thinking brought Seligman to reflect more deeply on his years of counseling and researching mental illness. In looking back at what had and had not worked over the years, he concluded:

> What progress there has been in the prevention of mental illness comes from recognizing and nurturing a set of strengths, competencies, and virtues in young people—such as future-mindedness, hope, interpersonal skills, courage, the capacity for flow, faith and work ethic. The exercise of these strengths then buffers against the tribulations that put people at risk for mental illness. Depression can be prevented in a young person at genetic risk by nurturing her skills of optimism and hope. An inner-city young man, at risk for substance abuse because of all the drug traffic in his neighborhood, is much less vulnerable if he is future-minded, gets flow out of sports, and has a powerful work ethic. But building these strengths as a buffer is alien to the disease model, which is only about remedying deficits.

Seligman's readiness to step back at a mature point in his career and challenge his ways of thinking and to take counsel from five-year-old Nikki are impressive. But the reason we mention Seligman goes beyond being impressed with him. As we have worked integrally with schools in various parts of the world and studied their successes, we have seen parallels to what Seligman detected in the field of psychology.

Over the years, the field of education has developed laserlike abilities to identify students' academic deficits so that proper remedies can be prescribed. Behavioral experts have created sophisticated systems for categorizing all types of defiant or disturbing student behavior so we can accurately identify and cure what ails them. Similar tools and tactics have been designed to measure and critique teachers' performances to increase their effectiveness. Indeed we have become quite adept at identifying "what is wrong" with students, adults, and schools—all with good reason and noble intent.

Such strategies and tools have their benefits. But in our pursuit to improve students' GPAs, have we perhaps become overfocused on students' GAPs (short for, Got a Pain)? In trying to improve teacher performance, have we turned into nothing more than a panel of critics in constant search of their "wrongs" so we can "right" them? Has the field of education become only about "remedying deficits"? Could anything be gained from stepping back, as Seligman did, to test the value of "identifying and amplifying [students' and adults'] strengths and virtues, and helping them find the niche where they can live these positive traits to the fullest"? Is there value in nurturing future-mindedness, hope, interpersonal skills, courage, the capacity for flow, optimism, and work ethic?

These and other questions have been on our minds as we approached this work. We hope you enjoy stepping back with us and exploring the education horizon in search of new ways of thinking relative to the three challenges.

Themes to Look For

As you progress from chapter to chapter, look for the following overarching themes:

A Whole School. *The Leader in Me* draws upon the talents of the whole school—*all* staff members and *all* students—and optimizes the support of parents and community.

When participants in a recent high-level leadership seminar were asked to name a person who had greatly influenced their lives, one immediately spoke up: "It was the cafeteria lady at my elementary school. School was hard for me. She was always there to ask how I was doing. She made me feel good about myself." Another said, "It was the playground supervisor at my school. One day she singled me out in front of a bunch of my friends and said I was honest. I have since tried to live up to that label." Equivalent remarks are said of librarians, custodians, aides, security staff, counselors, bus drivers, nurses, office staff, teachers, and others. Why would the talents and contributions of all staff members not be sought out when attempting to transform a school and better prepare a child for life? *The Leader in Me* sees all staff members as contributors—as leaders.

The same is true of students. Some school initiatives are designed for gifted students; others for those with special needs. *The Leader in Me* is not limited to any group of students. When Muriel Summers, principal of A.B. Combs, was asked by a parent, "Does my child have to be a strong leader to go to this school?" she responded:

This morning a special needs student who has an IQ less than 70 was assigned to welcome visitors to our site visit. He may not run a huge corporation one day, but he has unbelievable interpersonal relationship skills and there will be a job somewhere out there for him. He sees himself as a leader in manners. He is progressing. He feels so good about who he is despite his academic limitations. That is what this leadership model is capable of doing for all children.

> Everybody is a genius. But if you judge a fish by its ability to climb a tree, it will live its whole life believing it is stupid.
> —*Albert Einstein*

The Leader in Me sees all students as having strengths, as being contributors—as leaders.

A Whole Person. No two children are born completely alike. Their personalities are as diverse as their fingerprints. Yet almost as soon as they exit the womb their environment begins to shape them and they start taking on a cultural DNA, or *sameness*. When taken too far, that sameness can rob children of their unique identities, worth, and potential.

Some schools have become factories of "sameness." They operate like assembly lines for producing experts in two or three subject areas like reading, math, or writing. Each day, they essentially tell students to park at the front door their interests in art, music, computers, athletics, mechanics, drama, and so forth, and to then sit in straight rows, remain quiet, not wiggle, and somehow stay engaged. To add insult, their worth and potential are then judged largely by their test scores in those two or three subjects.

In contrast, *The Leader in Me* seeks to develop the whole person— mind, body, heart, and spirit. It starts with the belief that there is *greatness* in every student and every staff member. Greatness is not seen as attaining a high position or accomplishing a heroic feat, but as having strong character and unique talents which may or may not include the ability to read, write, or use a calculator. *The Leader in Me* searches out talents in each student and each staff member, and provides opportunities for using and nurturing those talents.

The Leader in Me seeks to discover, nurture, and honor greatness in all.

A Whole Lot of Imagination. *The Leader in Me* is not a program, it is a process. It is a process crafted by teachers for teachers. It is not a set of scripts that come in a box. Imagination is required—and lots of it.

The Leader in Me is like an operating system on a computer or smartphone. It is an underlying philosophy that impacts many aspects of a school. Staff members and students are free to utilize their talents and imaginations to design all kinds of curriculums, programs, activities, assemblies, and events to maximize the process, so long as they are suited with its principles and common language.

In fact, the real fun of *The Leader in Me* comes when walking through a school and seeing teachers' and students' imaginations displayed all over the walls. It comes when hearing a song composed by a teacher and her students that reinforces a leadership principle. It comes when observing a lesson a teacher has given ten times previously, only to see his eyes light up as he cleverly inserts a leadership concept for the first time. It comes when seeing a student's face beam as he sits down after speaking to an audience of adults. It comes when hearing a teacher say, "I've taught for thirty years and this brings me back to why I went into the field of education in the first place."

Our experience is that most educators like being challenged to re-think, redefine, and re-imagine their schools and classrooms from time to time. Some we know even refer to themselves as "re-imagineers."

Moving Forward

So there are a few themes to watch for: a whole school, a whole child, and a whole lot of imagination. Look for them on every page.

The remainder of the book is organized as follows:

Chapter 2 continues to set context as it describes how *The Leader in Me* got started—and *why*.

Chapters 3–5 delve into the *how*—how *The Leader in Me* helps schools address the three evolving challenges and how educators are seeing it as "not one more thing they have to do but a better way of doing what they are already doing."

Chapters 6 and 7 reveal how schools are engaging parents and community members to strengthen, lengthen, and widen the impact of *The Leader in Me*.

While most examples in this book come from elementary schools, the same process can be applied to secondary schools with some adaptation. That is described in Chapter 8.

Best practices for how to launch and sustain *The Leader in Me* over time are covered in Chapter 9. And by the time you arrive at Chapter 10, which is a summary reminder of why *The Leader in Me* is vitally important in today's reality, we hope you will have enough information to decide for yourself whether you think it is well matched to today's realities and pertinent to preparing young people for their todays and their tomorrows.

We also hope that as you reach the final pages you will have become as impressed with the educators described in this book as we are. They are modern-day miracle workers. They represent only a small portion of the tremendous stories and best practices that have transpired at the more than two thousand schools. We honor them for the everyday care they put into making a difference in young lives.

Finally, we hope that by the end of the book you will have come to the clear awareness that this book is as much about you and the engaging of your talents and energies as it is about releasing the potential of students. We challenge you to be open to new ways of thinking. Consider how you can apply what you read to your unique circumstances. Spend time at the end of each chapter seriously considering the "Personal Reflections" questions. Strengthen the greatness that is in you.

2

How It Started—and *Why*

For every thousand hacking at the leaves of evil, there is
one striking at the roots.

—*Henry David Thoreau*

A.B. Combs Elementary began its journey with the 7 Habits in 1999. A few years later, Principal Muriel Summers recorded a portion of how it started—and *why*. We begin the chapter with a few of her recollections, including the following personal introduction:

My name is Muriel Thomas Summers. I grew up in Lilesville, North Carolina. My father died when I was ten years old, and my mother raised my sister and me. She was an unbelievable role model.

I went to the University of North Carolina at Chapel Hill. My first years were challenging since I did not know what path I wanted to take. I recall sitting on a rock wall one day literally praying for someone to tell me what to do. At that moment, I felt a "calling," if you will, to go into teaching. I had always loved working with young children, and the moment I started my pursuit toward a career in education, I knew I had found my voice.

After graduation, I returned to Lilesville and taught for five years before moving to Maryland where I taught another seven years. There, I worked with many wonderful people, including Joann Koehler, who said she saw in me something that I had never seen in myself—the potential to become a school administrator. Before that time, I had never envisioned myself out of the classroom. Her faith in me inspired a master's degree.

Eventually my family returned to North Carolina to be closer to our roots. Year one was spent as a first-grade teacher. After that I became an instructional resource teacher. The position of assistant principal came next.

What makes Muriel's introduction relevant is the fact that the history and successes of any school are heavily rooted in the combined lives and philosophies of all who walk its hallways. Schools do not behave, people do. Thus it is Muriel's unique passions and energies, matched with the passions and energies of her entire staff, that have united to create the long pattern of successes at A.B. Combs. This becomes even more apparent as Muriel's narration continues:

Eventually, I became principal of A.B. Combs Elementary in Raleigh, North Carolina. A.B. Combs was a good school, but not a high-performing school. It was and continues to be a magnet school, which means there is supposed to be something unique about it that attracts students from outside normal boundaries. The particular magnet being promoted at the time was not attracting many students. Only 350 students were enrolled in a building sized to fit more than twice that number.

In 1999, I attended a seminar in Washington, D.C., led by Dr. Stephen R. Covey. I had been exposed to his work during my graduate studies in leadership, and was looking forward to hearing him in person. At one point during the speech I became very emotional. I was looking around the room and saw that it was full of people who looked very successful. Everyone was hanging on to every word. I believe they were sensing the same thing that I was sensing, which was that what Dr. Covey was sharing was a set of timeless, universal principles.

I found myself listening with the head of an administrator and the heart of a parent. The more I listened the more I kept thinking,

The 7 Habits of Highly Effective People

As Muriel sat among business leaders, she could not help but think, "If children learned the 7 Habits at an early age, how different their lives might be and how different our world might be." Read the following synopses of the 7 Habits in kids' language and see if you come to the same conclusion.

Habit 1: Be Proactive

I am a responsible person. I take initiative. I choose my actions, attitudes, and moods. I do not blame others for my mistakes. I can only be offended if I choose to be.

Habit 2: Begin with the End in Mind

I plan ahead and set goals. I do things that have meaning and make a difference. I am an important part of my classroom and contribute to my school's mission and vision, and look for ways to be a good citizen.

Habit 3: Put First Things First

I spend my time on things that are most important. This means I say *no* to things I know I should not do. I set priorities, make a schedule, and follow my plan. I am disciplined and organized.

Habit 4: Think Win-Win

I balance courage for getting what I want with consideration for what others want. I make deposits in others' Emotional Bank Accounts. When conflicts arise, I look for options that work for both sides.

Habit 5: Seek First to Understand, Then to Be Understood

I listen to other people's ideas and feelings. I try to see things from their viewpoints. I listen to others without interrupting. I am confident in voicing my ideas. I look people in the eyes when talking.

Habit 6: Synergize

I value other people's strengths and learn from them. I get along well with others, even people who are different than me. I work well in groups. I seek out other people's ideas to solve problems because I know that by teaming with others we can create better solutions than any one of us alone. I am humble.

Habit 7: Sharpen the Saw

I take care of my body by eating right, exercising, and getting sleep. I spend time with family and friends. I learn in lots of ways and lots of places, not just at school. I take time to find meaningful ways to help others.

"Muriel, if you could teach these principles to young children, they would not have to wait until they were adults to learn them. If they looked through the lens of the 7 Habits beginning at an early age and continued to look through that lens for the rest of their lives, how different not only their lives might be but how different our world might be."

At every break, I tried to muster up courage to ask Dr. Covey what his thoughts were about teaching the principles to young children. It took until the last break before I got my nerve up. I caught him as he was exiting the stage and asked, "Dr. Covey, do you think these 7 Habits can be taught to young children?" His response was, "How young?" I said, "Five years old." He paused briefly, then let out a smile and said, "I don't know why not." To that he added, "Let me know how it goes if you ever do it."

That was the end of our conversation. Little did I know of the influence that brief exchange would eventually have on my life.

What Muriel was sensing during her D.C. experience has been voiced by numerous parents: "If only my teen lived by these 7 Habits," or "Wouldn't it be great if my first-year college student exhibited these habits!" Many business leaders have expressed similar remarks: "We need our entire workforce to apply these habits." Yet Muriel was not thinking about college students, teens, or today's workforce. She was thinking about five-year-olds!

By the time Muriel returned to her office, numerous other things were already on her mind. So she did not think much more about her conversation with Dr. Covey or the 7 Habits until sometime later, when she was confronted with the following ultimatum:

A few months later, our superintendent called me in for a "reality chat." He informed me that our school was not attracting enough students, and either we had to come up with a new magnet theme or we would have to redefine the boundaries and go back to being a traditional school. In other words, "Reinvent yourselves or be de-magnetized." One week was the amount of time he gave us, and "you will have no additional resources to do it" was his parting encouragement.

My staff and I went to work trying to dream up the right school-saving solution. We talked to parents and to community leaders and asked them what they wanted from a school. What was interesting was that they all voiced the same types of things. They wanted children to grow up to be responsible, caring, and compassionate human beings who respected diversity and who knew how to do the right thing when faced with difficult decisions.

What else was interesting was that not once did we hear in all of our interviews and focus groups, "We want the best academics." It was all about building character and basic life skills.

So in short, Muriel and her team had one week to come up with a new theme to keep their magnet status alive. To their credit, instead of sitting around a table and trying to brainstorm in isolation, they had the humility and openness to approach their stakeholders and ask what *they* wanted most from a school.

What Teachers, Parents, and Business Leaders Wanted

As Muriel indicated, A.B. Combs was a good school in 1999. It had a decent staff and good students. But there were definite hurdles.

For starters, the neighborhood around the school was aging, and enrollment was in steady decline. This accompanied an equal decline in staff morale. No matter how hard they worked, nothing improved. Test scores were among the lowest in the district, and disciplinary problems were rising. While some teachers had independent projects going, there was no common vision or goals to unite the staff. They resembled a bunch of arrows going in as many directions as there are degrees on a compass.

The one thing that A.B. Combs truly had in its favor was the diversity of its students. Raleigh's Research Triangle and its universities attract people from around the world, and so students who attended A.B. Combs from outside the school's boundaries represented many countries. The staff prized that diversity, and wanted to do everything possible to preserve it.

A.B. Combs greatly prized the diversity of its students.

In brainstorming ideas for a new magnet theme, A.B. Combs's teachers were asked what they wanted in a school. Their first response, however, was what they did *not* want, which was "One more thing to have to do or teach!" They were already working very hard and bordering on burnout, so the new theme could not be one more burden plopped onto their overloaded plates. Once that was made clear, what the teachers said they *did* want was to be proud of their school. They wanted a magnet theme they could firmly stand behind, one that would set them apart. They wanted self-motivated students who liked coming to school. They spoke of becoming a staff that other schools envied in terms of knowledge, creativity, resources, and up-to-date methodologies. They spoke of collaborating and working as friends. They wanted to have their talents used and to go home each day feeling they had made a difference. They were passionate about these things, and Muriel and her team took careful notes.

The next natural step was to ask parents what they wanted from a school. Frank discussions followed. In short, the parents said they wanted their children to learn how to take care of themselves, to make responsible decisions, and to get along with others. They wanted their children to be tolerant of people's differences, to be problem solvers, to be safe, and to use time well. They wanted their children to grow up to make positive contributions to society.

A few of the parents were business leaders who saw a tremendous need for students to acquire the skills and traits that would make them most employable in the future. One parent even shared a list from an annual survey of businesses that identifies the qualities and skills that employers seek most. The list read:

- Communication skills (verbal and written)
- Honesty/Integrity
- Teamwork skills
- Interpersonal skills
- Self-motivation/Initiative
- Strong work ethic

- Analytical skills
- Technology skills
- Organizational skills
- Creative minds

Once again, Muriel and her team listened attentively. They hoped that something the parents and business leaders said would spark an idea for a new theme.

Today's Voices

At this point, we pause from A.B. Combs's story to note that what Muriel and her team were hearing from stakeholders in 1999 was in reality the early signals of a shift in what today's adults want from schools. The following sampling of research provides a glimpse into how that shift came about.

The 1990s were known as the "back-to-the-basics" decade in education. Emphasis during those years was narrowed to the three R's—reading, writing, and arithmetic—mostly at the insistence of parents. But as the decade and century came to a close, change was in the air. Some believe it was the deadly gunshots at Columbine High School in Colorado in 1999 that rattled parents and educators into thinking once again beyond the three R's. Many parents began to worry about their children's safety and emotional well-being at school more than their academics. Educators were left asking, "What can we do to prevent students from feeling so desperate as to commit such an act?"

In hindsight, the shift in adult attitudes started well before Columbine. In the early 1990s, University of Michigan sociologist Duane Alwin was revealing new trends in what parents wanted from schools. Whereas parents in the 1920s emphasized traits like obedience, conformity, respect, and good manners, Alwin's research indicated that what parents in the 1990s wanted foremost for their children was the ability to think for themselves, to take responsibility for their lives, to show initiative, and to be tolerant of diversity—much the same as what parents at A.B. Combs were seeking.

Toward the close of the 1990s, the United Nations Educational, Scientific and Cultural Organization (UNESCO) released the report *Learning: The Treasure Within*. Authored by fifteen global education experts, the report recommended four aims—or *pillars*—for educators to emphasize in the twenty-first century:

- *Learning to Know*: In addition to teaching facts, this pillar calls on educators to do more to teach students how to become lifelong learners by developing concentration skills, memorization skills, research skills, the capacity for abstract thought, intellectual curiosity, and logical problem solving.
- *Learning to Do*. This pillar challenges educators to do more to teach "personal competence" and not just "certified skills." Certified skills are skills needed for a specific job and are often taught in vocational schools. Personal competence includes certified skills but also encompasses general life skills and traits, such as initiative, the willingness to risk, time management, communication, innovation, leadership, and teamwork. The report insists that these skills "are not confined to highly qualified people," and therefore "ought to be taught to all people."
- *Learning to Live Together*. Noting the prevalence in society of prejudice, conflicts, gangs, and predatory behavior, this pillar calls on educators to instill in students from early ages "an awareness of the similarities and interdependence of all people," and to "teach them how to understand others by looking at things from their point of view. Where this spirit of empathy is encouraged in schools," it continues, "it has a positive effect on young persons' social behavior for the rest of their lives." It adds that students need opportunities to work together on projects with common goals. "When people work together on exciting projects . . . differences and even conflicts between individuals tend to pale and sometimes disappear."

- *Learning to Be.* The final pillar urges educators to recognize that "education should contribute to every person's complete development—mind and body, intelligence, sensitivity, aesthetic appreciation and spirituality," to the whole person. More is needed to equip students to "make up their own minds on the best courses of action in the different circumstances in their lives," and to take responsibility for their lives and education.

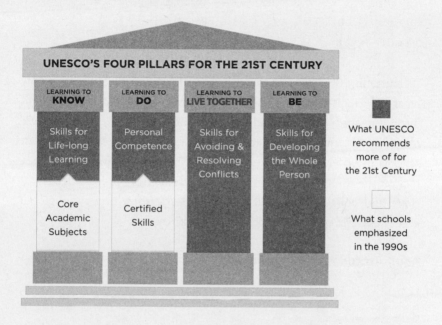

As the twenty-first century arrived, the shift in adult attitudes accelerated. Many educators were being influenced by Daniel Goleman's research on social-emotional learning (SEL). Goleman argued that Emotional Intelligence (EQ) is a better predictor of both academic and life success than is IQ. In terms of career performance, he asserted that "emotional competence is twice as important as purely cognitive abilities," and "for success at the highest levels, in leadership positions, emotional intelligence accounts for virtually the entire advantage." EQ is made up of *personal competence* and *social competence,* which are composed of:

Personal Competence	Social Competence
Self-awareness	Empathy
Self-assessment	Organizational awareness
Self-confidence	Service
Self-control	Inspirational leadership
Transparency	Developing others
Adaptability	Creating change
Achievement	Conflict management
Initiative	Building bonds
Optimism	Teamwork and collaboration

Then, in 2007, the Partnership for 21st Century Skills, a highly regarded coalition of educators and business leaders, released an intriguing study of U.S. adult attitudes on education. Titled *Beyond the Three Rs,* the study asked adults to rank various skills taught in schools in order of importance. Note in the table below where they ranked the three R's relative to skills such as problem solving, teamwork and collaboration, self-direction, leadership, creativity, global awareness, and ethics and social responsibility.

Adult Attitudes on Education

	% who rank this skill as a 9 or 10 in importance on a scale of 0 to 10
Reading comprehension	75
Computer and technology skills	71
Critical thinking and problem solving skills	69
Ethics and social responsibility	62
Written communications	58
Teamwork and collaboration	57
Oral communications	56
Lifelong learning and self-direction	50
Mathematics	48
Leadership	44
Creativity and innovation	43

Media literacy	42
Global awareness	42
Science (biology, chemistry, and physics)	38

In 2009, Edexcel, a worldwide education firm based in the United Kingdom, surveyed two thousand employers from twenty-four countries to ascertain what they wanted from the forthcoming workforce. Edexcel reported that the "most striking finding" was not any one particular item on the list, but "the commonality of the responses across countries." Topping their findings:

- Problem-solving skills
- Positive thinking
- Creativity/innovation
- Multitasking
- Initiative
- Cultural sensitivity
- Accepting responsibility
- Team working
- Empathy
- Communication
- Professional manners

In 2010, Tony Wagner launched his book *The Global Achievement Gap*, which he subtitled, *Why Even Our Best Schools Don't Teach the New Survival Skills Our Children Need—and What We Can Do About It*. In it he identified what he sees as the "new basic skills" for work, citizenship, and learning. What are they?

1. critical thinking and problem solving
2. networks and leading by influence
3. agility and adaptability
4. initiative and entrepreneurialism
5. effective oral and written communication

6. accessing and analyzing information
7. curiosity and imagination

And, finally, a 2013 nationwide Gallup poll of U.S. adults revealed that four out of five adults responded "strongly agree" that K–12 schools should teach critical thinking and communication skills to children. Sixty-four percent strongly agreed that goal setting should be taught, while a majority strongly agreed that creativity and collaboration are meaningful topics. The study concluded, "While student success may depend on mastery of content in core subject areas such as math and reading, it also depends on more than knowledge of core content. Critical thinking, creativity, communication, and other soft skills, as well as student physical and social wellbeing, are also necessary for future success in higher education and in the workplace."

The above reports are but a sampling of what parents, educators, thought leaders, and business leaders have been voicing in recent times. They trend with what Daniel Pink, Martin Seligman, Howard Gardner, and Paul Tough voiced in Chapter 1, and what others like Sir Ken Robinson and Carol Dweck have advocated as the new skills and mindsets for survival in the new reality. And they also match closely to what A.B. Combs was hearing back in 1999. It is a global call for educators to widen the lens beyond core academics. It is an outcry with which educators are very familiar, as they have heard it several times and want it for their own children. But the question that always arises is *How*? How to teach these skills and traits given all the other tasks and pressures already on their plates?

What Students Want in a School

In seeking a new magnet theme, A.B. Combs's main focus was on the input of parents, business leaders, and teachers. But what do students want from a school? How often do they get asked?

Some time ago, a young boy walked into Muriel's office wanting to talk. Soon tears were flowing. His father was serving in the military overseas and the boy missed him dearly. Through dripping eyes he said, "Ms. Summers, if everyone in the world lived like we are taught to live at A.B. Combs, my daddy would not be gone."

One does not need to travel to far-off war zones to find raging conflicts. Many neighborhoods, homes, and schools have become virtual battlegrounds. That said, we are convinced that most students are good in nature, and that what most of them want from a school is to get a good education, to be with friends, and to have a little fun—though not always in that order. But above all, they want peace of mind, and are quick to notice when it is missing.

Peace of mind shows up on students' faces, in their behaviors, and in their test scores. It comes when four basic needs are being met:

- *Physical* (safety, health, food, exercise, shelter, cleanliness, and hygiene)
- *Social-emotional* (acceptance, kindness, friendship, respect)
- *Mental* (intellectual growth, creativity, and stimulating challenges)
- *Spiritual* (contribution, meaning, and uniqueness)

These basic needs represent the body, heart, mind, and spirit—the whole person. Since not all four needs are met in every home, many students come to school hungry for them—in some cases practically starving. Educators like to imagine that their profession is focused solely on the mental need, but reality requires them to be attentive to all four.

In terms of physical needs, many schools have students who must first be fed breakfast before they can learn anything, especially in urban schools where "food insecurity" is often a concern. It is tough to learn on an empty stomach. Safety, fitness, hygiene, and good health are also ongoing physical needs for which schools must be concerned.

Likewise, most teachers can tell of the hours they spend mending social-emotional wounds. While some cases are trivial and even humorous in nature, others are outright tragic. The more students mature, the more relationships and emotional issues tend to matter to them, and the more concern there ought to be when students grow silent. When students feel no personal connection to school—through a peer, a teacher, or some other person they trust—chances of them doing well academically shrink, and their delinquency and drop-out rates increase. Relationships matter!

Perhaps the biggest need that staff members impact each day outside of the mental need is the spiritual need. The word *spiritual* gets its roots from *spirit,* for which there are many nonreligious definitions, including "disposition of mind" or "outlook characterized by firmness and assertiveness." Thesauruses feature many synonyms for *spirit,* such as *will, moral fiber, determination, courage, vigor, heart, enthusiasm, inner self, fortitude,* and *strength.* Teachers and other staff members play significant roles in nourishing or extinguishing the spirits of students. Countless students have their spirits lifted each day by a compliment, by being trusted, or by being shown their worth and potential by an adult at school.

In contrast, many students have their spirits trampled long before they exit the school system. Many come to school at a young age with

Many students' lives are changed for the good by adults who believe in them.

fire in their eyes, only to have those flames turn to ashes by the fourth grade, if not before. It is an oft cruel world that students face, and the crudeness of it can sap their feelings of self-worth very quickly. In fact, the most harmful form of identity theft in today's society is happening not in our economy but among our youth. Today's young people are constantly pressured by media and their peers into becoming something other than what they in their heart of hearts want to be. To be "cool" they are told they have to act a certain way or hang out with a certain crowd. To be "hot" they have to wear a specific fashion or indulge in daring behaviors. Some get labeled because of a low test score or one foolish mistake. Robbed of their unique gifts and identities, they become absorbed into the cultural DNA of the masses. Sometimes only a caring, perceptive teacher or staff member can prevent such a tragedy by giving them a sense of hope, vision, and optimism—a sense of their worth and potential.

The more students feel healthy and safe today (physical need), the more they feel accepted and appreciated for who they are today (social-emotional need), the more they feel their minds challenged and progressing today (mental need), and the more they feel their spirits lifted today (spiritual need), the more open they become to thinking about their tomorrows.

Developing Leaders One Child at a Time

Returning to A.B. Combs and their effort to select a new magnet theme, Muriel and her team were greatly influenced by the opinions of the teachers, parents, and business leaders. As they reviewed their findings, Muriel reflected back on her experience at the 7 Habits seminar in Washington, D.C.:

> As we listened to what parents, teachers, and business leaders were saying, I could not help but reflect on my experience with Dr. Covey and how closely the 7 Habits matched what everyone was wanting for us to teach students. I shared my D.C. experience with the staff and one

thing led to another. In short, the term that kept surfacing and seemed to capture what parents, teachers, and business leaders were all saying was "Leadership."

"That's it!" we thought. "We will use Leadership as our new magnet theme."

We quickly went to the Internet to see if there were other elementary schools using leadership as a theme. We found none. Our teachers started to work on ideas of what they could do with Leadership as a theme. They sensed they were on to something unique. By the time we took the Leadership theme to the superintendent a week later, there was so much energy coming from the staff that he could scarcely say no. And why would he? He too liked the idea—a lot.

And that is how "Leadership" became the new magnet theme at A.B. Combs Elementary. Before long, the school had a new mission statement: "To Develop Leaders One Child at a Time." The staff

After speaking with stakeholders,
A.B. Combs chose "Leadership" as a new magnet theme.

wanted each student to know that his or her worth exceeded any score on any test or any mark on any grade report. They wanted students to feel successful. They wanted all students to become not CEOs but leaders of their lives, leaders in the school, and leaders of their futures. Yet still there remained the nagging question of *How?*

Getting Under Way

The first order of things in starting out was getting everyone trained in the 7 Habits. They received the same quality of training as top corporate leaders receive. An important benefit of the training, led by senior lead consultant Dr. Nancy Moore, was the bonding that took place among staff members. Everyone left knowing each other better and sharing a common language. Right away they began looking for ways to apply the habits in meetings, in addressing challenges, and in improving their personal lives.

When it came to taking the 7 Habits to students, the staff decided to test the waters with one class per grade level. Lesson by lesson, the pilot teachers figured out clever ways to teach the habits, mostly by integrating the concepts into existing lesson plans. They discovered that it was not as hard as they thought it might be. The students enjoyed learning the habits. Before long, discipline problems dropped and student self-confidence rose noticeably in the pilot classrooms. Parents made positive comments, and at the end of that first year the pilot teachers summed things up by saying: "Every student deserves this!"

Something else happened that first year that caught the staff's attention. Aggregate scores on end-of-grade tests bumped from 84 percent to 87 percent. When analyzing the data, they found that the improved scores came from the pilot classes. The only thing they had done different from the nonpilot classes was to teach the 7 Habits. And that is when the staff began to think seriously that they might be on to something unique.

The next year the entire school took on the leadership theme, this time with added flair. Motivational displays and inspiring quotes went up in hallways. Assemblies and other school events focused on leadership. Songs the choir sang lifted students' visions of themselves and got them thinking of their futures. Students were given opportunities to be leaders in their class and in the school. As the year progressed, the 7 Habits language began to be heard in hallways, in classrooms, in staff meetings, and on the playground. Leadership truly became the walk and talk of the school.

Some staff members had been trained in Baldrige quality principles and tools. They saw how those principles and tools could help the school to better track and utilize academic data. So they looked for ways to incorporate them into the leadership theme. As part of that effort, students set goals and tracked their progress in personalized notebooks. Every student could tell where they stood academically, particularly in reading, writing, and mathematics. And at the end of that second year, the number of passing students took another impressive leap, this time to 94 percent—no small feat given the diversity of students.

Eventually test scores rose to a peak of 97 percent. As impressive as those academic improvements were, what really stood out was the new "feel" of the school. Students and staff wanted to come to school. Morale soared and so did the enrollment, which jumped from 350 to 900 students, with more wanting to get in. The magnet theme was attracting students. The superintendent could relax.

Each year thereafter, the teachers and staff have recalibrated their efforts to fit the challenges and unique situations of the coming year. A refresher visit from Dr. Moore or another consultant has inspired the staff to new heights. Each year they like to think it gets a little better. The continuous growth highlights the fact that *The Leader in Me* is not a one-time event but an evergreen process that continues to take shape and expand with each new year.

Rippling Across the Globe

When the first edition of *The Leader in Me* hit the bookstores, eight other schools were replicating what A.B. Combs had initiated and a handful of others were getting started. Five years later, those numbers eclipsed the 2,000 mark. Most of the schools are in the United States, though more than 100 are spread across Canada and another 200 are located outside North America. Much of the growth is grassroots in nature—parents talking to parents, teachers talking to teachers.

The majority of schools are public, although numerous charter and private schools have also implemented the process. Because the 7 Habits are based upon universal, timeless principles, such as responsibility and teamwork, they transcend differences of every kind—philosophical, cultural, political, religious, generational, lifestyle, socio-economic, and so on. Thus, *The Leader in Me* has been adopted by virtually every kind of school, including urban, suburban, rural, magnet, and independent schools, as well as religious, ethnic, and values-based schools.

In Brazil, more than one hundred schools have embarked on *The Leader in Me,* including some in the toughest neighborhoods. In Colombia, a local foundation has sponsored sixty schools with a goal of reaching one hundred. Mexico, Puerto Rico, Bermuda, Trinidad, Guatemala, Chile, Argentina, and other countries have schools in progress. Schools are under way in Asia in places like Singapore, Taiwan, Mainland China, Korea, India, and Malaysia. In Indonesia, ten schools have started. Thailand has six schools, including Satit Bangna, which received the King Royal Award of Best School—Elementary Level. Schools are also coming on board in Europe, particularly across the Nordic region, where in Sweden a handful of municipalities sponsored local schools. The Netherlands is under way, as are seven schools in Hungary. Australia has well-established schools, while Africa and the Middle East are getting started. Several of these schools are represented in this book; however, there is no way we could cover the full gamut. This is just a glimpse.

In observing these schools, many key lessons have come to the forefront. One is that the three challenges—academics, culture, and life skills—are highly interactive in nature. Many schools approach them as three separate challenges. They focus predominantly on academics since that is their major role. Then, if time permits or a crisis arises, they work on their culture. And finally, if any additional time or resources still remain, they take steps to teach life skills—or what we will from here on refer to as *leadership* skills, including the 7 Habits. However, what the schools have found is that by taking direct steps to improve any one of the three challenges, there are simultaneous improvements to the other areas. They are interactive—not separate— in nature.

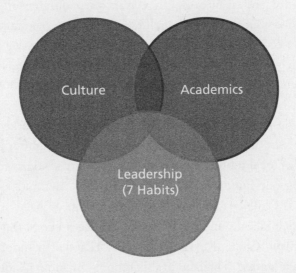

A second key lesson is that school transformation is a highly contextual process. No two schools or no two classrooms are completely alike, so no two schools or classrooms will implement entirely alike. Each school and class must examine its context and decide how—and how fast—it will implement. This turns out to be one of the most popular aspects of *The Leader in Me,* as it is not a canned program or script but rather a process that encourages staff members and students to add their talents, passions, and imaginations—to make it

Research Says . . .

Daniel Goleman and the Collaborative for Academic, Social, and Emotional Learning (CASEL) assembled an array of research showing the interactive nature of life skills, culture, and academics. These findings include:

1. Interventions that make the learning environment safer, more caring, more participatory, and that enhance students' social competence have been shown to increase student attachment to school. In turn, students who are more attached to school have better attendance and higher graduation rates, as well as higher grades and standardized tests scores.

2. When students are attached to school and to prosocial teachers and peers, they are more likely to behave in prosocial ways and to avoid engaging in high-risk behaviors (Hawkins, Catalano, & Miller, 1992).

3. Providing students with opportunities for participation may increase students' intrinsic motivation to behave in prosocial ways, thereby decreasing school crime and other forms of deviant behavior at school (Csikszentmihalyi & Larson, 1980).

4. In supportive atmospheres, students feel more comfortable approaching and interacting with teachers and peers, thereby strengthening their relationship skills. In essence, teachers and schools can improve students' social-emotional competence by creating a social learning context where such skills are frequently called for and positively reinforced.

5. Social-Emotional Learning (SEL) instruction provides students with basic skills, such as good decision making and refusal skills, which enable them to successfully avoid engaging in high-risk behaviors, and to participate in behaviors that support their positive development.

6. High-risk behaviors in students are associated with poor academic performance. Likewise, poor academic performance is a risk factor for a variety of high-risk behaviors, while academic achievement is a protective factor.

7. Social and emotional skills can significantly enhance learning when they are integrated into different academic content areas.

their own. We call it placing their personal signature or "heartprint" on it. Therefore, any ideas shared beyond this point of the book should be viewed as springboards to further creativity, not as methods set in stone.

A third key lesson learned is that school transformation works best from the inside out. As has been mentioned, ultimately schools do not behave, people do. School transformation is the outcome of individual transformation. So the place to begin a school transformation is with examining the paradigms—the ways of thinking—and the actions of the people, starting with the staff.

More key lessons will be shared as we progress through the book.

A Word about Leadership

So that is how *The Leader in Me* got started—and *why*. The next chapters cover how *Leader in Me* schools address the three challenges. Before approaching those chapters, a brief note is in order regarding what we mean by being a leader.

There are two general ways to be a leader:

1. *Leader of Self:* Leading one's life. Being self-reliant and in charge of one's choices, actions, and destinies. Being forward thinking. Having a plan and clear purposes, and the discipline to achieve them.

2. *Leader of Others:* There are multiple ways to be a leader of others, none of which requires holding a formal position. They include,

- Sharing knowledge or talents in a way that expands others' thinking or talents. *(Talent/Thought Leadership)*
- Inspiring others to see and rise to their potential. Being a role model. *(Inspirational Leadership)*
- Guiding a group—small or large—toward the accomplishment of a meaningful goal. *(Organizational/Team Leadership)*

While leadership can be defined in many ways and is described in more detail in Chapter 4, the definition that takes center stage in *The Leader in Me,* particularly as it applies to leading others, is Dr. Covey's favorite:

Leadership is communicating a person's worth and potential so clearly that they are inspired to see it in themselves.

Imagine what would happen in a school if everyone—every leader—led by that definition. That is why it is at the heart of *The Leader in Me.*

Clearly, the ultimate end in mind in working with students is not academics, school culture, or leadership skills. Those are all means. The ultimate end in mind is for students to develop the skills and mindsets that will allow them to lead their own lives, to be able to work effectively with others throughout life, and to make a meaningful contribution wherever they go in life—at home, at school, at work, at play. We want them equipped to make effective decisions today and into their futures. Academics, culture, and leadership skills are important means to those ends, so the hope is that schools will address all three challenges most effectively and in a balanced way.

In addition to helping students, *The Leader in Me* has as secondary ends: 1) enabling staff members to be more effective personally and professionally; 2) strengthening the home-school relationship, mostly by students taking the leadership skills home with them; and 3) improving communities, by providing a future workforce and citizen base that makes the community a more attractive and safe environment in which to live and do business.

To the extent that *The Leader in Me* contributes to those outcomes, it will have served its purpose.

Personal Reflections

A paradigm is a way of thinking, a mental map of how we view the world. A.B. Combs went to their stakeholders—teachers, parents, and the business community—to ask their views on what they wanted in a school. In essence they were given a chance to describe their ideal school. What is your paradigm of an ideal school? What is your paradigm of leadership? Does a formal leadership title automatically make a person a leader? In what ways are you a leader? In what ways can you become a better leader?

3

Teaching the 7 Habits

The 7 Habits are like vitamins. They can be found in all
kinds of places and are needed whether you are aware of it
or not. They can be mixed together, or taken one at a time.
You're healthier, happier, and more successful when the
habits are a daily part of your life.

—*Arlene Kai, elementary student from China*

The general subject being taught was science. The more specific
topic was seashells. It was a lesson teacher Mrs. Fowler had
taught her second-grade students multiple times over multiple
years. Yet on this occasion it was different.

At the center of the lesson was a basket filled with seashells of all
shapes and sizes. Their colors and curves were nearly irresistible to
little fingers. One by one, Mrs. Fowler plucked a shell from the basket, explained its parts, and described the critters that might venture
inside—the same way she had done in years past.

Then came the twist. This time, prior to putting each shell back in
the basket, Mrs. Fowler paused and pointed out a small nick, a little
scratch, or some other minor flaw in the shell. Once the last shell was
back in the basket, she calmed the children and said she had something to tell them. She explained how when she was in college she developed a habit of picking out other people's flaws, like she had done
with the shells. She said she became particularly adept at identifying
the weaknesses of her roommates—even their tiniest quirks.

One day an emergency arose. She desperately needed help. The only sources she could think to turn to were her roommates. When she called the apartment, the roommate with the "most annoying flaws" answered. Thankfully, the roommate responded, and the emergency was resolved.

Mrs. Fowler told her students how from that point on she started to focus on that roommate's strengths instead of her flaws. In fact, the roommate's flaws seemed to melt away as she and Mrs. Fowler became best friends. Mrs. Fowler said she learned from that experience that she would also be better off focusing on the strengths of her other roommates, instead of on their weaknesses. In time, she became good friends with those roommates.

From there, Mrs. Fowler transitioned to a handwriting exercise. She had each student select a classmate's name from a jar and write one thing they liked about that person—one strength. They needed to write the note in their neatest handwriting since it would be passed on to their selected classmate. Each student did his or her best to print very clearly. Yet when the time came to share their fine printing skills, the receiving students seemed far more interested in what their peers saw as their strengths than in evaluating how tidy the note was written. And that concluded the lesson, and the basket of shells became a memorable reminder she could refer to from time to time.

So with very little adjustment or added time, Mrs. Fowler had combined an existing science lesson and a handwriting exercise, and integrated a brief insight on Habit 6: Synergize, which focuses on valuing others' strengths. She did not see it as "one more thing," she saw it as "a better way of doing what she was already doing." She sensed it might help them to be happier in life.

A Case for the 7 Habits

Mrs. Fowler's way of integrating a short insight from one of the 7 Habits into an existing lesson plan is the primary method teachers apply to teach the 7 Habits in *Leader in Me* schools. We will share more examples of how it is done, along with other ways the 7 Habits are taught shortly, but first allow us to strengthen the case for why the 7 Habits are so relevant in today's world.

In 1976, the two hundredth anniversary of the United States, Dr. Covey was a university professor. He conducted an intense review of the "success literature" that had been published during that same two-hundred-year period. He pored through hundreds of books, journal articles, and biographies of respected individuals from history. His aim was to identify the most common traits and behaviors that lead people to be most effective. From that extensive literature review, he distilled *The 7 Habits of Highly Effective People*. He began teaching the habits first to college students, and later to corporate, government, and education leaders.

One of Dr. Covey's main discoveries was that the 7 Habits are based on timeless and universal principles. This means that regardless of a person's nationality, age, creed, ethnicity, health, or economic origins, the principles will apply to their varied circumstances. The principles existed centuries ago, and will exist far into the future. In fact, if anything, the principles seem to be becoming more relevant with the passing of time and the new realities.

Something else Dr. Covey discovered was that there is a practical sequence to the 7 Habits. The first three habits—Be Proactive, Begin with the End in Mind, and Put First Things First—help individuals to become more *independent*. They enable people to be more responsible, to take more control of their lives, to map out their future, to set priorities, and to achieve their goals by staying focused and disciplined. They include time management skills, planning skills, goal-setting skills, and other basic organizing skills that are foundational to independent living, or *personal leadership*. Doing them well leads to what Dr. Covey calls the *Private Victory*.

While becoming independent is important, neither business leaders nor parents see independence as the only "end in mind" for their employees or children. They want them to also be capable of working effectively with others. This is why the next three habits—Think

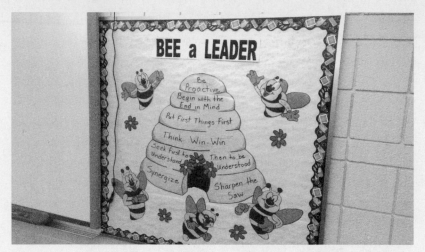

The 7 Habits are based on timeless, universal principles.

Win-Win, Seek First to Understand, Then to Be Understood, and Synergize—are so vital. They include skills for conflict resolution, listening, communicating, inspiring creativity, dealing with diversity, problem solving, and teamwork. They enable a person to become more *interdependent,* and culminate in a *Public Victory.*

Habit 7, Sharpen the Saw, sustains and enhances the first six habits, and focuses on the principles of renewal, continuous improvement, and leading a balanced life. It gives guidance for maintaining the "whole person" by staying fit in four critical areas—physical, social-emotional, mental, and spiritual—which are rooted in the four basic needs of individuals.

A review of the 7 Habits reveals two important points. First, the Private Victory precedes the Public Victory. To be effective with others, one must first be effective personally. Second, the 7 Habits contain many of the traits and life skills that parents, business leaders, and educators have been calling for students to be taught, as highlighted in the table below. Notice that under the heading of "What Parents, Teachers, and Businesses Want," the first column contains *competencies,* while the far right column contains *character* traits. This points

The 7 Habits	What Parents, Teachers, and Businesses Want	
Habits 1–3 (Independence) Be Proactive Begin with the End in Mind Put First Things First	• Goal Setting • Planning • Time Management • Organization	• Initiative • Responsibility • Vision • Integrity
Habits 4–6 (Interdependence) Think Win-Win Seek First to Understand, Then to Be Understood Synergize	• Conflict Management • Listening/Empathy • Speaking Skills • Problem Solving • Teamwork	• Respect • Ethics/Manners • Honesty • Openness • Valuing Diversity
Habit 7 (The Whole Person) Sharpen the Saw *(Care for Body, Heart, Mind, and* *Spirit)*	• Physical Wellness • Social Skills • Mental Skills • Emotional Stability	• Contribution/Meaning • Desire to Learn • Fun

out that while the 7 Habits do contain character traits, they are about more than character. They contain key workforce- and life-readiness skills, or what we again are calling *leadership* skills.

In years past, it was almost assumed that students would be taught these competencies and character traits at home. But nowadays nothing can be assumed. As Assistant Superintendent of Decatur City Schools Jeanne Payne points out, "Students don't always arrive at school with these habits. So why leave it to chance whether or not they learn these skills? Why not level the playing field and give every child the opportunity?"

But, again, where and when do teachers find time to teach such skills? How do they do it with everything else they have on their plates?

This is the point where if we could launch fifty fireworks to attract full attention we would. For what we are about to describe is clearly one of the most important components of *The Leader in Me*. It is that *The Leader in Me* takes a "ubiquitous" approach to teaching the habits. *Ubiquitous* means that the 7 Habits and other leadership lessons can be embedded into most any activity, any lesson, any counseling session, any newsletter, any assembly, any set of morning announcements, or any hallway discussion. Sometimes it happens in a planned-out manner; other times it occurs serendipitously. It is not a "theme of the month," nor is it a scripted curriculum. It happens in three ways:

1. Integrated instruction
2. Direct lessons
3. Modeling

Integrated Instruction

The most common way the habits are taught is through integrated instruction. In the same way Mrs. Fowler inserted a lesson on Habit 6: Synergy into a science and handwriting lesson, she could have taught any of the habits as part of any lesson and any subject: math, literature, science, history, art, music, technology, physical education, and foreign language—any subject.

We are always concerned about reading literacy. But we are also very concerned about students' character and social literacy.
—*Darcy DiCosmo, Principal, Cerritos Elementary, Phoenix, Arizona*

One of the simplest ways teachers integrate a habit into an existing lesson is through literature. Most books found on a classroom or library shelf offer examples of one or more of the habits. Some teachers, for example, use *Alexander and the Terrible, Horrible, No Good, Very Bad Day* to teach about Habit 1: Be Proactive. The class reads the book together and then students create skits to show how Alexander might handle the various "no good very bad" situations he encounters. First they act out possible reactive responses, and then possible proactive responses. Students learn how their choices in life determine their moods, attitudes, and actions. Other teachers utilize *The Little Red Hen* to illustrate Habit 4: Think Win-Win and to discuss how everyone wins when everyone helps. Many teachers are surprised at how often the habits appear in children's literature, and how often students are first to make the connections.

Some of the best lessons combine literature with writing assignments. At PSKD Mandiri in Jakarta, Indonesia, teachers assign books that involve young people who face tough life decisions. Students then write persuasive letters to the book's characters, giving them advice on how to resolve various situations they come up against by using one or more of the habits. When completed, students brainstorm ways they too can apply the habits to situations they encounter in life.

Another example of integrating the habits into existing literature and writing assignments comes from Sheila Aaldijk's fifth-grade class at Bessie Nichols Elementary in Edmonton, Alberta. Her class was assigned to lead a 7 Habits activity during a school assembly. Rather than viewing it as "one more thing," the class used the assignment to meet provincial poetry and history requirements. For history, the class was studying the life of Terry Fox, an athlete and national hero who ran across Canada to raise money

> A nation becomes what its young people read in their youth. Its ideals are fashioned then, its goals strongly determined.
> —*James A. Michener*

for cancer research while battling cancer himself. As part of their research, students sought out ways Terry Fox exhibited the 7 Habits. They then pooled their findings into a seven-stanza poem, and took turns reciting lines from the poem during the assembly. The assignment was fulfilled, and so were two provincial requirements—all while learning about how the habits can be applied to life.

During science, Mrs. Johnson at English Estates Elementary in Florida talks about Habit 4: Think Win-Win. She discusses the earth's environment and the scarcity of natural resources, and asks students what will happen if people think only of their wants being met. Students identify Win-Lose or Lose-Lose approaches to dealing with environmental issues and discuss the consequences of those approaches. Students then brainstorm Win-Win approaches. Similarly,

Ed Kelley at A.B. Combs uses a family connection to Albert Einstein to talk with his students about how scientist Albert Einstein applied the habits.

Math lessons encourage students to synergize as they solve word problems. Technology lessons involve students in designing projects that require students to "begin with the end in mind." History lessons are piled high with opportunities to discuss how historical leaders might have changed history by seeking first to understand or putting first things first.

Jacquie Isadore, Martha Bassett, and Debbie Powell of A.B. Combs deserve credit for pioneering ways to integrate leadership principles into music, art, and physical education lessons. Every year, Jacquie turns an average music class into a motivational experience. "Music teachers teach students to sing, play instruments, and appreciate music. It's what they do," she says. "So why not choose music that is inspiring, uplifting, and reinforces positive traits?" It brings a note of hope into every student's day.

Before retiring, Martha Bassett did the same with her art classes. Nearly every art project she assigned had a leadership connection. A favorite was for fifth graders to design a cover for *Time* magazine that included a self-portrait and a headline indicating something they might do in life that could someday land them on the cover of the magazine. So while learning art, students think of possible future goals and the type of person they want to become. By the end of each year, the school's hallways were literally filled with art—each piece having a leadership principle behind it. More important, Mrs. Bassett took time to get to know students' thoughts and the stories that went into each work of art. She was more into students' dreams and feelings than she was colors and shapes.

Meanwhile, Debbie Powell has physical education students "sharpening the saw," and setting and tracking goals for improving their eating habits and exercise routines. And all sports-minded students know that they cannot compete on school sports teams if they fail to exhibit 7 Habits during class. She reaches their hearts through more ways than aerobic exercise.

Each of these specialists knows how pivotal the specialist role is. Every student at the school passes through her influence on a weekly basis. They bring the habits to life and make them fun.

The more the 7 Habits are applied to authentic situations in a variety of subject areas, the more students experience how to apply the habits to real life circumstances. It can occur at any time or anywhere—during class lessons, assemblies, morning announcements, parent nights, and so forth. This is one of the main reasons why teachers say, "This is not one more thing. It is a better way of doing what we are already doing."

Art assignments are a colorful way for students to begin thinking about the future.

Direct Lessons

While the integrated approach is the most common way to teach and reinforce the habits, direct lessons—where the habits are taught as stand-alone lessons—also have their place. In fact, schools that implement *The Leader in Me* best are those that set aside consistent, ongoing times for brief but direct lessons.

Direct instruction is particularly needed when starting a new year. Many *Leader in Me* schools adhere to Harry Wong's approach of dedicating the first week to ten days of school to developing the culture and ground rules. They use a portion of that time to overview all 7 Habits. For first-year schools, this means starting from scratch. For schools in the second year or beyond, it means reviewing the habits. Eva McDorman, for example, a first-grade teacher, builds her first week of school around a Leadership Camp. Students participate in hands-on activities that teach the habits and what it means to be a leader. They create a class mission statement and work together to identify behavior expectations for the year. Students love going to camp and emerge understanding the basics of each habit. Other teachers prefer introducing one habit a week.

Many elementary teachers use *The 7 Habits of Happy Kids* book to get started. It covers a habit per chapter and contains fun-filled character illustrations that capture students' imaginations and enable them to acquire the language of the habits quickly. Numerous direct lesson plans and colorful resources are also available in *The Leader in Me* Student Journals and on *TheLeaderinMeOnline* website.

Direct lessons are a good way to deal with specific challenges a class might be encountering, such as bullying, or listening to the teacher without interrupting, or getting homework in on time. Fifth-grade teacher Brian Wenzell uses an interactive lesson on synergy to illustrate how working together to keep the classroom clean makes things easier and more enjoyable for everyone. The 7 Habits seem to always be at their best when they have a problem to solve.

As noted, opportunities for direct lessons can pop up at any random time, but most schools and teachers find it more practical to schedule consistent times for direct lessons. Beaumont Elementary in Waterford, Michigan, has lessons built into the start of every day. They call it LEAD time. Principal Jan McCartan explains:

> Every teacher sets aside the first 10–15 minutes to teach a LEAD Lesson. The lessons are the same for everyone for the first week of school. We then have an outline that takes us to the middle of the school year. From there, teachers decide what habits their class needs to work on most. The lessons can be anything they want—a book, song, discussion around a quote, an activity from *The Leader in Me* Student Journals, etc. LEAD time is primarily run by teachers with the exception of 5th grade, where students plan and lead their class LEAD time lessons and at our weekly Community Circle, where our student Lighthouse Team leads out.

It's encouraging that in response to the new reality, more and more countries are requiring schools to teach direct lessons around life skills. They have listened to parents, business leaders, and fellow educators and responded. Singapore, which is perennially a leading country in terms of education, requires that life skills and basic values be taught for a minimum of one hour each week. Chua Chu Kang and Horizon Primary schools have chosen to use that hour to teach the 7 Habits each week. First thing Monday, every class spends the first half hour learning a 7 Habits concept. Then, in the middle of the week, students attend a 7 Habits class taught by designated 7 Habits specialty teachers. The habits are then integrated ubiquitously throughout the remainder of the week.

In presenting direct lessons, teachers use all types of instructional strategies to make the learning fun and to address different learning styles. They use stories, games, toys, movies, drama, poetry, contests, writing assignments, art, dance, sports, etc. to make the lessons impactful. Class-created musical raps are a popular method of teaching the habits. Adjusting words to familiar songs is also a common technique. Try singing, or whistling, these Habit 1 lyrics written by teacher Paula Everett, to the tune of "Twinkle, Twinkle, Little Star":

Be Proactive Every Day,
Be Proactive, Stop and Think.
Even though it's hard to do,
I think you should try it too.
Be Proactive Every Day,
Be Proactive, Stop and Think.

At Chua Chu Kang Primary School, students worked together to write a play based on *Snow White and the Seven Dwarfs*. Each dwarf represented a habit and did his "hi-ho-hi-ho" best to help Snow White get her life organized. Fifth-grade teacher Rick Weber at A.B. Combs is a master at using clips from child-friendly videos to teach the habits. Students at English Estates in Fern Park, Florida, created a Trail Mix recipe where each of seven ingredients represents a habit. Examples go on and on. The point is that teachers use all "six" senses and a wide variety of instructional styles to teach the habits in ways that reach a variety of learning styles. There is no end to their innovation. And notice how several of the examples involved students coming up with ideas.

As with anything, there are cautions in teaching the habits. One is to not overdo it. Students have five or more years to learn the habits; they do not need to be taught everything at once, or even every day. Two, the habits should not be used as sticks to beat down children. If all they hear is "Why were you not proactive!?!" or "You need to put first things first!" or "You need to seek first to understand me," chances are students will steer away from, not toward, the habits.

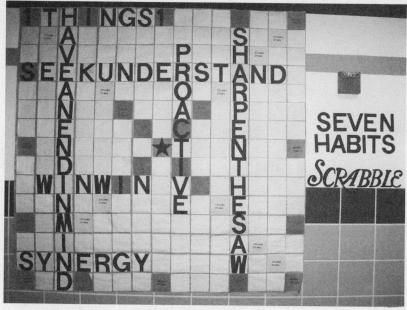

Creative teachers make a game of teaching leadership principles.

Modeling: Working from the Inside Out

The well-documented book *Teaching Practices from America's Best Urban Schools* shares accounts of urban schools that have defied the odds and performed well academically, and identifies the success factors that distinguish top-performing urban schools from mediocre-performing urban schools. What does it identify as the top factor? It is not the students and it is not the home environment. Rather it is the actions and practices of the adults in the school.

While integrated instruction and direct lessons are important ways to teach leadership skills, the highest order of teaching is always modeling. Not just talking the talk, but walking the walk. Students learn more from what staff members *do* than from what they *say*. It is the old adage, "What you do speaks so loudly I cannot hear a word you say." That is why after a group of local business leaders visited her school, fifth-grade Jocelyn turned to her principal and said,

"Not one of them shook my hand correctly. They didn't look me in the eyes."

This is why the first step in *The Leader in Me* process is to get all adults in a school trained in the 7 Habits. It is an inside-out approach. It starts inside with adults applying the habits, then works outside to students. As adults exemplify the habits and other leadership skills, their lives become the best lesson plans for teaching students.

As adults model the habits, they also reap personal benefits. A district administrator shared, "The leadership skills contained in *The Leader in Me* were exactly what our students needed. We have rising problems with gangs and increasing problems at home, and students need these skills to handle such situations." Then, without taking a breath, she said, "But the fact is that the 7 Habits were exactly what our staff needed. They have given them new ways of dealing with students and parents, and with each other." She then concluded, "The habits have helped me personally. This has been as timely for me as it has the staff and students."

> The nature of the relationships among the adults who inhabit a school has more to do with its quality and character and the accomplishments of its pupils than any other factor.
>
> —*Roland S. Barth*

When a first-year teacher in Iowa was asked what the habits had done for her school, she instantly replied. "They have helped me to become less reactive to students, to be more organized with my class time, and to listen more effectively to parents. Today, I responded calmly, proactively, and empathically to a situation involving a student that before I learned the habits I would have blown up over." Notice how each of the improvements to the school were actually improvements to her own effectiveness. Similarly, following a 7 Habits training in New York, a veteran teacher stood and thanked the district administrator: "I've been teaching for thirty years and this is the first time any professional development has been about me. It's already changed my life. Thank you. Thank you."

As adults learn and benefit from applying the habits, students benefit from seeing the habits modeled. Perfection is not required, but trying is.

Nonclassroom Teachers

With *The Leader in Me* there are no "non-teaching" staff members. Everyone is a teacher, particularly when it comes to modeling the habits.

The reality is that at A.B. Combs it begins with Susan and Mimi. At Crestview Middle School it starts with Kim, Julie, and Kathleen. Who are these individuals? They are the front office staff. They are the first points of contact. The language they use and the quotes and art they mount on office walls help everyone to learn and be reminded of the habits.

At Ruhkala Elementary near Sacramento, California, front office assistants Joyce and Shelley put together a colorful binder that describes one habit per page. When a student is sent to the office to speak with the principal for disciplinary issues, they have the student study the binder and think about how they might have used one or more of the habits to handle their particular situation differently. By the time the student sees Principal Melody Thorson, he or she already has ideas of how to better handle the situation.

In some schools, it is the school counselors who teach regular direct lessons. They go from class to class on a monthly basis teaching and connecting the habits to topics such as bullying, anxiety, stress, conflict management, dealing with loss, and so forth. The counselor can use the same language to counsel students across all grade levels or in working with parents. Counselor Dayle Gray at South Whidbey Elementary in Washington State ensures that lessons are taught in assemblies, and says that in counseling sessions she frequently asks students what habit they think will help solve their particular challenge, and that "most often they are spot on."

Librarians are another tremendous resource. Some librarians read stories to students with 7 Habits themes. Others find books with strong leadership connections and place them in reserved locations for teachers and students to access. One media specialist made colorful bookmarks to go with each habit to help students learn the habits.

The point is, teaching the habits is not a responsibility limited to classroom teachers only. It is a schoolwide effort. All staff can contribute to teaching the habits, if only by modeling and using the language. Parents too are great resources to guide once-a-week lessons, lead 7 Habits activities, or help students write a script for a fun 7 Habits play. It is a collaborative effort.

Student "Teachers"

To this point, the chapter has approached teaching leadership skills to students from the viewpoint of seeing students as "glasses that are half empty." In other words, the adults have knowledge and wisdom that the students do not have and must therefore fill the students' glasses with more knowledge.

Front offices are great places to reinforce the habits.

As the Pout-Pout Fish learned, part of being proactive
is choosing your moods and attitudes.

But what would happen if adults were to approach teaching leadership skills to students from the viewpoint of seeing students as "glasses that are half full"? In other words, what are some ways students can be utilized to teach the 7 Habits or other leadership skills to peers or younger students? Might they learn more if given that chance?

John C. Fremont Elementary in Taylorsville, Utah, led by Dr. Paul McCarty, utilizes students as teachers during what they call "Leader-Go-Rounds." Once per month, students from older and younger classes are matched, and the older students read a short book and do a related activity with the younger students. One time, they used the book *The Pout-Pout Fish* to highlight Habit 1: Be Proactive, specifically the concept of "Choosing Your Weather." The Pout-Pout Fish spreads frowns wherever he goes, claiming he cannot do anything about his gloomy nature. Yet by listening to the older students, the younger students learn that they, like the fish, can actually choose their moods and attitudes. The opportunity benefits older and younger students alike.

Similarly, Cunningham Elementary in Waterloo, Iowa, holds what they call "Family Time" once a week. One older class and one younger class are matched to form a family for about twenty minutes, and the time is spent discussing a 7 Habits concept. One "family," for example, projected a quote on the wall that talked about synergy and unity. During the discussion, a popular girl stood up without any prompting and addressed a behavioral problem she had observed repeatedly. She kept saying to the other students, "We can stop this ourselves. We don't need adults to stop it for us." It was a pep rally for change like no adult could have led, and the younger students—particularly the boys—listened intently. Sometimes students can say things in ways adults cannot.

Students can also help in teaching the habits to teachers. Shortly after attending the 7 Habits training, Trish Stehlin, third-grade teacher at Stanton Elementary in Fenton, Missouri, was hit by a car while jogging. When she returned to school after months of intensive physical therapy she wondered if she would be able to cope with the rigors of the job, both physically and emotionally. When she arrived for her first day back, she found her students had taped "Be Proactive" notes for her on a mirror. They used the language of the habits to encourage her to overcome her challenges. She said the students reminding her daily of the habits gave her the vision and energy to make her full return a reality.

Using students to research and teach the habits is more than a fun idea. Think about it. Who learns the most from any lesson, the teacher or the learner? It is the teacher. We call it "Teach to Learn." And the more mature students become, the more ready they are to teach, both the concepts and the applications. It empowers them to learn in ways that maximize their learning retention, transfer of learning, and self-confidence.

For All Students

Before concluding the chapter, we reiterate that the teaching of the 7 Habits and other leadership skills is intended to benefit all students. In fact, some of the most inspiring stories of what the habits can do for a child involve students with autism or other special needs. The common language and the concrete, directive nature of the habits provide a stable environment in which many of these students perform better.

One example is shared in an email from a parent, Frances Gardner, sent to Principal Julie Nolan of Scioto Ridge Elementary School (SRES) in Ohio. Mrs. Gardner has two daughters and a son at the school. For the two daughters, school and social skills come easy, but not for second grader Evan, who was diagnosed on the autism spectrum. As Mrs. Gardner relates:

> Prior to this year, Evan had only one birthday party with friends. He didn't like to have parties and had rarely been invited to them. When friends came to play, it was because I set it up, and I would end up playing with the friend more than Evan. I asked him a few years ago who his best friend was and he said it was me.
>
> When *The Leader in Me* was introduced, I saw how it might help Evan to be more focused educationally, and it has. What I didn't foresee was how much it would help him outside of school. His social life has blossomed. Evan has asked to have friends over to play this year, and recently asked to have a birthday party with friends from school. So I sprang into Mom-mode, and we decided to have it at Buckeye Bounce, where he and his friends could eat and jump on equipment.
>
> Evan and his dad drove around to hand-deliver invitations. At each home, Evan went to the door and talked with the friend or parent. When friends called to RSVP, he talked with them about the party and what presents he might like. Those may sound like everyday activities for many children, but for Evan, it was huge!
>
> I was nervous the day of the party. I wanted it all to go well for Evan.

He, on the other hand, was completely calm. We arrived early to set up the party room. He got the special jumping shoes on and off he went to play. I stayed by the door to greet his guests, and was totally stunned when his friends arrived to see Evan come out of the play area to greet each one. He shook their hands and thanked them for coming. He took them to get their jumping shoes and explained the rules. They jumped and played for the next hour so nicely.

That day I looked at Evan as a typical second-grade boy having a blast with his buddies on his birthday. At the end of the party, he hugged his friends and thanked them for coming. When we wrote out thank-you notes, it was more important to Evan to include thanks for coming to the party than to thank them for the gift they brought.

Is there a chance this may have happened without the 7 Habits? Yes, but I don't think so. *The Leader in Me* has given my son an opening to be himself with all of his little quirks and still be a part of the group. He is much more comfortable being himself socially. It has lit his fire.

I thought recently about asking Evan who his best friend is now, but I am afraid he will say a name that isn't Mom. To be honest, though, that news would make my day!

Again, the 7 Habits and *The Leader in Me* are intended for all students.

In Summary

The ultimate end in mind for teaching the habits is to prepare students for dealing with life. It is to help students become self-reliant (independent) and to work well with others (interdependent). It is to help students thrive as students, as parents, as members of the forthcoming workforce, and as community citizens. And the habits are not just for use in their distant futures; they are for their todays. The habits encompass many of the very same skills and traits that parents and business leaders are calling for to be taught.

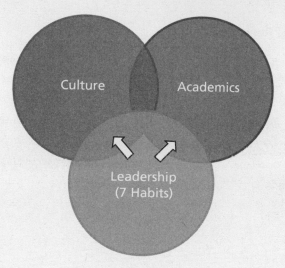

As students and staff apply the habits, indirect benefits also arise to the school's culture and to student achievement. When the principal of a tough urban turnaround school was asked if she had noticed any difference to her school after two months of teaching the 7 Habits, her very first response was "The way teachers treat each other in the teachers' lounge is so much better." She then went on to point out changes in playground behavior. The following year the school met Adequate Yearly Progress (AYP) for the first time in years. So not only were the habits developing valuable skills in students and staff, they were benefiting the culture and academics.

Teaching the habits is not a one-time event. It is not a one-time lesson; it is an ongoing journey of progression—starting from the inside out.

Personal Reflections

Habit 1: Be Proactive indicates that we are responsible for our actions and attitudes. In other words, we cannot always choose what happens to us in life, but we can choose our responses. If you could choose one thing that you would do differently in life to increase your effectiveness, what would it be? How might improving that one thing help you to be a more effective leader, or help you to improve your circumstances? How are you a role model?

4

Creating a Leadership Culture

The fact is that given the challenges we face, education
doesn't need to be reformed—it needs to be transformed.
The key to this transformation is not to standardize
education, but to personalize it, to build achievement on
discovering the individual talents of each child, to put
students in an environment where they want to learn and
where they can naturally discover their true passions.
—*Sir Ken Robinson,* The Element

Some people are surprised to learn there is an 8th Habit. It is called "Find Your Voice, and Inspire Others to Find Theirs." Olivia knows about it.

Olivia is a third-grade student at Winchester Elementary in West Seneca, New York. She is a bright, beautiful girl with above-average academic scores. She is also a selective mute.

Olivia speaks freely at home, but from the onset of kindergarten has chosen not to say a word to anyone at school beyond a once-a-year whisper to a teacher or friend. The exception has been in her younger brother's class, where she will read books to him and his friends.

So imagine the surprise on the face of Olivia's teacher, Mrs. Talty, when Olivia volunteered to speak at the school's Leadership Day. Mrs. Talty knew that it meant being in front of two hundred adults, and feared that if Olivia was given the opportunity and it went askew, it could have lasting effects. Yet she also did not want to miss the opportunity to have Olivia participate. So she again asked, "Olivia, are you sure?" Olivia responded with an affirmative nod that was less than convincing.

Mrs. Talty shared Olivia's willingness with Principal Kathy Brachmann. She too was both thrilled and surprised by Olivia's desire to participate in Leadership Day, and shared the concern about placing Olivia in a potentially detrimental situation. So she insisted that Olivia first be given a trial situation. She tried to talk with Olivia about it four days in a row, yet Olivia held her silence. Finally, on day five, a Friday, Mrs. Brachmann said, "Olivia, I know you want to speak at Leadership Day. If you will do the morning announcements on Monday and recite the Pledge of Allegiance over the speaker system, you can speak at Leadership Day. Will you do that?" Again, the best Olivia would offer in reply was a tentative nod.

On Monday, Mrs. Brachmann arrived at school following a district meeting to find her staff smiling through tears. They told how Olivia had arrived on time, had confidently taken the microphone, and in the sweetest voice said: "Good morning, I'm Olivia," and recited the pledge without any hesitation. The entire school roared with joy.

Eight students were selected to be Leadership Day speakers. Each was to describe one habit and how they applied it. At their first meeting, Mrs. Brachmann asked if anyone had a favorite habit they wanted to speak about. Up went Olivia's hand. When asked to identify her habit, out trickled a soft reply: "Habit 8: Find Your Voice." The choice caught Mrs. Brachmann off guard. Not only because of the irony of the habit Olivia had chosen, but because they had not really said much about the 8th Habit at school.

Olivia went to work. She researched the 8th Habit, and with a little help drafted an outline. When Leadership Day arrived, on cue she rose to the front of the auditorium and stood before the vast audience of adults. Gazing out at all the eyes fixed on her, she hesitated just long enough to put Mrs. Brachmann and Mrs. Talty on edge. "Come on, Olivia. We know you can do it!"

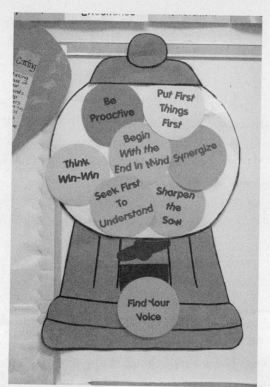

Some people are surprised to learn there is an 8th Habit.

Then, very calmly, and as if the entire day had been made just for her, Olivia began to speak:

Hi, my name is Olivia from Mrs. Talty's third-grade class. Habit 8 is Find Your Voice, then Help Others to Find Theirs. The essence of this habit is that you can say that you are one hundred percent involved in what you are doing with your life. By one hundred percent involvement I mean that your body, mind, heart, and spirit are all engaged in the adventure of your life.

To find your voice, you need to examine your natural talent. Everyone is good at something! Don't let anyone convince you otherwise. You can inspire others to do great things.

I practice this habit by reading books to my brother's kindergarten class. I also shared with his class the science unit we were doing on the life cycle of butterflies. I showed them all of our caterpillars. By doing this I shared my knowledge.

I am on to doing GREAT things. Thank you.

Most of the audience was unaware of Olivia's situation, yet her countenance let them know something special had just happened. Those who did know of Olivia's condition did all they could to restrain their emotions. Olivia's mother wept openly. She was so pleased that Olivia was in a learning environment where she was loved, respected, and given a chance to contribute—a place where she could find her voice.

Habits and Habitats

Whereas the previous chapter focused on teaching highly effective *habits,* this chapter focuses on creating a highly effective *habitat.* If students are taught effective habits but are then placed into a "defective" habitat (culture), one that is unfriendly, unsafe, or where they do not feel valued, they cannot be expected to fully develop their newly learned habits, or improve their academics. It is like taking a world-class seed, planting it in toxic soil, and expecting it to blossom to its full potential. It will not happen.

In contrast, miracles can happen when students are placed in a highly effective habitat, as occurred with one fifth-grade girl who was new to a school. She was sweet and generous as a little girl, but became angry and disrespectful as she got older. She sometimes got into fights. But then she moved in with her grandma and changed schools. In her own words:

My first day at school was not an easy one as I brought my old school side with me. Everyone was nice to me, telling me I was their friend. I was not used to that. I quickly learned that you don't "hit it out, you talk it out." I learned the 7 Habits from my teacher and class. I was

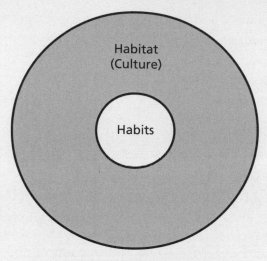

Habits and habitats are closely intertwined.

changed by the habits because I saw other people living the habits and I wanted to be like them, a leader.

I started using the 7 Habits by talking things out and knowing who I really was. I have a personal mission statement that I made and have it hung on my locker.

I am thankful for people in this school who have been here for me ever since I came to this school. They helped me see the leader that I am.

The same type of impact holds true for adults. Adults placed in highly effective habitats perform at higher levels than adults placed in highly "defective" habitats.

So there exists a reciprocal relationship between habits and habitats. Positive habits produce better habitats, and positive habitats produce better habits. The question therefore is: How does a school best go about creating a positive habitat, or culture?

Many schools take a reactive approach to improving their culture. They simply let it evolve or leap from crisis to crisis. When a problem like bullying arises, they form an action team, put out the fire (at least temporarily), and then dissolve the action team until the next crisis flares. In contrast, *The Leader in Me* is a very proactive, culture-by-design approach, as opposed to a culture-by-chance approach. It focuses primarily on three closely related areas:

1. The School Environment
2. Shared Leadership
3. Leadership Events

How Effective Is Your School Culture?

Highly ineffective people create highly ineffective school cultures, whereas highly effective people create highly effective school cultures. What kind of culture do you observe in schools?

Habit	Highly Ineffective Culture	Highly Effective Culture
1	**Be Reactive.** People make excuses, blame failures on others or policies, are moody, and focus outside their sphere of influence. They wait to be told what to do.	**Be Proactive.** People exert initiative, accept responsibility for actions, control their emotions, and focus on things they can influence. They make things happen.
2	**Have No End in Mind.** People lack vision and purpose. There are no common goals. Plans are constantly changing.	**Begin with the End in Mind.** People are in the pursuit of meaningful purposes with clear schoolwide goals and strategies. They have clear personal goals.
3	**Respond to Every Urgency.** People are constantly responding to crises. They have no time for planning or developing people. They lack discipline.	**Put First Things First.** People are focused on important priorities. They say *no* to frivolous requests. They make time for planning, preparation, and prevention.
4	**Think Win-Lose.** People go for win-lose or lose-lose. Trust is low. People battle over resources and do not share best practices due to worries that others might get ahead of them or be viewed as better.	**Think Win-Win.** People think win-win, are trustworthy. They balance courage with consideration, and look for ways to benefit the whole. Collaboration and sharing best practices is encouraged.
5	**Seek to be Understood.** People neither listen to others nor feel understood. They ignore others' feelings, and fear sharing their own feelings and opinions.	**Seek First to Understand.** People diagnose before they prescribe solutions. They are empathic, nonjudgmental, and feel free to express opinions freely.

6	**Work in Isolation.** People work by themselves or in cliques. They think their ideas are always best. They avoid people who think differently from them.	**Synergize.** People seek out others' ideas and value diversity. They are humble. There is high teamwork and creativity. People feel free to think outside the box.
7	**Stay Dull and Stagnant.** People's skills are outdated. They live unbalanced lives, neglect relationships, and often don't even know each other. They lack meaning.	**Sharpen the Saw.** People strive for continuous improvement. They are up-to-date, energetic, and enjoy a family feeling. They keep their spirits high.

The School Environment

A school's environment can be described by what is *seen,* what is *heard,* and what is *felt.*

What Is Seen—The Physical Environment

Other than a few portable trailers being added, the physical building at A.B. Combs has not changed much over the years. Yet step inside and there is an entirely new experience awaiting students. Entering the front doors, students immediately see a colorful tile mural depicting the school's vision statement. Former fifth-grade students created it as a legacy gift with the help of a parent. The main office to the left is so bright and inviting that it makes students want to be sent to the office.

Beyond the office is an intersection. To the left is a hallway with data charts displaying academic progress. In the hallway to the right are pieces of student art and a wall mural highlighting photos of leaders from around the world who have visited the school. Prominent for all to see is a sign that reads, "We honor the greatness in you." It is meant for students and adults alike.

From that point stretches a web of more hallways. Each is labeled with a street sign named after one of the habits or another leader-

What student wouldn't want to be sent to this office!

ship concept. The kindergarten hallway is filled with bulletin boards connecting various leadership concepts with academic topics. Each grade level has such bulletin boards. They change regularly, making it a living environment. A person could spend hours reading the student-created stories and insights posted on the boards.

Above the media center entrance are large block letters spelling out LEADERSHIP. A parent made that display. On various walls are quotations like "Leadership is doing the right thing even when no one is looking." On one wall hang photos of students involved in fun school traditions. It is a memory lane. Another wall displays photos of community and national leaders—astronauts, dancers, artists, etc.—who have spoken with the students about what it means to be a leader. In the cafeteria is a floor-to-ceiling painting illustrating the 7 Habits. Down a nearby hallway is a row of tall flags that celebrate the diverse nationalities of students. Across from the flags are personal commitments that each staff member has made for that year. High in the gym are motivational quotes related to athletics. Outside classrooms hang class mission statements. Some displays change frequently; others have been around for years.

Inside classrooms, the walls speak "Welcome." Many of the walls are covered with science, math, vocabulary, and history displays, similar to what is found in most any school. Yet scattered among them are friendly reminders of the 7 Habits, class goals, codes of cooperation, student leadership charts, and projects that students are currently synergizing on.

And so it goes. The entire building sends messages that say, "This is a place where expectations are high and where learning can be fun." Every piece of art, every data chart, and every photo reinforces that "everyone has talents and everyone can contribute to the success of the school." The goal is for the physical environment to communicate students' worth and potential without anyone needing to say a word.

Similar physical environments are showing up in schools across the globe. Indeed, we have seen some pretty amazing displays that inspire students and staff in many languages. While some of the displays are very professional and created by adults, the favorites tend to be those designed by students. In fact, in some locations, like Blessed Sacrament, a K–8 Catholic school in Quincy, Illinois, the walls start the year looking surprisingly bare. Then, day by day, display by display, students take over and create the physical environment the way they like it. They own it.

Some schools load their walls and ceilings, playgrounds, floors, and bathrooms with all kinds of displays. Others try for a more simplistic look. It is up to the staff and students to choose how they want it. Many choose to have students create two or three nice permanent displays each year, and in five years, "Wow, what a school." It is better to go slow and involve students than to go too fast or to have teachers do all the art. The goal is to build the culture and the students, not an art museum.

A school cannot change its culture merely by changing its décor—

what is *seen*. That said, the importance of the physical environment should not be underestimated.

What Is Heard—A Common Language

When asked about the impact *The Leader in Me* has had on their school, the most common response from teachers is "It gives us a common language."

The 7 Habits become the common language of a school as a natural outcome of staff members integrating the habits into lessons, using the language in meetings, activities, hallway displays, and assemblies. Students pick up the vocabulary of the habits as quickly as they do any other vocabulary. Once everyone knows the language, anyone can use it at any time. A first-grade teacher when encountering a misbehaving fifth-grade student they have never met can ask, "Are you putting first things first?" and that student knows exactly what is being directed.

> Treat a man as he is and he will remain as he is. Treat a man as he has the potential to become and you make him better than he is.
>
> —Goethe

School social workers and specialty teachers who work in multiple schools—some that teach the 7 Habits, some that do not—insist that it is far easier to work at schools that teach the 7 Habits, because they can use the common language with students at all grade levels, and regardless of what class they are in. They can even use the language with parents. "It simplifies things," they say.

The 7 Habits are not the only language of *The Leader in Me*. Other positive phrases are heard on a regular basis, such as "We dwell in possibilities here," "We focus on what students can do, not what they can't do," "Every child is important," "We tell students we love them every day." Or "It's amazing what these students can accomplish as leaders."

At A.B. Combs, a place and time when students hear a consistent stream of positive language is when they arrive at their classroom each day. Both their teacher and an assigned student greeter are there to meet them. They shake hands, look them in the eyes, say the student's name, and try to add something nice about how the student looks or something positive about the day. It is rare for a child to slip through a day without hearing his or her name in a positive way.

Being repeatedly referred to as leaders is by itself a powerful language for students (and adults) to hear and can have behavior-changing outcomes. A classic example involves a young man whose former principal contacted A.B. Combs to alert the staff regarding his nature. She revealed that the boy had recently knocked her unconscious, and warned that he would be a danger to the school. Many schools receiving such a student might react by putting the boy on some type of strict behavioral plan from day one. Muriel's recollection of how the staff chose to handle the situation instead suggests an alternative approach:

> We had just started this leadership theme and felt that if this process really did work then it would work for this young man. We never read his file, which in retrospect was probably not the wisest choice, but it was a choice from the heart to give this child a new chance.
>
> When he got off the bus there was no mistaking who the young man was. He walked with an attitude. I immediately went up to him and said, "You must be [name]." The guidance counselor was right beside me and added, "We're so happy you're here. I can tell you are going to be a leader." He responded, "Who the *!?*%# are you and get the *!?*%# out of my face." I said, "We don't use that kind of language here. We use a different kind of language. But we're happy you are here nonetheless."
>
> We began to build a relationship with him and could see that tough exterior slowly dwindle. We told him we loved him every single day. At first he would curse us. Other times he looked at us like we had two heads. Yet about a month later he began to tell us he loved us back.
>
> In November he ran for student body president. He did not win, though he became one of the more popular children in the school. He had a temper and had setbacks, but his life was forever changed. His grades went up and he made honor roll. He eventually moved and we

lost contact. But from that experience I knew the leadership theme could help all students.

Many educators are talented artists and can make beautiful bulletin boards and displays. They are *exterior decorators* and every school needs them. But the true artists—the true educators—are those who know how to inspire the beauty that is inside students. They are *interior designers*. Language is their primary tool. In a world where fear and despair shout loud and often, students deserve to hear positive affirmations and the language of hope on more than rare occasions.

What Is Felt—The Emotional Environment

Lee Ridge Elementary in Edmonton, Alberta, has been a *Leader in Me* school for four years and has seen numerous improvements. So it is interesting that when asked what the biggest difference was that *The Leader in Me* has made on the school, Principal Nigel Butterfield responded without hesitation, "It feels different."

In the teachers' lounge at A.B. Combs is a large quote that stretches across the width of the room. It reads: "In years to come, students may forget what you taught them, but they will always remember how you made them feel."

Indeed, when asked what impact *The Leader in Me* has had on their child, parents' first response typically regards how their child feels about school or how they feel about themselves. By far, their top comment is "It has really helped my child feel more self-confident." Many parents tell stories of how their child was struggling at one school and then moved to a *Leader in Me* school and ended up feeling more engaged and doing better socially and academically. They tell of shy children coming out of their shell.

Back at Olivia's school, another fascinating story regards a boy named Devon. The assistant district superintendent called Mrs. Brachmann and asked if she would consider taking in a student named Devon. Devon lived outside the school's boundaries, and would never physically attend due to extreme allergies. A robotic device that

Devon could control from home would allow him to view his class, and for his image to be viewed by classmates. He could even direct the robotic device to various parts of the school, and an audio system would enable him to ask and respond to questions. Not the typical new student.

Whereas other districts had turned Devon away, the Winchester staff saw it as an opportunity. "Of course, we'll take him," they said. In asking Mrs. Brachmann if the school would be willing to accept Devon, the assistant superintendent's observation was "Of all the schools in the district, I felt your school's culture and your students would be the most fitting environment for Devon." In other words, he was concerned how Devon would "feel," though he would never be on the campus.

A glimpse of what students feel in a leadership culture can be heard in a sampling of responses from students at Mukilteo Elementary in Washington State who were asked how the school has changed since starting *The Leader in Me*:

> In the high-trust classroom, the teacher is able to sense even the unexpressed needs of their students.
> —*Lonnie Moore,*
> The High-Trust Classroom

- I feel like I can do more at school.
- I've been more careful with people.
- I've started taking school more seriously now; I'm more honest now.
- I've been congratulating the other team if I lose in basketball.
- The 7 Habits help people be better listeners, make better choices, and get along.
- People remember to stop and think about how other people feel.
- Kids respect teachers and other kids more.
- Kids listen to each other more and play with each other, more, too.
- Kids at our school make plans before they put them into action.
- Everybody works together and synergizes even when no one's around to give them praise for it. They just know it's the right thing to do.

Many factors affect how students (or adults) feel at school. Recalling the four basic needs described in Chapter 2, students want to feel:

- Safe. None want to feel bullied or threatened. *(Physical Need)*
- Accepted, understood, and trusted. Mistrust breeds uncertainty, doubt, and inaction. Trust breeds stability, hope, commitment, and friendships. *(Emotional Need)*
- Vision, growth, and achievement. Students want to feel they are progressing, successful. *(Mental Need)*
- Meaning, contribution, and appreciated. William James, the father of American psychology, declared, "The deepest principle in human nature is the craving to be appreciated." *(Spiritual Need)*

Students lacking in one or more of the four needs feel insecure. Students feeling whole feel self-confidence. For some students, each of these needs is met often and easily. For others they come seldom. Students don't need to just hear about these things; they need to feel them.

Shared Leadership

An important part of what students see, hear, and feel every day is everyone being leaders. That includes all adults and all students.

The best way for students to learn to be leaders is by seeing all adults modeling leadership—not just the principal—everyone. When visitors to one *Leader in Me* school were taken on a school tour, at three different locations the name of Mr. Robert was mentioned. "Students love him," they said. "He treats them with total respect." "He involves them in projects. They love helping him." The visitors assumed Mr. Robert was the assistant principal or a favorite teacher. They were surprised when they finally met him and he was cleaning floors. He was the custodian. Another custodian, Mr. Baggett, at Wayne Avenue Elementary in Dunn, North Carolina, meets the car pool each morning to welcome students. He calls them by name, says encouraging things to them, and tries to cheer them up. His efforts help students feel connected. These custodians demonstrate that leadership is a choice, not a position.

And so it is meant to be with everyone. Classroom teachers are leaders of their classroom. Learning specialists are learning leaders. Some teachers are also grade-level leaders, Professional Learning Community leaders, or action team leaders. These same roles exist at most schools, but are not always viewed as leadership roles. And indeed, this would all be nothing more than a play on semantics if each staff member were not genuinely respected as a leader and empowered as a leader.

Research Says . . .

A six-year study funded by the Wallace Foundation revealed positive outcomes of shared leadership and its impact on student learning and staff morale. Jointly carried out by the University of Minnesota and the University of Toronto, the research conclusions revealed:

- When leadership is shared among the principal, teachers, staff, students, and parents (collective leadership), it has a stronger influence on student achievement than when the principal is seen as sole leader.
- Principals do not lose influence as others gain influence.
- School leaders impact student achievement more by improving teachers' motivation and working conditions than they do by attempting to increase teachers' knowledge and skills.
- High-performing schools award greater decision-making influence to teacher teams, parents, and, in particular, students, than do low-performing schools.

Of specific note is the study's finding that at higher-performing schools the sharing of leadership with students is particularly present.

When it comes to sharing leadership with students, there are at least three ways that *The Leader in Me* strives to involve students as leaders:

1. By giving them leadership responsibilities
2. By valuing their opinions
3. By helping them find their voice

Giving Students Leadership Responsibility

Most schools give students leadership responsibilities, but limit it to a select few who have proven themselves or were elected by peers. But what about the remaining students, the other 98 percent? Will they ever be given a chance to be leaders?

At the classroom level, giving students leadership roles begins with teachers asking, "What can students do that I am currently doing?" A teacher in Northern California asked that question of her students and the next thing she knew, students had put themselves in charge of shutting down computers, closing blinds, putting chairs on desks, emptying trash bins, sharpening pencils, and doing other tasks that used to take her twenty to thirty minutes at the end of each day. Her students loved it. Five minutes before the closing bell, she merely gives the signal and students get busy. "Why didn't I ask sooner?" she says. The key is not so much the jobs the students are doing, but the fact that they are taking ownership for the orderliness and success of the classroom. They are guiding the process.

At Janson Elementary in Rosemead, California, each classroom has a designated student technology leader. If the teacher has a problem with some type of technology, that student either fixes the problem or goes to the school's adult technology advisor. The advisor then either teaches the student how to solve the problem, or goes with the student to the classroom and they solve the problem together. The student learns new knowledge, and feels the responsibility, while the teacher keeps on teaching.

Giving students responsibilities for organizing books, announcing lunch menus, collecting homework, passing out supplies, greeting guests, taking notes to the office, leading the national anthem, dispensing hand sanitizer, and so forth, might not sound like major "leadership roles," but it is a starting place. It gives students an opportunity to *feel* what it means to be responsible, as opposed to just talking about what it means to be responsible. It teaches them that being a leader means being a contributor, and sometimes doing what others will not do. It allows students to feel regular successes. They feel of worth, appreciated. Most take pride in their responsibilities. Some chronically absent students have even turned into perfect attenders because they feel needed at school and do not want to miss a day. One boy woke up to find his mother drunk and passed out on her bed. He got himself dressed and to the bus. Why? He said he didn't want to miss his leadership assignment.

As students mature, so do their leadership responsibilities. With time they may be teaching lessons, leading projects, mentoring younger students, answering phones, or choosing books for the class to read. Several schools challenge older students to organize service projects that benefit the school or community. With teachers or parents as "guides on the side," students identify, plan, and carry out all aspects of the projects.

> Empathy is the one skill that most bullies lack. It also happens to be the one skill that has the greatest single-handed chance of eliminating bullying.
> —*Gary McGuey*, The Mentor: Leadership Trumps Bullying

At the school level, many opportunities are also available for students to be leaders well beyond the typical student leadership team. Students can give school tours, raise the flag, lead assemblies, help in the library, run recycling efforts, lead recess activities, help in the cafeteria, do safety patrol, lead morning announcements, be greeters, join the cleaning crew, make presentations, teach lessons, lead clubs, and so forth. When given the chance, students will come up with many of the best ideas for leadership responsibilities.

Fulfilling leadership roles, even simple ones, can be behavior

Assigning peer mentors is one of the many ways
schools ensure that students feel connected.

changing, if not life changing for students. At École Edwards, a K-5
French immersion school in Airdrie, Alberta, students apply for
schoolwide leadership roles at the start of each year. More than half of
the school's students receive assignments. An autistic boy with a history of not being able to track time was assigned to help in the nurse's
office, where he did simple daily tidying routines. Could the staff have
done them? Yes. But the young man was so excited to fill his leadership role that he began watching the clock like a hawk and was never
late to his responsibility. He sees himself as a leader.

At a school in South Carolina, a young boy was a known bully
and a loner. A perceptive staff member noticed that at lunchtime
he tended to sit near a group of special needs students. She asked
if he would like to help out and be a mentor for some of those stu-

dents. Overnight he went from being a bully to being a protector. He watched over those students carefully. When asked to write a paragraph about how he was helping the special needs students, he responded with a one-liner: "When I am with them I don't feel lonely anymore."

Mentoring is one of the more popular leadership roles students take on. Older students mentor younger students in academic assignments or in proper behavior. In some cases, entire classes of upper-grade student leaders are assigned to mentor a younger class. The McLees Academy of Leadership in Anderson, South Carolina, uses older students to mediate minor problems between younger students. They call them *Leadiators.*

Just as young students need an occasional visit to the playground or sandbox to release their energy and develop their creativity, all students deserve an occasional trip to the "leadership sandbox," a place where they can express their talents and develop their leadership habits. That applies to all students, not just a core few.

Seeking and Valuing Student Opinions

Shortly after A.B. Combs adopted the leadership theme, Muriel began inviting one student leader from each class to attend a once-a-month, thirty-minute chat session. Prior to each meeting, the student leaders were to ask classmates what they thought was going well at the school and what needed improvement. Month after month Muriel was amazed. Not so much by the problems students identified, but by the quality of solutions and ideas they generated. In one case, the school had developed a Code of Cooperation, or what many schools call a "code of conduct." They called it MAGIC, which stood for:

<u>M</u> odel expected behavior

<u>A</u> ccept responsibility

<u>G</u> ive respect

<u>I</u> mprove through goals

<u>C</u> ooperate

A young student during one chat session stood up and said, "Ms. Summers, what we do around here is not MAGIC. It is hard work." He suggested that a new Code of Cooperation be created, and even offered a new acronym, LEAD, which stands for:

L oyalty
E xcellence
A chievement
D iscipline

Muriel loved the idea and could tell he had put good thought into his suggestion. The problem was that a few days earlier she had hung MAGIC signs throughout the school. To change them would be a hassle and an expense. Nevertheless, the signs were changed. The student's opinion was valued.

How far A.B. Combs is willing to go in seeking student opinions is evidenced by the fact that each new staff member gets interviewed by students before they are hired. And according to the staff, student interviewers have a reputation for asking the toughest questions. They have a knack for picking out teachers who like (or do not like) working with children, something that is often difficult for adults to detect. One teaching applicant was graded low by student interviewers because, as they exclaimed with disgust, "She didn't even know we were a 7 Habits school. She didn't do her homework."

A more positive outcome occurred when Muriel received an outstanding application to fill a teaching position. The applicant, Rachel Smith, was invited for an interview and that is when Muriel discovered she was a "little person," a dwarf. Muriel could tell she would be a marvelous teacher, yet wondered how the children would respond. As it turned out, after the students interviewed her, not one word was

> It used to be that the only time we went to the office was when we were sent to the office. Now, when we think something needs to be changed, we go to the principal's office with a suggestion.
> —*Student, Huddinge, Sweden*

Be Careful What You Ask

Educators may want to be careful with how far they go in asking student opinions. Giles Junior School in Hertfordshire, United Kingdom, asked students to identify what they expected from their teachers. Their list included:

- Use the 7 Habits, be proactive
- Find the gift in everyone
- Show respect for us and other members of staff
- Be kind and helpful
- Think win-win when we are having problems
- Smile and look happy to see us, say hello
- Do the right thing even though no one is looking
- Tell us when we are doing well and how we can do even better
- Be very organised and tidy and make our classroom neater
- Help us to be leaders in our classroom by giving us leadership roles
- At the end of the day let us know who is doing well with our habits

said about the candidate's stature. That pleased Muriel, but left her curious. Eventually she asked the student interviewers, "Did you have any reservations about her height?" With totally perplexed looks on their faces the students looked at Muriel and returned the question, "Ms. Summers, do you have a problem with her height?" Today, the new hire stands tall and is loved and looked up to by students and staff.

The spirit of why it is important to listen to students is captured in an incident at Heritage Elementary in Highland, Michigan. The school was only three months into implementation when nine principals and an assistant superintendent from the district arrived for a visit. Students led the tour. At the conclusion, the group gathered in the foyer to ask questions. The principal, Dr. Deirdre Brady, invited the students to do the responding. One visitor asked, "What is different in your school now that you are doing *The Leader in Me*?" A fifth grader stepped forward. Using his hands to motion, he said, "It used to be the principal was up here (raising his hand above his head), and the teachers were here (putting his hand chin high), and the students were down here (his hand now belly-button high). Now," he continued, "It's the principal, the teachers, and the students (sliding his hand horizontally at chin height) and we are all at the same level. We all work together." If students can go from thinking they are belly buttons to thinking they are chins in less than three months, now that is progress!

> The woods would be silent if no bird sang but the best.
> —*Henry David Thoreau*

Students have many valuable ideas for assemblies, service projects, improving classroom behavior, activities, and so forth. Why not seek their opinions?

Helping Students Find Their Voice

Sharing responsibilities is one level of student leadership. Utilizing students' opinions is an even higher level. Yet the highest level of giving students leadership opportunities involves helping them to find their "voice."

In Olivia's case, her teachers and principal literally helped her find her voice by persistently looking for ways for her to share her talents and be a leader. But Olivia is not alone. Winchester Elementary looks for ways to help all students find their voice. Remember Devon, the boy with the robotic device? He may not attend the school physically, but that does not keep Winchester's staff from finding ways to help him find his voice. Devon is assigned as a regular class greeter. Each morning he is at the classroom door with his face lit up onscreen welcoming students by name. He takes notes and attendance to the office. He calls out bus times. He is sensitive to people in need and is often the first to contribute to class service projects. And he does it all from home. This is because Winchester dwells on what students can do more than what they can't do.

The most fundamental assumption of *The Leader in Me* is that every child is important, every child has gifts. Some students may find their voice in art, in science, in technology, in sewing, in serving, in cooking, in coaching, in dance, in math, in inventing, in writing stories, in being kind, in listening, or in drama. One young student who had a series of discipline problems literally found her voice in singing. At first, her voice was a little rough, but after a few lessons and opportunities to be in front of audiences, she blossomed. It hoisted her confidence and greatly reduced her outbursts.

Others may not fully find their voice until high school, or university, or later in life—like after they become a teacher. More worrisome is that some may never find their voice because no one ever helped them to see it in themselves. Teacher Pam Almond poignantly captured the spirit of helping students find their voice when she said, "I see every child as having something special about them that nobody else has, and I might be the only person in their life that sees that gift in them, and it is my responsibility to show it to them."

Winchester Elementary helps all students find their voice.

Leadership Events

Any typical school or classroom event—assemblies, parent nights, field trips, dance festivals, concerts, class meetings, award ceremonies, plays, sports competitions, classroom meetings, and so forth—can be turned into a leadership event. The primary purposes for holding leadership events are to build a sense of community, to create vision, and to establish a culture of trust. Leadership events are also excellent opportunities to teach the 7 Habits, to give students opportunities to apply their leadership skills, and to celebrate successes, but those purposes are secondary.

Schoolwide assemblies are a common example of an existing event that can be turned into a leadership event. Typical agendas for school assemblies are 80 percent adults talking and 20 percent student participation. When turned into a leadership event, those percentages are reversed, if not entirely student led. In some cases, it may be a class or grade level that takes on the planning and delivery roles, with students from those classes in charge of planning, greeting, emcee duties, activities, etc. But the more significant key is that a portion, if not all, of the assembly is geared toward building a community feeling by reinforcing the mission statement, celebrating leadership accomplishments, or sharing what is happening with the upcoming service project. Fun activities can be carried out that involve students in interactive games that build camaraderie or teach teamwork skills. So it is not much different from a typical assembly. What is different is that when planning the agenda those doing the planning put on their leadership glasses and view the agenda from a leadership perspective. "How do we build community and trust?" The same can be done for any school event.

Some of the most productive leadership events happen in the classroom. Most classrooms have consistent times each week when they get together to talk things over or do something fun to celebrate a success. For example, some classrooms have regular class meetings, or "circle time," where they do sharing time, celebrate the star student of the week, go over rules, or work on an interesting project. *Leader in Me* schools simply look at those times through the lens of leadership and turn them into leadership events. Instead of the teacher doing all the leading, students take turns leading discussions, planning projects, practicing public speaking, or teaching the 7 Habits. The objective is to build a community, family feeling; to establish a common vision; and to build trust among class members.

A common practice in weekly class meetings is for students to reflect on what went well that week and what they can do to improve their class atmosphere the next week. Several teachers have even found it valuable to bookend leadership moments at the start and finish of each day as a way of talking about how things went that day, what goals they want to achieve that day, complimenting positive leadership behaviors that were spotted during the day, and so forth. Such moments are great opportunities for teachers to model and use the 7 Habits as a framework for problem solving.

A schoolwide leadership event that has become a favorite tradition at A.B. Combs is called Leadership Day. It began almost out of self-defense due to so many people asking to visit the school. Muriel and her team had the idea to set aside a day twice a year for visitors to observe the school in action. It was a way of consolidating visitors. Before long, 150 visitors were showing up to each event, with more being turned away due to space restrictions. But with time, the purpose of the day has turned from merely trying to consolidate visitors to truly giving students an opportunity to develop their leadership skills and celebrate their achievements. Students do most of the speaking parts, some dance, some sing, some have art displayed, some do skits, some do booths, some play musical instruments, some are guides, some are greeters, some serve food, and some share other talents. All are given the opportunity to participate. Students come away feeling excited and confident about themselves. Teachers likewise enjoy hosting guests in their classroom and showcasing their creative ideas. It gives everyone a chance to tell a part of their story. Students help with planning, invitations, thank-you notes—the whole works. This tradition has since spread to hundreds of other schools.

Students in Korea hold a class meeting.

A Leadership Paradigm

To this point, this chapter has highlighted three key components for creating a leadership culture: working on the school environment, engaging students in leadership roles, and optimizing leadership events. When coupled with individuals applying the 7 Habits, the three components have the potential to make a significant impact on a school's culture. Underlying the success of each of these components, however, is a need for people to work from a leadership paradigm first, a management paradigm second.

Leadership is about effectiveness, *doing the right things.* Management is about efficiency, *doing things right.* Leadership is about building relationships; management is about making schedules. Leadership is about innovating and thinking outside the box; management is about executing goals and meeting deadlines. Leadership is about inspiring people; management is about optimizing things. Leadership is about building complementary teams; management is about building complementary systems. Leadership is about teaching principles; management is about improving practices.

Leadership Days offer students the chance to share their talents and become comfortable presenting in front of adults.

Leadership	Management
Effectiveness: *Doing the right things.*	Efficiency: *Doing things right.*
Relationships	Schedules
Innovation	Goal execution
Inspiring people	Optimizing things
Building complementary teams	Building complementary systems
Teaching principles	Improving practices

Leadership and management are both important. Yet most organizations (including schools) tend to be overmanaged and under-led. Efficient management without effective leadership is like straightening the chairs on the deck of the *Titanic*. Everything may be tidy, but who is looking ahead? Who is watching out for dangers? Who is setting direction?

Educators as a whole are excellent managers. They must be efficient and organized just to keep all the records in order, plan out the various schedules, file all the lesson plans, make sure all the standards are met, and complete the multitudes of other daily tasks. It is a matter of survival.

Numerous educators are also stellar leaders. They inspire people. They establish a common vision and communicate meaningful goals. They optimize people's potential and get diverse groups of people to work together in collegial ways. They give their all for students and staff. They turn around schools. They lead by example and truly make a difference in the lives of students and staff. They are amazing leaders.

Yet in a spirit of being frank, it must be said that there are many schools where leadership is marked absent on a daily basis. Many educators are so overburdened by management tasks that they find no time to even think about leadership. Many have never been afforded leadership training. They were great teachers so everyone assumed they would automatically make great school administrators. And when they do get summoned to attend leadership training, they discover that in reality it is nothing more than management training: hiring policies, new laws, upcoming curriculums, and so forth. All this happens despite everyone knowing that sitting behind a certain office desk no more makes a person a great leader than sitting behind a certain classroom desk makes a child a great student.

As a result, many schools have developed strong management cultures. They are into efficiency, managing budgets, conducting assessments, filling out paperwork, attending meetings, sifting data, and so forth. Likewise, many classrooms have strong management cultures. They are focused on maintaining control, checking off standards, finishing before bells, collecting homework, tracking attendance, and identifying high and low achievers. Again, all that management is necessary and important, but what about the leadership?

If it is any consolation, the same lack of leadership resides in corporate and government sectors. It is also true of many homes where parents are trapped in management paradigms, thinking only of control and rules, with little thought of setting direction, finding purpose, building a family feeling, or being role models. Leadership is also lacking in many individual lives. People are so busy managing schedules, checking off tasks, and putting their noses to the grindstone that they seldom pause to clarify their values or spend time building their most meaningful relationships.

One area where the absence of "leadership" is most apparent is in dealing with student discipline in the classroom. It is even commonly referred to as "classroom management." How might it be handled differently if it instead was called "classroom leadership"? A partial answer to that question can be felt in the following example, shared by parents Gayle Gonzalez and Eric Johnson:

> When our daughter was in fourth grade, a new boy came to her classroom with significant anger issues. The way the teacher handled him was inspiring. The teacher visited honestly with the children one afternoon when the boy was not in class. She said, "The recent blowups in our classroom are not working for us to make a good learning environment."
>
> > When you make a mistake, a friend tells you how to fix it and they don't raise their voice. They do it with kindness. We synergize to fix it.
> > —*Josh, first grader*
>
> The children understood that much of the problem was this new student. On their own, they formed a support team. They said they could help this new boy even better than the teacher. The young man responded well and was making great academic progress for the first time in his life. When he moved away, students in the class cried. They had learned to love him.

The teacher could have "managed" the new boy, had him reprimanded, sent to the office, or disciplined in some other typical way. Instead her humility and foresight led her to take a leadership approach, not the least of which involved enlisting students' help.

When Justin Osterstrom was hired as a fourth-grade teacher at A.B. Combs, he learned firsthand the difference between a leadership versus a management approach to discipline:

A boy in my class had behavior issues. Poverty, low socio-economic status, and other such factors were hurting his school progress. Still he had so much good about him.

He ended up in the office for discipline issues one day. Instead of punishing him, Muriel truly took the time to understand him. She ended up giving him the responsibility to speak at Leadership Day and to tell visitors about the student data system. I remember thinking, "What is that going to do for him?"

Giving him that responsibility totally changed his maturity. He blossomed and started hanging out with peers that were good for him. His grades improved. The positive influence of the school culture on him was incredible. I learned what a moment of leadership can do for a child. I feel privileged that I got to see the shift. He makes me smile.

Whereas many teachers and administrators might have gone after the boy with a management mentality—"How do we control him?"— Muriel approached him from a leadership paradigm—"How can we help him see potential in himself so he will not feel a need to act out?" In other words, "How do we communicate to him his worth and potential more clearly so he will see in it himself?" In the words of Booker T. Washington, "Few things help an individual more than to place responsibility upon him and to let him know that you trust him."

The important thing to point out is that in each of the above situations, what changed first was the educator's paradigm of their role and the paradigm they had of the student. Instead of seeing themselves as a manager—a controller—they saw themselves as a leader— one who releases students' talents and energies. Sometimes we work so hard and long to change students, when in reality the more powerful, lasting step is to first change our paradigms. Lead people, manage things.

Olivia Is Not Alone

In summary, a school's culture deserves proactive attention and needs to be consistently nurtured. When left to chance, a school's culture can become management heavy, leadership light, and grow stifled almost overnight.

Taking intentional steps to create a leadership culture brings direct effects. Students and staff become more engaged. Parent involvement increases. The physical environment becomes a more vibrant, pleasant place to learn. Students' desire to be in school and on time increases. Students feel safer physically and emotionally. Trust goes up. These are some of the direct impacts that can come from proactively working on the culture.

Indirect effects also come from creating a highly effective leadership culture, not the least of which involve academics. A recent "Quality Counts" report from *Education Week* reveals that 74 percent of school-level administrators now recognize improving school culture as "very important" to improving student achievement. The report also indicates that administrators see that "students are important allies in improving schools." "Students want to feel respected," they said,

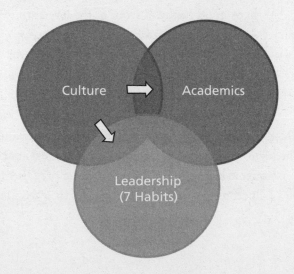

and fundamental to making students feel respected is finding ways to allow their "voices to be heard." All this bodes well for academics and for building students' self-confidence—both of which are aims of *The Leader in Me.*

All this takes us back to the conclusion of Dr. Martin Seligman cited in the opening chapter that "raising children . . . [is] far more than just fixing what [is] wrong with them. It [is] about identifying and amplifying their strengths and virtues, and helping them find the niche where they can live these positive traits to the fullest." And we add that the same holds true for staff members. Remember Mrs. Brachmann, Olivia and Devon's principal? Not long ago she was giving a presentation about *The Leader in Me* in front of a large group of educators an hour from her school. At one point she glanced over and saw her husband, Bud, who had come along to support her. Tears were trickling down his face. "Why the tears?" she thought.

Mrs. Brachmann was approaching her sixtieth birthday and Bud had known her since she was fifteen. Throughout her entire career she had been terribly mortified when presenting in front of adults. Whenever such a presentation would come up, she would obsess about it for weeks. It would affect her eating and sleeping patterns, and when the time to present finally arrived, her hands would tremble. Yet on that particular day, there stood Kathy in front of the large group of strangers speaking freely and passionately about *The Leader in Me.* She hardly had a note to follow and was entirely calm. She was confident, convincing, and enjoying every second. Bud had never seen her like that in forty years of marriage. He could hardly believe what he was seeing. His thrill came out in tears.

Mrs. Brachmann has since presented in front of several more adult groups. She loves to tell about her school and her great staff. She says, "By helping students learn the 7 Habits and by helping them find their voice, it has helped me to find my voice, and it is a wonderful place to be."

Personal Reflections

Habit 2: Begin with the End in Mind teaches that for every creation there is first a "mental creation," then a "physical creation." If you were to imagine a mental image of your ideal culture of a school, what would that culture look like, sound like, feel like? Are there things you do that can just as well be done by a student? What have you done recently to build a sense of community in your school, your home?

5

Achieving School Goals

Every enterprise requires commitment to common goals
and shared values. Without such commitment there is no
enterprise; only a mob.

—*Peter Drucker*

As an *indirect* result of teaching the 7 Habits and working on their culture, numerous schools have seen simultaneous bumps in academic scores. It is always a pleasant bonus. But there are additional leadership skills that at numerous schools have brought *direct* benefits to student achievement. They are part of a proven goal-setting process, one that can be seen in the story of Colby, as told by his teacher, Melissa Brinson, at Beaumont Elementary in Waterford, Michigan:

Colby entered the fourth grade feeling defeated as a reader. He had struggled with reading from the time he entered school, and had a consistent record of losing ground over the summer breaks. Fourth grade was no exception.

When Colby and I sat together at the beginning of the first marking period to set an academic goal, we looked over his reading pre-tests. We could see his patterns and decided that what was most holding him back was his word accuracy. He would notice the beginning blend, or *digraph,* and from there take a guess at a word. Poor guesses were at the root of his low scores.

We set Colby's goal to move up two reading levels by the end of the first marking period. Together we crafted an action plan for how that would happen. His action plan involved meeting with me each day and reading a few pages out of his "Just Right" independent reading books. If he read with four or less errors, he earned a star in his planner that his mom saw each night at home. His mom followed a similar process at home using books sent home from school. This helped keep open communication between myself and Colby's mom.

Tracking and seeing progress on the "Reading Graph" in his Leadership Notebook made Colby push himself. It truly empowered him. By the end of the first marking period he had already surpassed his goal. He was elated! He could see that not only had he reached his goal, but he had helped his entire class reach its goal of increasing the number of students reading at grade level. He loved contributing to the class goal.

With each success, Colby felt more and more confident. He caught fire. By the end of the second marking period, he was already at grade level, an accomplishment he had never before met so quickly. He is now in fifth grade and did not have any "backslide" during the summer, which was another first. I truly believe it resulted from tracking his data, seeing his success, believing in himself, and feeling part of a team. I am so proud of the way he has learned to take responsibility for his progress.

Seeing a student like Colby shift from being a "defeated" to an "elated" reader is any teacher's dream. The trajectory of his life will be forever changed as a result of being in Mrs. Brinson's classroom. And the great news is that Colby is merely one example. Several students—and Beaumont Elementary as a whole—have seen marked improvements to student achievement.

Aligning for Results

To fully appreciate Colby's and Beaumont's stories, it is helpful to reflect back on A.B. Combs and what it was like prior to implementing the leadership theme. Recall that Muriel described the school as a scattered mass of arrows pointed in as many directions as there are degrees on a compass. Several teachers had individual projects in motion, yet none of them was linked to any common school vision or goal. Everyone was doing their own thing. They lacked alignment.

> Far and away the biggest mistake [leaders] make is ignoring the crucial importance of alignment.
> —*Jim Collins and Jerry I. Porras, Built to Last*

As with wheels on a car or vertebrae in a person's back, any time a school lacks alignment there is pain—sometimes severe pain. It was not until *Leadership* was chosen as the new theme, and *Developing Leaders One Child at a Time* was targeted as its new mission statement, that the A.B. Combs staff truly began to be aligned as a team. It put them in a position to pursue meaningful goals, including improving academics.

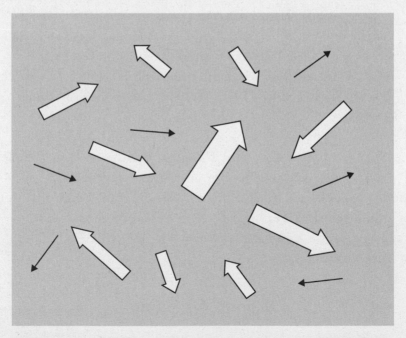

Prior to their new theme and mission statement, A.B. Combs resembled a bunch of arrows pointed in as many directions as there are degrees on a compass.

Beaumont Elementary went through a similar transformation. The year prior to implementing *The Leader in Me,* the culture at the school was toxic. Several teachers were embattled in contract negotiations. They wore matching shirts on Fridays as a sign of solidarity and paraded in front of parents at drop-off and pickup times in hopes of gaining their support. Not all teachers supported the tactics, however, and that brought an element of friction. And while some parents did sympathize with the protesting teachers, others were disturbed by their actions. So not only did the school resemble a bunch of arrows pointing in random directions, some of the arrows were rather sharp and directed at each other.

In the midst of the tensions, teacher Heather Nuckolls came across *The Leader in Me* book. In it she saw teachers engaged in the same types of methods and activities she wanted to be involved with as a teacher, including focusing on the whole child. She mentioned the book to Principal Jan McCartan, who happened to be near a bookstore that evening and grabbed a copy. It was at the start of a holiday, and before the break was over

> When people comment on the joy they feel when they are in this building, and the happiness that we feel, it is because we are a team with a common mission and a common vision.
>
> —*Martha Bassett, art teacher*

she had read it from cover to cover and felt it could help her school. But how could she get her staff to climb out of their current depths to turn things around?

Mrs. McCartan purchased additional copies of the book and circulated them to a handful of staff. She asked for honest opinions. The more the staff read and spoke among themselves the more they recognized how much they had in common. Everyone's highest interests were in helping students, yet they had let themselves get caught up in a quagmire of issues that had little to do with students.

To their credit, the staff had the humility to step back and look at the bigger picture. They agreed to disagree on the contract issues and to not let those differences thwart their desire to benefit students. Not all staffs have that kind of strength.

Before long, the entire staff was trained in the 7 Habits, walls were painted, motivational quotes were placed on walls, and a ribbon-cutting ceremony welcomed students back to a new year. Within days there was a whole new feeling. The staff decided to capture that feeling in the form of a new school mission statement. It read:

At Beaumont, we are a community of leaders. We recognize, honor and celebrate the leaders within us! We . . .

> Love learning
> Excel in all we do
> Achieve goals together
> Do what is right

The new mission statement brought clarity and direction. More important, the staff began to own it and to live it. It was more than a plaque on the wall. It focused them on key stakeholder needs, and gave them something compelling toward which to align their arrows. Soon similar mission statements began popping up for each classroom, each staff member, and each student—including Colby. Everyone was becoming clear about their highest priorities.

With the improved alignment came the fruits of their efforts. Staff camaraderie improved immensely the first year. Students picked up the language of the habits quickly and loved being given leadership responsibilities. The new, colorful environment brought a welcoming atmosphere. By the end of the year things were looking up, and students were made to feel even better when it was learned that their overall scores on state exams also improved.

Having established a clear *why*—a clear mission—and having re-established a culture of trust, where people were collaborating and getting along, Beaumont was now in a position to more deeply address other important issues, not the least of which was academics. They did so by applying the following four-step process.

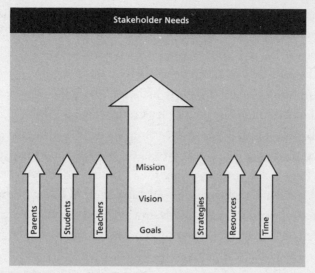

Bringing the arrows into alignment keeps the focus on highest priorities.

1. Setting Wildly Important Goals (WIGs)
2. Translating Goals into Meaningful Action Steps
3. Keeping Scoreboards
4. Establishing a Cadence of Accountability

We will first use Beaumont as an example of how schools apply the four steps, then share other examples of what schools are doing to apply the process.

Setting Wildly Important Goals (WIGs)

Whereas a mission captures the purpose—the *why*—goals define the *what* and *when*. "What do we want our school to look like and feel like five years from now?" "What goals will our class achieve this quarter?" "What will I personally accomplish by the end of the term?" Broad goals are sometimes described as visions—both long- and short-term visions—but eventually visions need to be turned into specific, actionable goals if they are to have any chance of coming to fruition.

Year two was when Beaumont was trained in the four-step process, beginning with setting one or two Wildly Important Goals (WIGs). WIGs are the highest-priority goals, which if not accomplished in due time will result in significant pain. WIGs are more important than Pretty Important Goals (PIGs), which are also important but if not achieved will result in less pain or frustration than a WIG.

The Beaumont staff chose to center their WIGs in two areas— reading and writing. They also set goals for improving their teaching of the 7 Habits and for improving their culture, but those goals were PIGs. A challenge they faced in pursuing their WIGs was that their population of economically disadvantaged students had grown from 31 percent to 54 percent in the three previous years, so just keeping academic scores flat was going to be a feat.

Half the challenge of achieving a goal is stating it right in the first place. Goals like "we will do our best" or "we will be number one" give little tangible direction and can in some cases be achieved merely by the failures of others. In contrast, goals stated in specific terms are very useful. Specific goals provide clarity around where an individual or organization is at currently (X), where they want to be (Y), and a target date for *When* the goal will be achieved. We call such goals "X to Y by When" goals.

Recall how Colby was pre-tested in reading at the beginning of the school year. That gave him and Mrs. Brinson a solid baseline (his X). From there they talked things over and identified a goal for Colby to move up two reading levels (his Y). He was to achieve it by the end of the first marking period (his *When*). This resulted in Colby having a clear target—a WIG.

Involving Colby in the process gave him an appropriate level of buy-in. In fact, the real power of the goal-setting process at Beaumont is as much about how students are involved in setting goals as it is in how specific its goals are. No adult likes it when somebody "up above" writes a goal that they "down below" have to achieve without any input. Students are no different. If students are expected to achieve a goal, they deserve to be involved in setting the goal.

Some adults question students' abilities to participate in goal setting. Such adults must first develop the belief that if a student is old enough to attend school, he or she is old enough to participate in setting goals. Younger students might start out with goals like the kindergartner who set a goal to blow a bubble using bubble gum by the end of the term. But as they mature, their goals will also mature, as will their ability to set goals on their own. The caution with most young students (and some adults) is that they tend to shoot for the stars, so need coaching around being realistic. According to Harvard's Tal Ben-Shahar, the best goals fall within a student's "stretch zone," which he defines as "the healthy median between their comfort and panic zones."

Translating Goals into Meaningful Action Steps

Before Colby and Mrs. Brinson chiseled their goal into stone, they were wise to first talk about action steps. Action steps involve determining the specific tasks that need to be done, the resources that will be required, and the barriers that need to be overcome to achieve the goal. Some older students need only to have a clear understanding of a desired goal—the end in mind—and then everyone needs to get out of their way and allow them to determine the action steps on their own. For most young students, however, research suggests they must be able to see up to 90 percent of the path that leads toward their goal. In other words, setting a reading goal with a youngster like Colby that says "You will jump two grade levels by the end of the first marking term" will mean little to Colby unless he can see 90 percent of what he needs to do to achieve that goal.

That does not mean that a second-grade student should be given a goal that requires 100 tasks, and as long as he can envision 90 of the tasks he will be fine. In fact, just as the number of goals should be limited, so the number of action steps should be limited to only the highest leveraged steps—as few as two or three. Making sure they are the right action steps requires effort, and is often the most important and challenging aspect of goal setting.

In Colby's case, his action steps were based on a "data dig" of his pre-test results and his previous year's work. He and Mrs. Brinson discovered that he needed to work on his word accuracy, and so Mrs. Brinson helped him to come up with a few action steps to improve his accuracy. For other students, the action steps may have been entirely different. But again the key was that Mrs. Brinson worked this out with Colby. No involvement, no commitment.

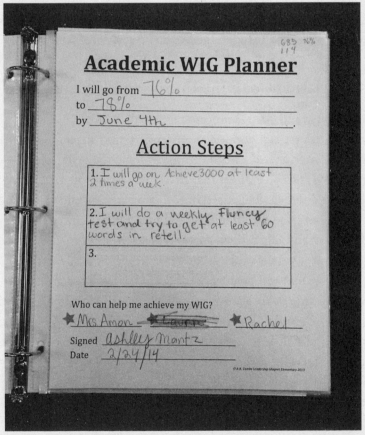

Students like Colby and this student turn their goals into doable action steps.

Keeping Scoreboards

The next step in helping Colby achieve his reading goal was to identify how and how often he would track his progress. Without good measures and timely tracking, how else would he know if he was moving in a forward direction or at a timely pace? How else would he know when his goal was achieved?

Watching children play games reveals that students can be very motivated by scoreboards. Remove the scoreboard on a pinball game and see how long a child continues to stare at a silver ball being rocketed around. Take away the flashing lights on a video game so a child cannot sense the feeling of progression, and see how long he or she keeps playing.

Indeed, watching children react to tallies and bells as they near a new level of a video game tells us a lot about what keeping score and scoreboards can do to excite youngsters. The challenge is to capture that same excitement in an academic goal.

Typically it is only "above-average" students who get excited about academic scores. Not many want to be told they are "below average." Yet what students like even less is not having any idea at all where they stand. Imagine a basketball team allowing only the coach to know the score of a game, and then that coach only telling players the score between quarters. Sound ludicrous? It may also sound familiar. It is the standard mode of operation in many classrooms. Students work all quarter without knowing where they stand, and then at the end of a quarter, or term, the teacher sends a report home letting parents know their child's scores. Only if parents choose to say something does the student learn how he or she is doing, and often it is only the "bad" scores that are brought to their atten-

> When success in the classroom is defined in terms of competitive status with others, only a few students can be successful. However, when individual growth is the criterion for success, then all students can experience success regardless of their comparative status.
>
> —*Robert J. Marzano,*
> *What Works in Schools*

tion. No wonder why some students don't like the game of school. No wonder why some quit.

Something else "below-average" students do not like is being constantly compared to others. Imagine showing up to work every day and being told you are a below-average employee. Or going home every night and being told you are a below-average family member. Even if you agree, you don't want to hear it.

At a minimum, students want to feel they are making progress against themselves and improving with time. They want to celebrate what for them is an above-average day, regardless of how it compares with others. For Colby, keeping a personal scoreboard and seeing his

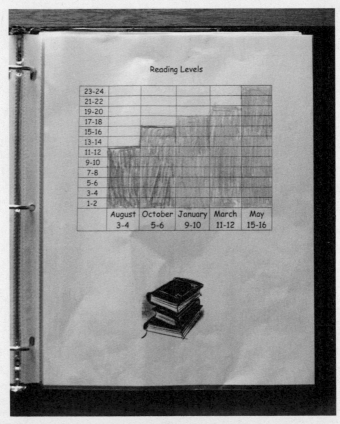

Personal scoreboards helped Colby track his progress.

test scores improve at regular intervals turned out to be a great motivator and confidence builder. He could see his progression.

Sometimes the scores that are heralded most in schools are end-of-year scores. End-of-year scores are helpful, especially at administrative levels where strategic decisions are made regarding curriculum and district-wide trainings. Yet as vital as they are, end-of-year scores are "summative" measures and are considered to be *lagging indicators* because they arrive after the work is completed. They are measures of hindsight more than foresight. As such, they arrive too late for students like Colby or anyone else to make adjustments during the year. That is why it is important that "formative" measures, which are predictive in nature and considered to be *leading indicators,* are provided at regular intervals throughout the year. Mrs. Brinson had Colby charting his progress on his reading accuracy on a near-daily basis, and other measures on a more weekly or monthly basis. That way there would be no end-of-the-year surprises, and time to course-correct as needed.

> Autonomy must be balanced by accountability.
> —*Richard DuFour and Michael Fullan,* Cultures Built to Last

Establishing a Cadence of Accountability

Someone once said that goals should be stars to steer by, not sticks with which to beat ourselves. And that is how *The Leader in Me* views accountability. It is a positive opportunity to review progress and say, "Hey, look at what I did!" It is a time for Mrs. Brinson to express her confidence in Colby. It is also an opportunity to recalculate goals or refine action steps. And with *The Leader in Me,* accountability is a two-way encounter.

People are far more likely to achieve a difficult goal when a trusted person checks in with them on a consistent basis. "How's it going?" "How can I help?" How and how often accountability is best handled is unique to each situation.

Setting regular "check-in" times is what we call establishing a cadence of accountability. In Colby's case, Mrs. Brinson set up daily visits. Other students may require only weekly visits. Teachers can be creative as to when visits occur, but most try do it during an already-designated time slot, such as when students are scheduled for a large block of quiet reading time. Some follow a five-students-per-day rotation. For most students, it takes only a few minutes to give constructive feedback or discuss a new strategy.

Some teachers use parents to help with accountability sessions. Others use older students. Mrs. Brinson involved Colby's mother. At a minimum, enough time should be afforded for students to self-reflect on the progress they have made. In fact, the more the student owns of the accountability process the better. The teacher's (or other accountability partner's) role then becomes that of a cheerleader, a sounding board, a motivator—a leader.

Another role the accountability partner fills is to help remove barriers. In the case of a teacher, this may include getting students extra resources, finding tutors, moving seating locations, etc. We call that "clearing the path." It is where the two-way accountability comes in. Did the student get the help and resources they needed? For Colby, this included Mrs. Brinson arranging additional reading resources for him to take home, and for her to make time to visit with him each day.

Classroom WIGs

To this point, we have briefly described four steps for setting and tracking goals: 1) Setting Wildly Important Goals (WIGs), 2) Translating goals into meaningful action steps, 3) Keeping scoreboards, and 4) Establishing a cadence of accountability. Student-level involvement is central to all four steps if the goal is to be achieved.

Another key to achieving academic progress is classroom goals. Classroom goals are far undervalued in many classrooms, but not in Colby's case. His class applied the same four steps, and it turned out to help motivate Colby in achieving his personal goal.

Step 1: Setting WIGs. Colby's class had a classroom WIG focused on reading, and all the students knew what it was. The class worked together to come up with the WIG by taking the aggregate scores of all the students on the pre-test to determine the class's X. They then used the aggregate of all the students' goals to determine a class Y; the *When* had been predetermined by Mrs. Brinson.

Step 2: Translating Goals into Action Steps. The students and Mrs. Brinson next worked together to identify three action steps that would help the class achieve their goal. Students went through the nameless data with Mrs. Brinson to identify the greatest overall needs of the class and then worked with Mrs. Brinson to select what they felt were the three highest leveraged steps that would help them achieve the goal. Mrs. Brinson guided the choices based on sound reading strategies and principles.

Step 3: Keeping a Scoreboard. Colby's class had fun creating a class scoreboard for reading. They called it their "data board." It was mounted in a visible place where all students could see it from their desks. Whenever they took a reading test or got a new score, they updated the data board to mark their progress. So when Colby did well on his reading tests, he could see his score impacting the class reading score, which he loved.

Step 4: Establishing a Cadence of Accountability. Throughout the year, Mrs. Brinson visited with students as a class during regular weekly meetings about how they were progressing, what they could do differently, and so forth. Class members encouraged each other. Some volunteered to stay in at recess to help students who were struggling. The students truly took ownership to motivate and help each other to achieve the goal.

Colby and his classmates put a lot of thought and energy into achieving their class goal and took great pride when it happened. It was something they had accomplished together—a team effort. In fact, it was clear that Colby and his classmates put more energy into their personal goals because they were trying so hard as a class to achieve the class goal. Personal achievement seemed almost secondary to class achievement.

Scoreboards show up in every classroom at Beaumont.

Schoolwide WIGs

Beaumont as a school approaches goal setting and tracking using the same four-step process that Colby and his class used. In fact, it was at the school level that Colby's and his class's goals had their origins. The staff had examined the prior year's test scores and determined that the highest leveraged academic improvements they could make were in reading and writing. So they focused their school WIGs in those two areas, but particularly in reading.

Thus it was all classes, not just Colby's class, that had a reading goal. Each classroom also had a class reading scoreboard to track progress. Each grade-level team was given the freedom to decide how they would approach their goals, what action steps would best fit their students, how they would measure and track progress, and how they would handle accountability. Once the classroom goals had been set, the school set a schoolwide reading goal based on real live data and real live input from staff and students. Scoreboards were put up in high-traffic areas so everyone could see how the school as a whole was progressing.

With time, Beaumont also set aside a "staff only" room to track and discuss academic progress. One wall was dedicated to their reading WIG, and one to their writing WIG. A third wall tracked math goals. The fourth wall became a data wall that displayed where every student was in their reading progress. The reading specialist and grade-level teams used the room and charts to review goals, to reevaluate action steps, and to collaborate to ensure that no child fell through the cracks. It was a team effort.

In addition to the academic goals, Beaumont continued to set goals for better implementing the 7 Habits and improving their school culture, but those goals were relegated to PIG status. Some of those goals were delegated to students. For example, the staff noticed that there

Beaumont's "Success Room" helps staff track progress toward goals, one child at a time.

were recurring problems with hallways getting messy. Rather than distracting teachers from their academic goals, they turned the challenge over to the student leadership team. The student leaders made a rubric and set a goal for achieving a "Total Cleanliness" score by the end of the term. Students introduced the goal during the weekly Friday assembly and asked everyone to help. A scoreboard was posted in a main hallway for all to see. Student leaders reported progress and suggested improvements on a weekly basis, again during the Friday assembly. Once that goal was met, the student leaders picked another goal. One term they worked on classes putting chairs on top of their desks to make it easier for the custodian to vacuum. Another term they had a goal for forming straight, quiet lines when walking as a class. Each time a rubric and a scoreboard were made for all to see. Students set the goals, and were the judges and scorekeepers.

Celebrating Successes

To this point we have focused on setting, tracking, and achieving goals. But when do the celebrations occur? When is the party?

Particularly with younger students who seek external cues, celebrations can be a great way of reinforcing desired behaviors and outcomes. That is why in most *Leader in Me* schools there is a lot of celebrating for personal and group achievements. They especially celebrate small wins—the milestones. The refreshing thing is that the majority of celebrations involve *intrinsic* rewards. There tend to be less *extrinsic* rewards—prizes or parties—though those do have their place.

Beaumont enjoyed immediate rewards upon implementing *The Leader in Me*. When the staff got together in the summer with their spouses to paint walls and spruce up the building, it turned out to be a lot of fun and removed a lot of the existing tensions. That was a reward. Many staff members viewed the 7 Habits training as a gift and huge reward. Seeing students apply the habits and being leaders gave staff members the satisfaction of feeling they were making a difference—another reward. Students were rewarded with a nicer physical environment and happier teachers, as well as the chance to be leaders and to feel of worth. For Mrs. Brinson, her reward was in knowing she had a central role in Colby's progress. Those are all natural consequences, which tend to have the most lasting and meaningful value.

Compliments are a great way of celebrating. Mrs. McCartan says, "We are constantly pointing out students' strengths and progress. We do lots of verbal pats on the back during class and during assemblies, but mostly during one-on-one visits. We do this for students and for staff. We don't use a lot of extrinsic rewards. Students get so much out of simply achieving a goal and feeling good about themselves." And Colby would agree. His biggest reward was becoming a better reader and contributing to his class goal. He feels better about himself, and has even been heard to proudly tell people, "I'm a leader of reading." That is a natural consequence with lasting value.

Some researchers discourage extrinsic rewards. The biggest problems with extrinsic rewards are how frequently they are overused and

Rewards can emphasize teamwork and leadership skills in addition to academics.

Research Says . . .

In *Visible Learning*, John Hattie summarizes eight hundred meta-analyses tied to student achievement. We have applied his findings specific to goal achievement to *The Leader in Me* goal-setting process, with which they match up well.

Setting WIGs

- Goals are critical for enhancing performance, and have major effects on the development of self-efficacy and confidence, which in turn affects the difficulty level of future goals.
- Goals should be specific, rather than "do your best," which can easily be attained since anything can be defined as "your best."
- Goals should be challenging, even for special education students (Fuchs, 1986), though not so high that the goal is seen as unattainable.

Translating Goals into Action Steps

- Students must be able to see a pathway to attaining a challenging goal—which can include strategies for understanding the goal and implementation plans to attain it.
- Goal achievement is highest when 90 percent of tasks needed to accomplish the goal are known; far lower when less than 50 percent of tasks are known. (Burns, 2002)

Keeping Scoreboards

- Trying to beat "personal bests" motivates students and increases their enjoyment of school, participation in class, and persistence on the task. It helps students to compete against their previous performance (Martin, 2006, p. 816).
- Self-evaluation and self-monitoring helps students to have a reasonable understanding of where they are, where they are going, what it will look like when they get there, and where they will go next.

Establishing a Cadence of Accountability

- Feedback is among the most powerful influences on achievement.
- Regular, timely feedback helps students set reasonable goals and make adjustments in effort, direction, and even strategy as needed. (Locke & Latham, 1990, p. 23)
- Many teachers claim they provide ample amounts of feedback but, at best, students receive only moments of feedback in a single day. (Nuthall, 2005).
- Feedback about the task itself, the process, or the effort is more effective than providing a nonspecific character description such as "you are a good student."

Celebrations

- Extrinsic rewards (stickers, awards, etc.) often undermine intrinsic motivation, and can be viewed as a controlling strategy. (Deci, Koestner, and Ryan, 1999, p. 659).

how often they are used in isolation from intrinsic rewards. Some teachers hold a party for every outcome. Young sports teams get loaded with after-game treats whether they won the game, played fair, or worked hard, not to mention whether or not the treats are healthy. In such cases, the natural consequences get diluted or forgotten, and the attempt may be more harmful than rewarding.

The best use of extrinsic rewards is when pairing them with intrinsic rewards. There is a gaping difference between "You got a one hundred percent on your spelling test, here's a sticker, now go sit down," versus "Way to go! You earned a one hundred percent on your spelling. Here's a sticker. Every time I see that sticker I'm going to remember how hard you worked to achieve that score. I also admire how you went the extra distance to print your letters neatly. I bet you keep your room clean, too. Good spelling is going to help you throughout life." Okay, that may be a little overboard, but notice how the student's internal qualities are recognized and reinforced—and all tied to a little sticker. So when giving extrinsic rewards—young students love them—always remember to pair them with intrinsic rewards. And rather than the staff trying to figure out what the best extrinsic rewards will be, students really are some of the best sources for ideas, especially inexpensive ones. High-fives with a compliment cost nothing.

Three Tools

Three tools augment the goal-setting process. Variations of the tools have been around education circles for years and are not unique to *The Leader in Me*. However, portions have been adapted to the leadership theme, and those applications are unique. The three tools are Leadership Notebooks, student-led conferences, and quality tools.

Leadership Notebooks. One of the most powerful tools of *The Leader in Me* is a Leadership Notebook. It offers a single location for students to house their WIGs, track personal scoreboards, record leadership reflections, and showcase best works. Most schools use a simple three-ring binder with tabs. Leadership Notebooks help students keep the highest priorities—the end(s) in mind—at the forefront.

An impressive experience is to have a young student share his or her Leadership Notebook and explain its contents. It quickly becomes clear that the child owns the goals and data, and is proud to share his or her progress. It is important that teachers also feel ownership for the notebooks. From a custom cover to the individual sheets that fall within the tabs, teachers design the notebooks to meet the needs of students and achieve grade-level goals.

Student-Led Conferences. Many schools have migrated to student-led parent-teacher conferences, where instead of the teacher or parent doing the talking, students lead the discussion. In the case of *The Leader in Me*, students share with parents their WIGs and how

A student in Taiwan shares her Leadership Notebook with a guest.

they are progressing. They outline their strengths and steps they can take to improve. As they talk their parents through their Leadership Notebook, parents and teacher listen and ask questions. This keeps students in charge of their learning.

Student-led conferences also have benefits for teachers, who once they have the routine down, find it easier in terms of preparation. A side benefit is that since implementing the student-led format, the percentage of parents attending conferences at Beaumont has gone up from 74 percent to 98 percent. Students prod their parents to attend because they are eager to share.

Quality Tools. The third tool is actually a set of tools. Teachers commonly refer to them as graphic organizers. They include Venn diagrams, force-field analysis, Gantt charts, fishbone diagrams, affinity diagrams, bubble maps, plus-delta charts, and lotus diagrams. Entire books are written about these tools, but suffice it here to say that students enjoy using them to problem-solve, brainstorm ideas, analyze stories, plan projects, set goals, and establish classroom protocol.

Kindergartners use force-field analysis,
a quality tool, to define expected behaviors.

What About the Results?

What Beaumont has done sounds good, but at the end of the day is it really making a difference? A partial answer to the question is revealed in what parent Rochelle McGee shared during a Leadership Day:

Two years ago I attended an international executive development program focused on getting "back to the basics." What were those basics?

- Setting goals for ourselves
- Setting goals for our companies
- Working on the corporate culture
- Clearly communicating goals and encouraging collaboration
- Tracking progress, and predicting and analyzing our failures

A few months later, I was in a Parent Teacher Association (PTA) meeting and Mrs. McCartan suggested introducing the 7 Habits to the school. I thought, "I remember taking the 7 Habits workshop when I worked for a marketing company. How can those habits apply to kids?"

Soon the school began getting a facelift: quotes on walls, new bulletin boards, flags in the lobby, and a front entrance rug that said, "Together We Lead." It didn't happen overnight. The changes were staggered over the months. The kids were engaged. The staff was engaged. And whether I knew it or not, I was becoming more and more engaged.

Each class made mission statements and set classroom goals, copies of which were brought home for students to explain to us parents. It was great that we knew what kind of classroom community the kids and teachers were going for, and even more compelling was the fact that a fourth grader could explain how the class mission supported the school's mission.

The students were seeing their teachers set goals. When teachers fell short on goals, they analyzed why the goal was missed. Did the goal change? How do I make a better goal next time? This was the same stuff I'd been taught by expensive consultants!

My husband and I were impressed that the parent-teacher conferences were entirely student-led. My son was excited to show us his Leadership Notebook. I was curious what kind of data a fourth grader would keep. He was able to answer questions about his grades, knew which test it was that he did poorly on, remembered *why*, and explained the difference between pre- and post-tests. We were blown away.

My son's ability to communicate has jumped about ten levels. When our friends, grandparents, and neighbors comment on how articulate our nine-year-old is, that he actually converses rather than merely answers questions with a yes or no, I can't help but think it's the confidence he has built as a by-product of living the 7 Habits.

The leadership Beaumont exudes does nothing less than set our students up for success. I hope they'll always set goals, track progress, hit their milestones, and celebrate.

As a parent and business leader, Mrs. McGee sees the benefits in students learning how to set goals, in making changes to the culture, and in learning the 7 Habits—the whole package. And the Beaumont staff seems to agree. When asked on a staff survey whether they would prefer to go back to the way the school was prior to *The Leader in Me,* not one staff member responded "agree" or "strongly agree." There was 100 percent agreement that things had changed for the better.

But what about academics? The state of Michigan ranks schools by percentiles according to their performance on state exams. When Beaumont started *The Leader in Me* it was ranked at the 23rd percentile in reading, the lowest quartile in the state. One year into the process, it was ranked 29th. Two years in it was ranked 42nd. And the next ranking is expected to be even higher. Particular growth has happened with writing, going from 36 percent of students passing the state exam to 67 percent, a 31 percent increase in just two years. That is in spite of the introduction of several state and district initiatives and the high influx of low socioeconomic students.

Other Schools

As mentioned, Beaumont is not the only school having success with the goal-setting process. Numerous other schools tell similar stories. A good example is Stanton Elementary in Fenton, Missouri. It was already a high-performing school prior to *The Leader in Me.* Principal Matt Miller is an expert in Professional Learning Communities, and with the help of an outstanding staff had the school in good order. In fact, first-grade teacher Mrs. Weis says that her biggest surprise with *The Leader in Me* has been how much it improved the school. "We were already a great school. So I can't believe how much better it has made us."

Mr. Miller is a firm believer in focusing on only one goal. One year, the school chose to focus its one schoolwide Wildly Important Goal on reading. The school's reading scores were already admirable, but the district had sent them two hundred new low-income students from outside their boundaries, and the staff felt a need to focus on the reading skills of those students, particularly the younger grades.

Each grade-level team got together to choose a reading WIG. They determined what measure they would use for a pre-test to identify their X, and based on those scores set their goal (their Y). A post-test was to be conducted toward the end of the year prior to state exams (their *When*). They also identified the formative measures they would collect periodically. They created class and grade-level scoreboards in their hallways so each class and grade level could see how they were progressing.

Grade-level teams designed colorful covers for their Leadership Notebooks, and determined what pages would go behind each tab, including scoreboard pages for reading. One resource that was used to track progress throughout the year was Accelerated Reader (AR) books. Once students had read a book they could take an online quiz to show comprehension. Kindergarten classes posted a round circle in the hallway for every hundred AR books they passed off as a class. The circles formed the shape of a caterpillar, and before long, the students had that caterpillar winding its way down the hallway and around the corner. They celebrated each time a circle was added, and teased about how big the butterfly was going to be.

> Don't be afraid to give up the good to go for the great.
>
> —*Jim Collins,* Good to Great

First graders had their own AR scoreboard in their hallway. It showed that the first year of doing the goal setting process they passed off 5,500 books in the second quarter alone. That far surpassed the prior year when they had taken a full half year to reach 5,000. Meanwhile, a colorful thermometer near the front of the school captured the total number of books read by the entire school. Students got a thrill out of making the temperature rise, and eventually broke the thermometer when they surpassed the school's reading goal.

Reading specialist Mary Jo Barker designed a special personal scoreboard for remedial students to track their reading progress. The

This caterpillar motivated kindergartners
to read more and with greater comprehension.

scoreboard was in the shape of a hand. Each finger represented a specific component of reading. When students demonstrated they had mastered one of the components, they got to color in the associated finger. Whereas the average number of students to advance out of the remedial program in the four years prior to using the goal-setting process was 7 students per year, that first year of goal setting they advanced 48 students.

Stanton Elementary also assigns older students as reading mentors for younger students. They call them "accountabili-buddies." Once a week, the older students read with the younger students and cheer progress. For the older students, a group of mentors from the high school visit once a week.

After two years of implementing the goal-setting process, fifth-grade teacher Julie Arth indicated, "We are miles ahead in goal setting from where we were five years ago. We as teachers used to set goals for the students and they didn't track them at all. Now students are accountable for setting and tracking their goals. They like to advance in a public way." Peer teacher Shannon Gruzeski adds, "With students being responsible for their goals, they are much more interested when we ask, 'Is that a good choice of book? Will it help you toward your goal?' They aren't trying to get a pizza party, they are trying to become better readers."

Other Goals

To this point we have emphasized how the goal-setting process is applied to academic goals. But the same four-step process can be applied to any goal. Schools use it to reduce discipline referrals, improve parent involvement, reduce tardiness, improve bus behavior, or to inspire other desired behaviors.

Principal Kim Cummins of Martin Petitjean Elementary in Rayne, Louisiana, observes, "Once teachers get familiar with the process and the value of goal setting they realize how much easier it makes things." In addition to academic goals, her school applies the goal setting process to:

- *Health and fitness.* Every month students set health and fitness goals, and track progress in their Leadership Notebook. Some track how many miles they walk during PE with the goal of walking the equivalent of a marathon. Each mile they walk results in a paper shoe being placed on the class scoreboard. Student leaders also talk about goals for eating right as they review the food being served in the cafeteria that day.
- *Attendance.* Personal, class, and schoolwide attendance is tracked every day. When the school averages 97 percent attendance three days in a row, students get an extra five minutes of recess. Of the twenty-seven schools in their district, Petitjean ranks second in attendance and 10 points higher than other schools in their immediate area, which is up significantly since prior to setting and tracking goals and in spite of a high-risk population.

- *Speech*. The speech therapist has students set goals and track progress relative to their special needs, such as articulation. Students keep progress charts in their Leadership Notebook, and have shown markedly higher progress than students at equivalent schools in the area.

As noted previously, schools use the process for many other non-academic purposes, such as hallway behavior, fund-raisers, cleanliness, and so forth. And aside from what the schools are doing, it is worth noting that numerous staff members have found ways to apply the goal-setting process to personal goals. PE teacher Cheryl McCabe, for example, used the process to train for a marathon. She posted her goals in the gym and put up a workout scoreboard so she could model the goal-setting process and so students could be her accountabili-buddies. We know of two educators who have used the goal-setting process to lose more than one hundred pounds. Way to go!

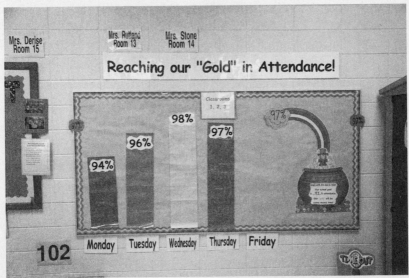

Martin Petitjean students keep a close eye on their daily attendance.

It Starts with Paradigms

What the schools mentioned in this chapter have demonstrated is that, if applied with fidelity, goal-setting can have positive direct effects on student achievement. Of course, it is a challenge to demonstrate cause-effect relationships with academic achievement given all the variables that go into measurement—changing exams, demographics, varying cohorts, and so on. Nevertheless, several schools have reported improvements, particularly in terms of students taking responsibility for their learning.

The goal-setting process can also have indirect impacts on school culture and students' leadership skills. As Mr. Miller at Stanton Elementary indicates, "As much as anything, the goal-setting process has helped our students learn to work together. Students are focused on team academic goals and work together to achieve them. If our students were tested on people skills and teamwork skills on state exams, they would be way ahead. It has taken them to a whole different level."

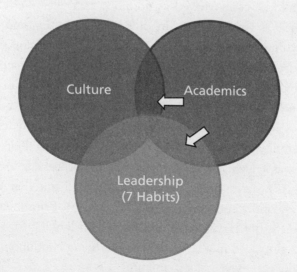

But for as much potential as the goal-setting process holds, it could easily fall flat or even have opposite effects if not implemented with proper levels of thinking—the right paradigms. In fact, the goal-setting

A warm greeting awaits Beaumont students every day
to let students know the entire staff cares.

process could be easily viewed as no more than what we referred to in Chapter 1 as GAP finding. In other words, testing and retesting students to find their GAPs (Got a Pain), then analyzing their data to decipher what is "wrong," and then working hard to "remedy" it.

In Colby's case, he knew Mrs. Brinson cared about him and was not just pursuing his fault lines. She used him in class for other leadership roles and knew well his strengths in other areas. He felt a sense of responsibility to his class, and liked contributing to their progress. His input was valued as he was involved in the process. He felt he was seeing steady progress on his personal scoreboard, and that made him feel good and more confident. So, yes, he and Mrs. Brinson were looking for GAPs, but it was in combination with looking for strengths, and it was all placed in a larger context of being continuously recognized for the greatness that was in him.

As with teaching the 7 Habits and creating a culture of leadership, the key to setting, tracking, and achieving goals has much to do with relationships—about caring.

• • •

So as we arrive at the halfway stage of the book, let's pause and look back to give context for what is ahead. The first five chapters have explored the origins and the primary content of *The Leader in Me:*

- Too Good to Be True?
- How It Got Started—and Why
- Teaching the 7 Habits
- Creating a Culture of Leadership
- Achieving School Goals

The book could stop here and schools would have plenty to consider. However, the schools that have truly shined with *The Leader in Me* are those that have engaged the help of family and community members in the process. Therefore, Chapter 6 describes how schools have involved families in *The Leader in Me* process, and Chapter 7 shares examples of how and why communities are getting involved.

Furthermore, Chapter 8 gives an introduction to what is happening at middle and high schools, and takes a brief look at college levels, and Chapter 9 shares vital insights for sustaining the process over time.

Finally, Chapter 10, "Ending with the Beginning in Mind," overviews key aspects of the book, and challenges you to see yourself as a leader and to live your life in crescendo.

Personal Reflections

Habit 3: Put First Things First teaches that effectiveness (doing the right things) comes before efficiency (doing things right). Once A.B. Combs and Beaumont identified their highest-priority goals, they improved in effectiveness and efficiency. Thinking of your own life, what are your one or two highest priority goals—your Wildly Important Goals? For each goal, what is the one thing you can do this week that will have the most impact on achieving the goal?

6

Bringing It Home

When our five-year-old son started coming home and using phrases like "Win-Win" and "Begin with the End in Mind," it hit home with me. So I decided to take the training, and now we're putting it into place 24/7 as a family. It helps my son's daily routines, my daily routines, my wife's daily routines, and our family's daily routines.

—*Dean Harrison, Parent, Medicine Hat, Alberta, Canada*

If any successes trump the outcomes being reported by *Leader in Me* schools, it is the stories coming from home. Consider three short examples.

The first comes from Canada, where a father showed up to school one day with his son. He was a kind man, though some of his kindness may have been initially camouflaged by his bulging muscles. His son had been diagnosed with a cognitive delay and oppositional defiance, and the father had been told the school had a behavioral program that could help him.

Soon the son was enrolled and learning the 7 Habits with all the other students. Within days the father noticed changes in his son's demeanor and attitude about school. Occasionally, he came home with a homework assignment to teach one of the habits to a parent or sibling. He taught his dad. A few months later, the father attended a parent night and, during a question-and-answer period, stood and asked permission to say something. "What this school is teaching students has changed my life," he said. He then sat back down.

A few weeks later, the father returned. He revealed that years earlier he had been caught in a drug sting in the United States. While awaiting a court date, he fled to Canada and went into hiding. There he eventually married, had a child, and was trying to live a productive life. Yet he could never shake the feeling that law officials were one step behind him. He said his son's lessons about taking responsibility, having goals, and putting first things first had pricked his conscience and made him want to set things right so he could be the kind of dad he wanted to be. He had contacted authorities to turn himself in, and pointing to his son added, "This boy's my hero."

The father was told to expect to serve a prison term of up to two years. As it turned out, a sympathetic judge examined the evidence of what the father had done during his years in hiding. Included was a letter from the principal emphasizing the importance of the father's relationship with his son. Ultimately, the judge concluded, "This man doesn't belong in jail costing taxpayers money. He needs to be with his son and continuing to make a difference in his community." A solution was worked out that allowed the father to remain at home and pay his penitence in other ways.

The second story also comes from Canada, where a single father who is striving to raise a family and maintain his profession shared how he organized his children's after-school chores and activities. Each day he makes a First Things First chart of things his children need to do when they arrive home. As soon as they walk in the door, they look at the chart, see what is expected of them, get it done, and then go off to play, all while the father keeps working. He got the idea after observing a First Things First chart in one of his children's classrooms.

Lastly, when we asked a teacher at a rural school how the 7 Habits had benefited her school, she responded rather casually with a few examples. But when asked if the habits had impacted her personally, no words came out, just tears. It turned out that at the same time she was going through 7 Habits training, her family was going through hell. Two teen sons were in a mess. Her husband was out of work and depressed. Divorce was a steady topic. So all she could think about during the training was how much her family needed the habits.

She decided to take her 7 Habits training manual home and began teaching the habits to her family. They covered one topic per evening and discussed how they could apply the concept as a family. They were some of the most constructive, forward-thinking conversations they had experienced as a family. It gave them a language to explain their feelings and tackle their challenges. Two years later, all she could say through her tears was that the training had saved her family, and maybe even a life.

Literally hundreds of such stories come from homes around the globe on a steady basis. Our favorites refer to times when students use the habits to give their parents advice. Like the father who confessed that he was driving home from a sporting event when someone cut him off and his temper flared. His young daughter kindly remarked, "Daddy, I wonder how we could have been a little more proactive in that situation."

The Home and School Relationship

Society is filled with turbulence. For some students and staff, home is their one refuge from the storm. For others, home is the storm.

What happens at home is important to schools for at least two reasons. First is the impact that home has on students. Many of the behaviors, knowledge, and mindsets students carry with them to school each day come right out of the home. For better or for worse, those influences impact the culture of the school, the atmosphere of the classroom, and a student's yearning for learning. Karen L. Mapp of Harvard University's Graduate School of Education reports that when the home and school staff work together, "students earn higher grades, perform better on tests, and have better social skills and behavior. There's also a link to students finishing high school and heading to college." Home clearly impacts student performance.

Second is the impact that the home has on staff members' effectiveness at school. Like students, staff members carry remnants of home with them to school each day. What went on "last night" or what parting words were spoken "this morning" can make or break a staff member's moods and actions for the day. Any extra stress, conflict, or ineffectiveness that staff members bring from home can impact their ability to concentrate and perform on the job. So the better things are at home, the better things go at school.

The same way a home can impact what happens at school, a school can have impact on what happens at home. Students spend more than six hours a day at school for upwards of nine months each year—more than a thousand waking hours. The friends they meet, the teachers they receive, the opportunities they are given, and the knowledge they attain all have potential to wiggle their way into the home for better or for worse. The same is true at the staff level where a rotten day at school can make for a surly night at home.

As tempting as it may be at times, most schools do not want to be in the business of telling parents how to raise their families. Neither do most parents want to be in the business of telling schools what to do. But to the extent the two can help each other, why not work together?

This chapter shares how homes and schools are working together using *The Leader in Me* as a framework. It looks at:

- Students taking the 7 Habits home
- Parents and families engaging at school
- Ways of applying *The Leader in Me* @ home

In discussing these topics, we acknowledge that families and homes come in all shapes and sizes. No two families are alike. We make no attempt to define a family or differentiate between "good" or "bad" homes. We know that all homes have challenges and some are in virtual disarray. Nevertheless, as you might suspect, *The Leader in*

Parent buy-in and involvement has given heart to the
sustained success of *The Leader in Me*.

Me operates from the paradigm that there is greatness in every home,
every parent, and every child, and seeks to nurture and optimize that
greatness.

Students Taking the Habits Home

It has been the source of great entertainment as parents have come
to school and asked with puzzled looks on their faces, "What are you
teaching my child? He keeps saying things like, 'Momma, can't we
synergize around this?' or 'Why don't we ever Sharpen the Saw and
do something fun?'" As delightful as it is to see those astonished looks
on parents' faces, the intent is for parents to be informed about the
7 Habits and *The Leader in Me* well before their child begins speaking
the language at home.

There are several ways that schools inform parents about the

7 Habits and *The Leader in Me*. Some of the more common ones include:

Letters Home. Many schools send a letter home at the beginning of the year to inform parents of *The Leader in Me*. In most cases, it is a simple one-page overview. On the back or on a separate page is a summary of the 7 Habits for parents to place in a visible location for all to see.

Welcome Packets. For new students who arrive during the year, some schools create a packet with photos and examples of what the school is doing to implement *The Leader in Me*. Success stories, testimonials, and answers to frequently asked questions are included.

Newsletters. Many schools and classrooms send home weekly, monthly, or quarterly newsletters. A portion of the newsletters can highlight a habit or share a success story. It can be as simple as a single quote.

Website. Schools with websites often post information about *The Leader in Me* on their site. The site can be updated regularly with new photos, traditions, or insights for parents to enjoy and apply at home.

Books. Some schools set up a family library for parents to check out resources. Books and audios like *The 7 Habits of Highly Effective People, The 7 Habits of Highly Effective Teens, The 7 Habits of Happy Kids,* or *The 7 Habits of Highly Effective Families* are valuable resources for parents to acquaint themselves with the habits. Berrian Elementary in Quincy, Illinois, used grant money to purchase a *Happy Kids* book for every family and asked them to read it and discuss the end-of-chapter questions with their children at home.

Students Teaching. One of the most effective ways for parents to learn about the habits is for students to take home assignments to teach the habits to parents and siblings. Such assignments can contain a short story or lesson followed by a discussion on how the child or family can apply the concept at home.

Transfer of Learning. The best way, of course, for students to take the 7 Habits home is to apply them. Some parents are literally stunned with their child's understanding of the habits. One dad was

Signs at this school help parents learn the habits
when picking up or dropping off students.

surprised when his first-grade son began washing dishes without being prompted, and asked him, "What are you doing?" The son responded, "I'm being proactive and helping without being asked." The father, a corporate executive, said, "You don't even know what the word *proactive* means." At that, the father sat in awe as his son taught him all about Habit 1.

> Where a school cannot change the income, education, or occupation of adults in the home, it can have a potential impact on the atmosphere in the home.
>
> —*Robert J. Marzano,*
> What Works in Schools

Such stories of students bringing the habits home are common, like this nugget emailed from a parent in Florida:

One night I came home and my daughters were busy cleaning their rooms—an event not too common without prodding. I kept asking, "What's going on here?" The girls said, "We're synergizing. We're thinking win-win." They were doing it all on their own. The 7 Habits are now integrated in a lot of our home activities. We ask, "What's First Things?" and then we focus on those things. It has reduced a lot of stress in our home. I learned these concepts as a manager after college. I wished I had learned them as a child.

The important thing is that lives are changing and homes are being improved as students bring the habits home. Children can do impressive things when taught principles and trusted to contribute.

Engaging Parents and Families at School

Another way to expose parents and families to the 7 Habits and *The Leader in Me* is to invite them into the school for events. Schools already host family-friendly events, so it is a matter of finding ways to integrate an overview of the leadership principles into those events or some related activity. Again, consider a few examples:

Back-to-School Night. Most schools host back-to-school evenings for parents prior to the start of school. Those nights are good opportunities to inform parents about *The Leader in Me* and to give them a preview of the types of things their children will be experiencing.

Cunningham Elementary in Waterloo, Iowa,
celebrates fun memories of Dads and Donuts.

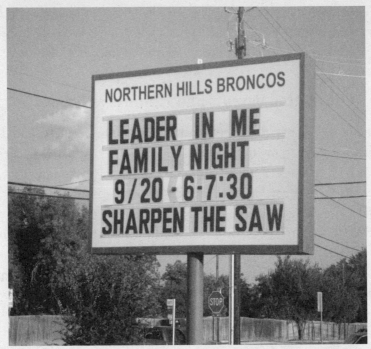

Family nights are fun times to engage families in leadership activities.

Family Nights. Some schools set aside a special parent night for a one-to-two-hour overview of the 7 Habits. The goal is to familiarize parents with the language and basic concepts. Wilderness Oak Elementary in San Antonio, Texas, has a night where the whole family is invited and can rotate from habit to habit, hallway to hallway, as students demonstrate the habits by grade level.

Dads and Donuts or Moms and Muffins. Numerous schools enjoy the tradition of inviting dads or moms to read with their children on a designated day. The Cunningham School for Excellence, an elementary school in Waterloo, Iowa, invites dads (or an uncle, grandpa, or other male role model) to read with their children about someone who is a leader. Dads then spend time telling their child what characteristics they feel are important to being a leader and describing the leadership characteristics they see in their child. The donuts are merely a tantalizing sideshow.

Grandparents Day. Some schools similarly invite grandparents to read with their students. Some add a twist to those occasions by having students write letters and draw pictures about how they think their grandparents are leaders.

Student-Led Conferences. As described in Chapter 5, student-led conferences provide students the opportunity to teach their parents about the habits and their leadership roles. Many schools see a significant increase in parent attendance when turning the conference reins over to students.

Leadership Day. Some schools hold Leadership Days and large audiences of fellow educators show up. Other schools do not have many outside guests so they look to parents or grandparents to be their main audience, or at least their dress-rehearsal audience. Parents and grandparents love it. Every child deserves an audience.

Parent Classes. Several schools offer opportunities for parents to go through the same 7 Habits signature training that they experienced as a staff. Others offer *The 7 Habits of Highly Effective Families* workshop. Some hold evenings to focus on a single concept, such as at Junction Elementary in Roseville, California, where Principal Carrie Vincent organized a parent night on "Creating a Family Mission Statement."

Virtually any school event that typically involves families—concerts, plays, field days, etc.—can be turned into opportunities for families to become familiar with the habits. Some parents have even commented how their child began kindergarten already knowing the habits as a result of having attended school activities and seeing older siblings teaching the habits or being leaders.

Along with holding events, another way to get parents exposed to the 7 Habits is to invite them to volunteer. Examples include:

* Some classrooms invite a parent per month to share what they have learned about leadership in their careers. One parent taught students what firefighters need to know about leadership.

- Some schools organize mini job fairs where students rotate from parent to parent learning about different careers and how leadership is important in those careers.
- Some parents volunteer their skills to help students create art displays, write songs, or write plays that integrate the habits.
- Some parents teach students how to lead real-life projects. One parent, an architect, led a fifth-grade grade class through the process of designing their ideal classroom. They began with the end in mind by making real blueprints. Another parent, a graphic designer, taught a class how to design amazing art for their room using professional equipment.

Parent volunteers can also be responsible for getting the word out to other parents about *The Leader in Me*. They can create Welcome Packet materials, organize parent volunteers, help the librarian identify books by 7 Habits categories, and so forth. Several schools, like PS 133, William A. Butler Elementary in Brooklyn, New York, have a Parent Lighthouse Team that sends home regular notes about 7 Habits concepts. Horizon Primary School in Singapore has a Parent Lighthouse Team that helps arrange leadership events for students and families. The right parents can lift a lot of effort from staff members' shoulders while bringing a variety of new talents.

The Leader in Me @ Home

Now that we have shared ideas for students taking the habits to homes and families, we turn the focus to staff members applying the habits at home. While most of the examples describe homes with children, the same concepts can be adapted to homes without children.

Our experience is that most parents are doing better at parenting than they give themselves credit for. Nevertheless, parenting can be overwhelming at times. Indeed, we have spoken with corporate CEOs who masterfully lead multibillion-dollar enterprises and yet, in private, confide that their toughest struggle is in trying to lead their family.

Mukilteo Elementary enjoys the sun as students share their Leadership Notebooks during its Family Leadership Day.

We have talked with high-ranking military officials who command thousands with precision yet readily admit that their troops at home are in disarray. And, yes, we have spoken with teachers who say, "I can manage any classroom size and gain the respect of students, but once I arrive home, all the glory and honor disappears. It is out of control."

While the 7 Habits may not be the remedy that mends all ailments in a home, our experience is that they can have a significantly positive influence. Over the past few years, Robyn Cenizal has led a community initiative in Jacksonville, Florida, that has overseen 7 Habits training for more than four thousand parents. Many of those parents come from extremely challenging homes, while others come from homes that society might label ideal. Through it all, Robyn has been continuously amazed at how the habits apply to any type of home. "The best to the worst can benefit from the habits," she says.

Rather than create a new process for bringing the habits home, parents can apply many of the same *Leader in Me* concepts used at schools by:

- Teaching the 7 Habits @ home
- Creating a leadership culture @ home
- Achieving family goals @ home

Teaching the 7 Habits @ Home

In teaching the 7 Habits, schools take three general approaches: direct lessons, integrated approaches, and modeling. Each can be applied at home.

Direct Lessons. At the beginning of the chapter, we cited the example of the teacher who took her 7 Habits training manual home and taught the concepts to her family. Her approach was exactly what her family needed. But most parents do not go to that length in teaching the habits to their families. Most start simply by using the language of the habits with their children, or reading a book that includes a 7 Habits concept.

Many parents lean on one or more of several 7 Habits resources available for families. Sean Covey has authored a handful of books appropriate to children. *The 7 Habits of Happy Kids* is a starting point for young children. Each chapter has a Parents' Corner that includes discussion ideas and activities for a family to talk about and apply. Parents with teens find *The 7 Habits for Highly Effective Teens* a useful resource. *The 6 Most Important Decisions You'll Ever Make* applies the habits to major choices teens face on a regular basis, including what they will do about drugs, sex, school, parents, peers, and dating. Each book is written in child- or teen-friendly language and comes with practical life applications. *The 7 Habits of Highly Effective Families,* by Stephen and Sandra Covey, is loaded with ideas for families and marriages.

Just as teachers use different approaches for teaching the habits, parents use a variety of teaching approaches to match a child's maturity and personality. For young children, leadership-based bedtime stories are an opportune time and method. For teens, less structured approaches are typically better. Sometimes inserting an audio version of one of the teen books during a long drive on a family vacation creates a captive teen audience. Inserting a brief "life lesson" during a dinner conversation may be another occasion. Many teens resist requests for one-on-one conversations but are open to chats at times when a parent is helping them do a chore, like washing dishes, or while doing an activity like bowling. Lessons may need to be restricted to thirty-second sound bites—and that is okay.

One of the best ways to provide direct lessons is to have children do the teaching. Ask them to teach a habit to a younger sibling or to you. They can use skits, art, music, or other creative means to make their point. Children can be surprisingly creative in how they teach.

Integrated Approaches. Many parents find ways to teach or reinforce the habits during activities or tasks that are already being done in the home. Just start using the language. The safest way is to begin by applying the language to yourself: "I'm sorry, I should have sought first to understand," or "Hey, does anyone want to come sharpen the saw with me and go swimming?" The more they hear the language applied to authentic situations, the more well-rounded understanding of the habits they will attain.

> The greatest gifts you can give your children are the roots of responsibility and the wings of independence.
> —*Denis Waitley*

Parents who read with their children regularly can challenge them to spot one or more of the habits during reading times. Many movies or newspaper articles illustrate the use or abuse of a habit and the resulting consequences. Parents can share stories from family histories that support a leadership principle, or go places on family vacations or weekend activities that stimulate thinking about leadership. Some parents take their child to meet a friend, relative, or neighbor who is a leader in a company or volunteer organization, or who has exhibited excellence in a particular talent, and ask the person a lot of questions so their children also learn good question-asking skills. If a child likes

Key Actions to Conflict Resolution

Be Proactive

- Pause, gain control of your emotions. Stay apart until tempers cool.
- Stop and think. What do you feel is the *right* thing to do?
- Remember, people cannot "make" you mad; anger is a choice.
- Focus on matters within your influence, not on matters outside your control.
- Take responsibility for actions rather than blaming others or making excuses. Apologize.

Begin with the End in Mind

- Choose your battles. Do not contend over matters that have no relevance to what is truly important.
- Focus on what you want your relationship with your child or spouse to "feel" like once the disagreement is resolved.
- Tell the person from the start you value them and want to make things right.

Put First Things First

- Act on problems in a timely manner; do not allow them to fester or grow.
- Be true to your values.
- Speak only words that will communicate the other person's worth and potential. Don't say things you will regret.

Think Win-Win

- Balance courage with consideration. Be considerate of others, but not afraid to express your own feelings.
- Make meaningful "deposits" in the person's Emotional Bank Account.

- Seek mutually beneficial outcomes. Say NO to outcomes that would help you but not help the other person in the long run.
- Avoid comparing a child with other children.
- Forgive.

Seek First to Understand, Then to Be Understood

- Give your undivided focus. Say NO to television, cell phones, or other trivial interferences while talking it out.
- Listen with your ears, eyes, and heart until your child or spouse feels fully understood.
- Be open to feedback; correct inaccurate feedback.
- Clearly, concisely, and calmly communicate your feelings.

Synergize

- Optimize the other person's strengths and perspectives to resolve the issue.
- Be humble. You do not have to be the one with the right answer.
- Look for third alternatives, solutions that are better than either party has previously suggested.
- If needed, seek out other people who might have a more objective or educated view, and who might provide a better solution.

Sharpen the Saw (the great conflict preventer)

- Get rest, exercise, and eat right so you feel good. Fatigue and stress feed conflict.
- Build the relationship with a child or spouse in calm times.
- Learn stress reduction techniques.
- Learn about basic human psychology to help you understand why a child or spouse might think or behave in certain ways at different stages of life.
- Engage in meaningful activities in life so your confidence and esteem will be impenetrable. Avoid entering conflicts feeling vulnerable and weak.

a particular sport or hobby, parents can ask them who the leaders in that field are and what makes them a leader. These are all nonintrusive ways to integrate a brief lesson into day-to-day family activities.

Modeling. If ever there is a place where there is a need for fewer critics and more models, it is in the home. Homes are in constant need of modeling and remodeling.

Home brings out the best and worst in people, parents included. Just when parents think they are at the pinnacle of being the captains of their emotions and models of the habits, a child does something irritating and they lose it. Or just when they think they have mastered the habit of listening, their spouse breaks their trust and everything falls apart. Applying the habits is an ongoing process of learning and growing. Parents' ability to model the habits is often determined by how they treat the child who tests them the most.

Indeed, the actions of a single child or a spouse can put every parent and every habit to the test. The next time a disagreement arises with your teen, spouse, or other close relation, try walking away and reading the following list of possible action steps for resolving conflicts.

Temper gets us into problems; pride keeps us there. Teaching the habits at home—especially in challenging times—always works best when it starts from the inside, with modeling.

Creating a Leadership Culture @ Home

The framework for creating a leadership culture at school provides a template for how to create an effective culture at home. This includes working on:

- The Home Environment
- Shared Leadership
- Leadership Events

The Home Environment

As with schools, there are three parts to the home environment. The first is *what you see*.

One of FranklinCovey's consultants was sharing photos of school hallway displays and asking a group of teachers, "What do your school walls communicate to students?" when the thought crossed his mind, "What do the walls of my home say to my children?" Before long, he and his wife had removed some of the nice store-bought wall hangings they had mounted on a large wall in their home, and turned the wall over to the children to redecorate. What went up was a bulletin board full of photos of fun family memories and close friends. Now when friends come to visit, guess where the children always take their friends. They own that wall. It is theirs.

One parent worked with her boys and plastered the entire bathroom with leadership quotes. "They're all going to spend time in there eventually, so they might as well be thinking positive thoughts," she said. A single mom turned one room into an art gallery of sorts for her children's colorful arts and crafts. Chances of children liking the décor and feeling at home go way up when the decorations are their own handiwork.

> The 7 Habits was for us like the missing piece of a jigsaw puzzle that we didn't even know we were looking for. As good as we felt our family was before we were introduced to the 7 Habits, we're even better now.
> —the Wall family, Mukilteo, Washington

Parents can also benefit from what is placed on walls. One parent was very forthright about a personal drug usage problem. She placed a list of the 7 Habits on her bathroom mirror and read them every morning. "I needed them as a daily reminder, more than my kids," she said. An Asian CEO took down a painting from one of his walls at home and replaced it with a photo of his father. "That photo is my mission statement," he said. "I want to be the type of father and leader he was."

The main question to ask in creating the physical environment of a

One family's backdoor exit to greatness.

home is "What do the walls communicate about the worth and potential of each person who lives here?"

The second part of the home environment is *what you hear*. What is the language of your home? Is it affirming? Or is it condescending?

One parent told how some of his mother's last words before dying were "You're a good boy." He said those words have stuck with him for forty years. If the last words your child or spouse heard from you this morning were the last words they would ever hear from you, what lasting message would those words portray? What lasting message would you want them to portray?

What if the first words every child heard from a father or mother each morning were positive affirmations of their worth and potential, and the last words they heard before going to bed at night were compliments?

When speaking the language of leadership at home:

* *Don't* use the habits as whipping sticks. If all a child hears is "You're not being proactive . . ." or "Why didn't you put first things first like I told you to . . . ?" chances are they will develop an allergic reaction to the language of the habits.
* *Do* use the language as a positive affirmation, "I was so impressed with how proactive you were when . . ." or "I was amazed at how you put first things first and did you chores before going out to play." Use the habits as healers. "I'm sorry, I didn't seek first to understand . . ." or "I apologize."

The third aspect of the home environment is *what is felt*. Much can be said on this topic. Suffice it to say that home is intended to be a place where the four basic needs are felt and fulfilled: *mind, body, heart, and spirit*. Entire books can be and have been written on each of the four needs.

What they point to in essence is that there is a difference between returning each day to a house and returning each day to a home. The difference is not in the size or furnishings, but in the relationships and feelings.

Shared Leadership

With schools we identified three ways to involve students in leadership: 1) giving them worthwhile responsibilities, 2) valuing their opinions, and 3) helping them find their voice. Again, all three apply to home.

Most parents post job charts or give regular assignments to children. In addition to those valuable "chores," children can take on additional assignments that build skills, raise confidence, and demonstrate trust. One educator had his thirteen-year-old son ask to replace the garbage disposal that had broken on their kitchen sink. "No way" was his first thought. "Why not?" was his second. "It will give us time together and I·can teach him how to do it right when he gets it wrong." The father then watched as the son did the entire thing correctly without help. It was a real confidence builder for both son and father. Giving children responsible roles to play breeds responsible children. It is difficult for children to feel of worth if they are not given opportunities to do things of worth.

In the same vein, listening and allowing children to have a voice in family matters can bring surprises. One energetic principal was taking her family to Disney World as a Christmas gift. The family was on the way to the airport when her small sons spoke up from the backseat, "Mom, do we have to go to Disney World?" "What do you mean?" she asked. The boys wanted to go to Legoland. It was an easy switch, and a gentle reminder that children do have opinions. Another set of parents were about to rent a home at a vacation spot that would cost about $750 for three days. The children said, "What if we go to the campground nearby instead, and put the money we save toward a new TV?" The parents had planned to buy the TV anyway, so in spite of a few mosquito bites they were pleased to have the children learn the value of budgeting and working together.

> Don't define your child by their weaknesses, define them by their strengths.
>
> —Dr. John and Jane Covey

- Children have opinions about chores, about plans for the week, about meals, about consequences, and so forth. They want to have choice and voice.

Parents who hover over their children, doing all their jobs for them or making all their choices for them, are either servants or managers, not leaders. Too many families are overmanaged and underled. Sometimes parents think they are doing something *for* their children when in fact they are doing something *to* them.

As for helping children find their voice, think of a child who you know fairly well—if not a child of your own, then perhaps a relative or neighbor. Ask yourself:

- What talents does this child possess naturally?
- What interests, skills, or traits does this child possess that if nurtured could turn into talents?

Now consider: What have I said to this child within the past three days that has communicated my recognition of his or her current or potential talents? What have I done lately to nurture those talents? What will I do for or say to her or him within the next three days that will communicate my recognition of and admiration for those talents?

Children deserve opportunities to be leaders in the home. They want to contribute more than child labor—to have their opinions valued and to find their voice.

Leadership Events

Dr. John (Stephen's brother) and Jane Covey have devoted a significant portion of their lives to teaching the 7 Habits to families across the world. They identify three family events that create leveraged outcomes—high returns to the family from small investments. Each is a reminder of the power of "One":

One meal together. Mealtime is "sacred time" in John and Jane's book of life. Busy schedules make it easy for a family to live in the same house and never communicate, like passengers in an airport coming and going with no meaningful interactions. One meal a day together can bond a family. It may last only twenty minutes, but that is ample time for parents to hear things that need to be heard, share a positive idea, or communicate a child's worth and potential. Before sitting down, a parent can pause and think: "How can I best use this time to build family ties and trust?" Mealtime can provide nutrients for minds, hearts, and spirits—in addition to what it does for bodies.

One night per week family time. Setting aside one night (or one day) each week as family time makes room for meaningful interactions. It is time to do something fun, work on a project, or do service as a family.

Some find it helpful to schedule the same night every week so children learn to plan on it—it becomes habit. When it is not scheduled, chances of it happening are in jeopardy.

One-on-one conversations. Every child is unique; each deserves personal attention. Young children thrive on one-on-one time, whereas teens are prone to resist it, particularly if it feels "planned" or they sense it is an "I'll fix you" session. One busy father with a large family made it a habit to wash dishes with each child on an assigned night. His teens never turned down the help, nor did they know it was dad's built-in way of ensuring he was spending weekly one-on-one time with each child. "How's school going? What fun things are you learning? How is [friend's name] doing?" Similarly, a mother designated brushing teeth time as one-on-one time with her young children. She committed to saying only positive things about them during that time. Other times were set aside for lengthier one-on-one visits. Such visits are great times for offering intrinsic motivations and talking about long-term goals.

Like these three events identified by Dr. John and Jane Covey, any family activity or project can be turned into a leadership event. Even driving a child to school can be a leadership event. They are opportunities to build a family culture, create a vision of the future, and establish trust while doing everyday, normally occurring tasks.

Achieving Family Goals @ Home

FranklinCovey works with thousands of organizations across the world. Most have a mission statement, along with a strategy for what they want to accomplish over a year's time. In fact, some top organizations set aside weeks out of each year for strategic planning and goal-setting purposes.

Yet when it comes to families—the most important organization in the world—relatively few have a clear set of goals they plan to achieve together. Even fewer have a mission statement.

Why would parents want to begin a year with *no* end in mind? Why would they want their family life to happen by chance, without any vision or intentional plans?

If you are a parent—and are willing to risk that your children will think you have totally lost your mind—gather them together and follow three steps for writing a family mission statement:

First, *explore what your family is all about*. Ask questions such as:

- What is the purpose of our family?
- What kind of family do we want to become?
- What are our family's highest-priority goals?
- What are our unique talents, gifts, and abilities?
- When are we the happiest?
- What do we want our home to look like, feel like, and sound like?
- What kind of home do you want to invite friends to?
- What makes you want to come home? What would make you want to come home even more?
- How can I/we as parents be more open to your influence?

Initially your children may look at you very strangely as you begin asking such questions. But in a high-trust situation, most children will warm up and even like discussing such issues—especially if their opinions are valued. They like to have a say in family matters. If and when they open up about their feelings, listen. Do not criticize. Respect their choice and voice.

Second, *write it down*. There are fun ways of creating a family mission statement, such as cutting out pictures or words from magazines to make a family mission statement collage. Some families have made up a family song. Written mission statements do not need to be lengthy or perfectly written. In fact, what is written is less important than what is felt. A few tips include: 1) Write it as though you intend to live it. Be realistic. 2) Consider all four basic needs: physical, social-emotional, mental, and spiritual—thinking about the whole child, the whole family. 3) Keep in mind the various ages in the home so that the language and concepts are meaningful to all.

Third, *use it*. Once a draft is written, try living up to the mission statement as a parent first. Use the mission statement to make decisions. Plan specific activities that reinforce the mission statement. A mission statement is meant to be a source of inspiration, not a rulebook. Use it to course-correct as needed.

Once you have a clear idea of your mission, set specific goals that align to it. Identify the action steps and who will do what. When appropriate, create a scoreboard to show progress. Hold each other accountable. Then celebrate, while remembering the value of intrinsic over extrinsic rewards.

Great peace comes from having a place family members like to call home. As with schools, that feeling comes from proactive, intentional planning and goal setting. It does not happen by chance.

Go Easy

A former colleague of ours liked to tell the story of his dog bouncing out of a lake with a ball he had retrieved. He was one excited dog! As he dropped the ball at his owner's feet and barked delightfully, he vigorously shook his fur, spraying water in every direction. Everyone within reach of the dog dove for cover, not sharing the dog's excitement.

Sometimes people come out of 7 Habits training pumped up and ready to change the world. Figuratively speaking, they begin spraying everyone with their excitement. Not everyone receives the spray with an equal level of interest. Some may even dive for cover when they see the person coming. Without having been through the 7 Habits training they do not grasp its value. So a parent may want to check family members' interest level before spraying leadership ideas on them. It may take time. It may need to start with small steps.

A few tips for getting started at home:

Make a plan. Look over the suggestions in this chapter and choose a few activities or ideas to work on. Spread them out over a year's time so you do not try to do too much at once. If you ever feel your plan is too slow paced or overambitious, adjust. A yearly plan followed by weekly planning brings perspective, order, and balance.

Learn to say NO! Examine your current calendar and daily activities to see if there are things that can be removed. If yes, replace them with more worthwhile activities. Be honest. Are there things you are currently doing that in the grander scheme of things are a waste of time? Big blocks of television or video games are time fillers—can they be replaced with mind fillers? It is easier to say no when there is a deeper yes burning within.

Keep it simple. Think of how teachers say, "This is not one more thing, it is a better way of doing what we are already doing." That is also a good way to approach *The Leader in Me* at home. Look at what is already being done and add a leadership twist to it. If you are already eating dinner as a family, use the time to intentionally build relationships rather than to discuss minutiae. If you are already exercising regularly, take a child on a walk and use the time to tell stories of people you know who exhibit leadership qualities. In other words, keep doing what you are already doing, just do it through a new leadership lens.

Have fun. If you feel tensions rising because a son is ruining your great plan to discuss a habit as a family, back off. If you are irritated because your daughter is singing away while you are trying to get her to listen to *The 7 Habits of Highly Effective Teens* audio, hold your tongue. The suggestions in this chapter are intended to make things at home better, not to start a war. Make learning about leadership fun, not one more chore.

Start with yourself. Most important, win your own battles of effectiveness first, then help others win theirs. The only thing we can control is ourselves, so why not start there? As you model and live the habits, family members will be more inclined to follow your lead.

A Final Word on Taking It Home

Leadership in the home sets the first patterns and foundations for leadership in society. That is why one of the most gratifying rewards of working with *The Leader in Me* has been the stories that have come our way telling how schools and homes are working together for mutual benefit.

Schools and homes need to be about the business of doing more than remedying deficits in children. They need to be about the business, as Dr. Seligman learned from his five-year-old daughter, Nikki, "of recognizing and nurturing a set of strengths, competencies, and virtues in young people—such as future-mindedness, hope, interpersonal skills, courage, the capacity for flow, faith and work ethic." They need to do less "fixing" and finding out what is wrong with children, and more "identifying and amplifying their strengths and virtues, and helping them find the niche where they can live these positive traits to the fullest." Isn't that what home is all about?

This is why *The Leader in Me* prefers to approach home not from the vantage point of "What is wrong with the home, and how do we fix it?" but rather "What is right with the home, and how can we optimize and nurture those strengths further?" For this to happen in the most effective manner, it needs to be a planned effort, not a lofty set of ideals relegated to chance.

Personal Reflections

Habit 4: Think Win-Win involves seeking mutual benefit. What a boost educators would feel if all home-school relationships were win-win, where people truly strive to help each other. If you could somehow improve the home-school relationship, what steps would you take? What steps in this chapter could you apply to your home setting? Is your home in need of more modeling or remodeling? Do you spend more effort trying to remedy deficits in your family or discovering strengths?

7

Engaging the Community

The research is abundantly clear: nothing motivates a
child more than when learning is valued by schools and
families/community working together in partnership. . . .
These forms of involvement do not happen by accident
or even by invitation. They happen by explicit strategic
intervention.

—Michael Fullan

Donnie Lane, CEO of Enersolv Corporation in Decatur, Alabama, was intrigued when learning of A.B. Combs. The 7 Habits had greatly impacted his life and the way he led his company, so he couldn't help but wonder, "What might this do for students?"

Donnie went to nearby Chestnut Grove Elementary, where his children had attended school, and spoke with Principal Lauretta Teague about the possibility of visiting A.B. Combs. Lauretta recalls:

Mr. Lane called me on the phone. He indicated that having parental and community support was important to the success of our school and that there were people in the community who wanted to make a difference. We later met in my office and he showed me a short video of A.B. Combs Elementary. He felt our students could benefit from learning the *7 Habits* and that we should visit Combs. A few of us went with him, including one of our parent volunteers. After seeing A.B. Combs, the teachers all turned to me and said, "Mrs. T, we can do this."

Upon their return, the teachers who visited A.B. Combs made a presentation to the remaining staff about how the 7 *Habits* could benefit students. The staff grew excited, yet wondered how they would pay for the training. Again Donnie Lane stepped in. He covered expenses for getting the entire staff trained in the 7 *Habits*. He wanted it done in a special way, so he paid for them to go off-site to a resort location. The retreat provided an opportunity for the staff to bond and to develop a new vision for the school.

Donnie's vision, however, went well beyond Chestnut Grove. He felt that if all students in Decatur received the 7 Habits throughout their thirteen years of schooling, then Decatur would be a different type of community. When things went well the first two years at Chestnut Grove, other people began to share Donnie's vision, and the Decatur Public Schools district began looking for ways to make the offering available to all twelve of its elementary schools. But again, how would they pay for it?

Donnie Lane took a proactive step to influence his entire community.

Donnie was highly involved in the local Chamber of Commerce, so he teamed with Chamber executive John Seymour and began holding information meetings with influential leaders from local businesses. In the ensuing months they received sponsorships from several businesses, and with their help the district was under way.

Decatur had the fortune of being home to one of FranklinCovey Education's top consultants, Dr. Jane Knight. Jane had spent years in Alabama schools and was well respected. When her good friend Charlotte Feigley, supervisor of the training center at Athens State University, saw what was happening in Decatur, she called Jane and offered to host regional trainings in the 7 Habits and *The Leader in Me*. Before the two of them could catch their breath, more schools in the region had embarked on *The Leader in Me* journey, and numerous other schools across the state were taking notice.

Meanwhile, John Seymour contacted Mick Fleming, national director of the American Chamber of Commerce Executives (ACCE), about inviting Stephen Covey to speak at their national conference. As fate had it, that year's conference was held in Raleigh, North Carolina, home of A.B. Combs. At the event, Dr. Covey and Muriel Summers took turns sharing the keynote stage in front of one thousand Chamber executives before turning the microphones over to ten A.B. Combs students, including a few first graders. Chamber executives watched in awe as the students spoke about the habits and their leadership responsibilities with more confidence and stage presence than would be expected of most adults. The students stole the show, and within a year approximately thirty schools had embarked on *The Leader in Me* with support from local Chambers.

Today, what started as one man's vision for a local community has spread to Chambers across the United States and touched upwards of 200 schools—approximately 100,000 students and 800 staff. Thank you, Donnie.

Bringing Schools and the Community Together

Indeed, nearly half of *The Leader in Me* schools have enjoyed some form of corporate or community sponsorship. This chapter shares only a fraction of what has happened and how *The Leader in Me* schools and community members are working together to benefit students. But first a little context.

To say that relations between schools and businesses have been less than synergistic over the years is an understatement. Many educators will tell you they dislike businesspeople meddling in their affairs. They feel that too many businesspeople talk about students as if they are widgets that can be mass-produced with zero defects. They point out that while businesses can hire whomever and whenever they want, schools are compelled to accept almost anyone who walks in the door at any time. It does not matter if a new student speaks only a foreign language, just came from juvenile corrections, has a learning disorder, or flat out does not want to be in school; schools are obligated to give them every chance to receive a proper education. This means that schools do not have the luxury of laying off 30 percent of their lowest-performing students to improve their end-of-year, bottom-line results. So educators are wary of businesspeople (or politicians) who act like experts in saying, "Let us tell you how to educate kids."

At the same time, many business leaders are frustrated with schools. They view schools through bifocals, one lens being the view they get as parents or grandparents, and the other being the lens through which they view the coming workforce. Through either lens, they are not seeing what they want to see. For years, they have been content to remain at arm's length and merely point fingers, but that is changing under the new reality. Invited or not, a good number of them are getting off their spectator chairs and becoming involved. The reasons *why* are reflected in the following excerpt from an annual U.S. Chamber of Commerce report card on schools, called *Leaders and Laggards*. Catch their tone:

It has been [more than] a quarter century since the seminal report *A Nation at Risk* was issued in 1983. Since that time, a knowledge-based economy has emerged, the Internet has reshaped commerce and communication, exemplars of creative commerce like Microsoft, eBay, and Southwest Airlines have revolutionized the way we live, and the global economy has undergone wrenching change. Throughout that period, education spending has steadily increased and rafts of well-intentioned school reforms have come and gone. But student achievement has remained stagnant, and our K–12 schools have stayed remarkably unchanged—preserving, as if in amber, the routines, culture, and operations of an obsolete 1930s manufacturing plant. . . . Only about two-thirds of all 9th graders graduate from high school within four years. And those students who do receive diplomas are too often unprepared for college or the modern workplace.

Despite such grim data, for too long the business community has been willing to leave education to the politicians and the educators—standing aside and contenting itself with offers of money, support, and goodwill. But each passing year makes it clear that more, much more, is needed.

In essence, business leaders are feeling the pressures of global competition and are becoming more and more vocal about schools and what they perceive as serious shortcomings with the forthcoming workforce. What this leads to in many communities is a business world that is frustrated with schools, and educators who are annoyed with what they view as arrogant, naïve business leaders. Fingers are being pointed in both directions.

In contrast, neither A.B. Combs nor its community of business leaders is pointing fingers at anyone. Rather they are putting their heads and hearts together to focus on the common goal of helping young people. Muriel sees her business community not as ornery customers but as friends and partners. They in turn are applauding what is happening and are offering to help. It is a synergistic, friendly relationship.

With that as context, we will now share more of how business leaders, community leaders, and educators are coming together to bring similar levels of progress to students the world over.

Individual Contributors

In the early stages, most sponsors were individual contributors, like Donnie Lane. They were individuals with love for children and minds for what *The Leader in Me* can do to elevate a workforce and community. Andrew Cherng, founder of Panda Express restaurants, was among them.

For a number of years, Mr. Cherng had passionately worked to find ways to better integrate the 7 Habits into his rapidly growing business. So when he was in Raleigh on a business trip he visited A.B. Combs to see how they were doing it. What he saw, he said, "was beyond any preconceived expectations." What impressed him most was what happened toward the end of his visit. He explains:

> I was asked to speak to the students, and was telling them a number of things that really impressed me about them and their school. It was a lengthy list. At one point, one of the students, I believe he was a third grader, raised his hand and politely asked, "Mr. Cherng, you have told us about the good things we are doing at our school, but what about the deltas? You know, the things we need to do better."
>
> The young man was totally serious. He sincerely wanted to know how they could improve the school. He spoke as though he was one of the leaders of the school who could potentially enact the changes. And the great thing is that he was, as were all the students at A.B. Combs. They are all leaders, and all are taking ownership for the school.

When he returned home to California, Mr. Cherng was quick to share his experience with his wife, Dr. Peggy Cherng, co-CEO of the business. Before long, she too had the opportunity to visit

A.B. Combs. Speaking from the perspective of years of leading a successful organization, she observed:

> When we recruit leaders, we like to see people who are able to project their passion, who have self-confidence, and who have the right attitude to truly face the unknowns and the uncertainties that we all face every day in our personal and professional lives. I saw all those traits in the children at A.B. Combs.

Before long, the Cherngs had generously sponsored six schools near their corporate headquarters in Rosemead, California. Inspired by Panda's spirit of giving, employees went the extra mile to organize with the partnering schools' read-alongs, beautification projects, and leadership recognition events.

After launching *The Leader in Me* in those initial local schools, the Cherngs expanded their commitment to impact even more schools throughout the country, particularly in communities in which Panda

Peggy and Andrew Cherng, founders,
Panda Express and Panda Charitable Foundation.

Express operates. First, through their Panda Charitable Foundation, they sponsored an additional thirty schools in the western United States. Then with time, they became the founding donors for the "I Am A Leader Foundation," founded by Boyd Craig. Its mission is to unlock the potential within young people to lead by offering grants to highly qualified, committed public schools in financial need to launch a long-term implementation of *The Leader in Me*. To date, the Cherngs' contributions have enabled more than 250 schools across the United States to embark on *The Leader in Me*. This sets them apart as the largest single contributors to *Leader in Me* schools, touching the lives of more than one hundred thousand students.

Similar altruistic individual sponsors have offered caring support, including:

- Allan Markin of Alberta, Canada, who is the former chairman of Canadian Natural Resources Limited. He has taken a keen interest in Canadian education, with a particular eye for reversing negative health trends in youth. He funded fifty-seven schools in implementing the Alberta Project Promoting active Living & healthy Eating (APPLE) in Schools, which aims to help elementary students start out with the right health and fitness habits. When he learned of *The Leader in Me,* he saw it as a natural companion to his APPLE efforts. So in 2012 he began funding efforts to integrate *The Leader in Me* into the APPLE schools. His kindnesses have launched more than fifty schools in the Edmonton area, and reached out to urban, rural, First Nations, Métis, and Inuit students.

- In Lehigh Valley, Pennsylvania, two private visionaries are touting *The Leader in Me* like professional cheerleaders. But there is no fluffy rah-rah in their message. Al Douglas is a highly successful local investor, while Glen Bressner is a think-tank guy who runs a marketing business and spawns entrepreneurial ventures in the community. They play golf together a lot, but far more than talking about their golf swings they discuss ways to enhance the expanding

Lehigh Valley region. Together they have sponsored multiple
schools and have drummed up sponsors for additional schools from
their pool of friends.

* Marty Carver of Muscatine, Iowa, used the 7 Habits to turn his
tire retread company, Bandag, into a hallmark success. He says the
7 Habits played a pivotal role in changing the company's culture
and making it an attractive acquisition when it was purchased by
the Bridgestone-Firestone Corporation. Afterward, Marty and
his wife, Ruth, wanted to give back to their home community and
could think of no better way to do it than through sponsoring *The
Leader in Me* in all eight local schools via the Carver Foundation. In
doing so, the Carvers exemplified proper respect for the educators.
They did not force the idea onto the schools, nor did they dictate
how things were to be done once the offer was eagerly accepted.

These are but a few of the many individuals who have risen to sponsor schools.

Foundations

Several foundations that are not tied to individuals but rather to specific agendas for building their communities have also joined in. The
Staten Island Foundation in New York, for example, has a mission
to combat "big picture" challenges common to any sizable community, including racial bias, substance abuse, and general civility. Betsy
Dubovsky, executive director, says the foundation saw an immediate
connection between *The Leader in Me* and the foundation's mission.
Over the past few years it has contributed toward helping eight
schools get started, along with supporting student and faculty training
in the 7 Habits at the College of Staten Island.

Similarly, the John Deere Foundation has sponsored ten schools
in the Quad Cities area, which borders Iowa and Illinois. Drawing
no attention to itself, it saw *The Leader in Me* as compatible with its
mission and as a way of giving back to its loyal customers and commu-

nities. The Honda Foundation, based in Southern California, the Ford Motor Company in Florida, and so many others have also contributed to schools.

Outside North America, several foundations have also engaged. In Indonesia, where some of the kindest people in the world reside, the Dharma Bermakna Foundation, led by Chairperson Laurel Tahija, sponsored the first school to bring *The Leader in Me* to Indonesia. That school, PSKD Mandiri in Jakarta, became the first to receive the Lighthouse Award outside the United States and Canada. Nearby, the honorable Ny. Rosfia Rasyid funded the first Islamic-based school, An-Nisaa', to become a *Leader in Me* school. The GarudaFood Group and the Dunamis Foundation have likewise helped to get a few public schools started. In Colombia, the Terpel Foundation has funded sixty schools, with a vision toward funding one hundred schools. Several of the schools are housed in some of the neediest communities.

Again, these represent only a small sampling of foundations and individuals that have stepped in to lend a hand in an effort to better their students and communities. We honor all who have been so kind.

Students sponsored by the Terpel Foundation in Colombia
are finding their voices using handcrafted instruments.

Community Efforts

In several locations, it is not individuals or foundations that are sponsoring *The Leader in Me*. It is entire communities working together. They have taken the expression "it takes a village to raise a child" to a new level.

Most communities have high hopes for the well-being of all students and truly want to provide the education they need to be successful in life. And that is their primary motive. But there are practical interests beyond student welfare that also attract the attention of the wider community. Good schools produce good workforces and attract outside businesses, investors, and home buyers. Good schools also produce good citizens and community volunteers, which equates to a safer and friendlier community. Everyone wins.

Some community leaders even see *The Leader in Me* through the lens of cost savings. One county's juvenile rehabilitation administrator noted, "You save me one child and you save me six hundred thousand dollars in court fees, incarceration costs, and rehabilitation expenses." An assistant county attorney said that whenever his department confiscated property in connection with crimes or drug raids, any goods turned over to the county would be sold and the money given to the school for 7 Habits training. The rationale was that by the time the county investigated a murder or drug scene, pursued, arrested, prosecuted, incarcerated, and rehabilitated the offender, it cost the county up to a million dollars. Another state in which we are heavily involved reports the average annual per-juvenile cost for rehabilitation to be above the eighty-thousand-dollar mark. So regardless of the price tag, if *The Leader in Me* saves one child, these leaders see a return on their investment.

Whether their intent is to help children, to improve the workforce and community, to save costs, or all of the above, several communities have become involved. Again, we share only a handful of examples, including ones that involve Chambers of Commerce, the United Way, and municipalities in Sweden.

The Chambers of Commerce

In attendance at the national American Chamber of Commerce Executives convention were nearly a thousand Chamber executives from around the United States. Chambers have a real interest in schools. So, after the conference, a number of Chamber executives returned home and gathered their resources to consider bringing *The Leader in Me* to their community.

The largest Chamber initiative currently under way is in Bowling Green, Kentucky, where at a fund-raiser, a local business leader stood and said, "I could interview three hundred adults for a line position at my factory and not one of them would shake my hand and look me in the eye like the young student who greeted me at the door tonight. If that's what this process does for kids, I'm in." Ron Bunch, Bowling Green Area Chamber CEO, says, "We got involved because our businesses said the workforce lacked basic social and life skills. We see it as strategic for economic development, talent innovation, and matching people with jobs." The initiative involves districts from ten counties, as well as mayors, university administrators, and several businesses. Tonya Matthews, the Chamber's vice president of Partnering Services, recognizes that many relationships between schools and businesses across the world are disconnected or even contentious. "Yet this project," she says, "it is a symbiotic relationship. Everyone is working together." So far twenty-four schools are under way.

In Iowa, Bob Justis, CEO of the Greater Cedar Valley Chamber, returned from the national conference on a mission. He teamed with local businessman Tom Penaluna, CEO of the CBE Group, to start a pair of schools in the Cedar Falls and Waterloo districts. Tom went so far as to have all his employees trained in the 7 Habits. Things went well enough with those first two schools that Bob Justice eventually hired a former principal to oversee the rollout of additional schools. To date, twelve schools are started, and Cedar Valley is gradually becoming known as Leader Valley. Across the state in Council Bluffs, the

Chamber led by Bob Mundt sponsored the Titan Hill Intermediate School.

In North and South Carolina, CEO David Bradley of the Greater Statesville Chamber worked with his community to sponsor five schools in its award-winning district that is led by North Carolina's Superintendent of the Year, Brady Johnson. Mr. Bradley says that one of his biggest roles as CEO is to continuously demonstrate how the chamber is relevant, and he insists that *"The Leader in Me* is as relevant as anything our Chamber has ever done since it strengthens the youth of the community and supplies our future workforce with practical skills and critical life habits." The local police chief agrees and used a drug-free grant to fund one of the schools.

In South Carolina, Principal Lori Dibble at Summerville Elementary reports, "Not only have our teachers embraced *The Leader in Me* but our community has as well!" She adds, "The Greater Summerville/Dorchester County Chamber of Commerce and its CEO, Rita Berry, have walked hand in hand with us on the journey. Together we are creating a stronger workforce, stronger families, and a stronger community and region." The Chamber has helped start three schools, and annually hosts a combined educator, business leader, and parent 7 Habits training. Rita also partnered with David Bradley to feature *The Leader in Me* and Sean Covey at the bistate convention of the Carolinas Association of Chamber of Commerce Executives.

Chambers have been wise not to force *The Leader in Me* on schools. Marvin Jones, Chamber executive in Chillicothe, Ohio, was excited about the program but knew it had to be a school's choice. So he invited local schools to an overview. Initially, only one school was keen to embark, but gradually others became comfortable and now all four elementary schools and the middle school are implementing, with more than twenty local businesses contributing support.

Additional Chamber initiatives are under way in other parts of the United States, and in each case the overarching desire is to get students the skills they need to be successful. CEO George Swift and

Nancy Kelley of the Southwest Louisiana Chamber–Economic Development Alliance have worked hard to get the initiative started in Lake Charles. Nancy points out, "Many children have loving homes but share their parent(s) with two jobs. As a result, not all of them get the character and life skills training necessary to take care of themselves or make right choices." Similarly, Christi Kilroy of the Vicksburg–Warren County Chamber in Mississippi sums up the reality that, "*The Leader in Me* fills in an enormous missing void. The people funding the initiative in our area are the employers who are struggling to find people with basic skills, like getting to work on time. We can teach them technical skills, but we cannot teach them how to get along with people, to get to work on time, or to have a plan. We wish students were getting these skills at home, but many are not." Fortunately, students are now learning the needed skills, and people are noticing. The governor of Mississippi awarded the chamber and Vicksburg Warren County School District the Governor's Award for Excellence in Education, and one of the schools they sponsored, Bowmar Avenue Elementary, was recognized for the top reading scores in the state.

The United Way Leading Out

Similar to what is happening with Chambers are the efforts of local offices of the United Way. Two stand out: Quincy, Illinois, and Lafayette, Louisiana.

Quincy is tucked between beautiful farm fields and the banks of the Mississippi River. Its story began with Dr. George Meyer, a former teacher, school administrator, and district superintendent. Upon retiring, he joined the staff at Quincy University where he became dean of the School of Education. While there, he came across *The 7 Habits of Highly Effective People*. He became a certified 7 Habits facilitator and began teaching the habits to education students. He then partnered with Principal Christie Dickens of Dewey Elementary to bring the habits to her school.

Things went well. Tardiness dropped 35 percent. The number of parents attending PTA meetings more than doubled. Disciplinary referrals dropped 75 percent, and referrals of students for completion of work declined 68 percent. Within two years the percentage of students passing end-of-grade reading tests jumped from 57.4 percent to 89.7 percent and the percentage of students passing math jumped from 77.4 up to 100.

About that same time, the United Way of Adams County was researching ways to contribute to the community. After reviewing several proposals and visiting Dewey, it determined to take the *7 Habits* to all ten thousand students in the county. As United Way of Adams County's executive director Cheryl Waterman describes it:

The United Way of Adams County was seeking to take a position on an issue in the community, and to really put forth an effort to engage the community in something that would truly make a difference. We examined a number of underlying challenges in our community, such as poverty, and considered how it was leading to other things like teen pregnancies, substance abuse, and underemployment. We knew that if children succeed in school and in life they are more likely to avoid a lot of those other problems. So after doing our research we decided to take the *7 Habits* to all students in the county. Once we stepped up and made a three-year commitment to doing this, it was only a matter of time before local businesses were willing to step in and help with funding, to provide training space, or do whatever they could do.

Within their boundaries were the Quincy Public School District and the Adams County schools. Pat Heinigen of the United Way took a lead in working with the schools, while Cheryl and others set out to raise funds. Six years into their efforts, eighteen schools and more than eight thousand students in the county have been introduced to the 7 Habits.

In Lafayette, Louisiana, Sarah Berthelot is chief operating officer for the United Way of Acadiana, which covers four parishes. She says their mission is focused on three pillars: education, raising income, and health care, and that *The Leader in Me* matches perfectly with their education pillar. They started by sponsoring one school, Martin Petitjean Elementary, which quickly began to see transformational changes. Attendance was up. Academics were up. But what Sarah and others saw as "even more noticeable were the intangibles, like the relationships between faculty, parents, and students." So they combined efforts with local civic leaders, the Chamber of Commerce, local businesses, the school districts, and the I Am a Leader Foundation to fund eight additional schools. Dr. Jason Huffman, director of Impact Strategies for the United Way, has led the effort and played a synergy role in getting the various schools together once every five weeks to share best practices at the United Way offices.

Swedish Municipalities

In many parts of the world, school systems are under the governance of local municipalities, giving residents a voice in what their children learn at school. Sweden is one example where a number of municipalities have chosen to offer schools the opportunity to implement *The Leader in Me*.

In the municipality of Karlskrona, for example, three schools have started: Jämjö church school, Jändel school, and Tornham school. The schools already had good cultures, but were striving for an even better staff feeling and overall culture. Sixty staff members were trained in the 7 Habits and before the training was over they were already seeing positive changes in staff camaraderie.

Benefits also quickly spread to students. One example was a student who was very afraid to speak in front of people, even classmates. Before the school's first Leadership Day, however, the principal asked him to be the one who got up first and welcomed guests. He thought about it a few days before agreeing to do it. When the day arrived, he was well prepared, and none of the guests sensed any nervousness. He even had the confidence to slightly alter his speech midway, just enough to add, "It's my birthday, today."

Two young girls were tour leaders on Leadership Day. They took their roles seriously and led their group from location to location with excellent communication skills. One member of their group happened to be the head principal, and at one point she overheard one of the girls whisper to the other, "Could you please go behind the group and make sure our principal stays where she is supposed to be. She keeps wandering away and we will lose her if we don't pay attention." The principal was full of smiles later when sharing, "This is what happens when children understand what responsibility is and are given the lead over handling difficult situations, even when it involves a wandering principal!"

These types of improvements in student self-confidence and social skills, along with the increases in staff collaboration, were exactly the types of outcomes the municipality desired. The other municipalities are seeing similar positive results, and in each case there is the hope that the benefits will ultimately spill over into other interests of the community where they are trying to improve workforce readiness and deal with social issues commonly tied to highly transient populations.

These are a few examples of how communities are getting involved. In each case, someone from the community is leading out to champion the effort.

In other cases, the schools have championed the process themselves and engaged the community. At Heritage Elementary, Principal Dr. Deirdre Brady organized the campaign. She lacked funding, but felt strongly about bringing *The Leader in Me* to her students. Her proactive philosophy is: "Money is not the reason we don't do something." So she and the staff and even a few parents went to work fund-raising. Some businesses chipped in. Some parents gave donations. They received a few community and state grants. They went to the Rotary Club and one of its members organized a raffle. The Parent Teacher Organization contributed. And the school contributed a portion as well. Even students helped by going to some of the businesses and getting donations. It was truly a grassroots, community effort, and it raised enough money for the school to get under way.

Dr. Brady insists the effort was worth it. In the few years they have been engaged in the process, the school's behavioral referrals are down 85 percent. Dr. Brady says she seldom sees fourth and fifth graders any more for discipline issues. Either they take care of them on their own or the fourth- and fifth-grade peer mediators handle them. But even they have been complaining about a lack of "business." Academics have also improved steadily, and they have dropped 7 percent of students off the resource needs list, partly due to their goal setting efforts. Parent satisfaction is up. Teacher turnover is rare. Parents outside the boundaries are trying to enroll their children. All of which is what the community was anticipating.

An Investment in Our Future

In some countries, businesses have become so invested in helping students that they have made it part of their business to get involved. A few examples include:

- *Brazil.* The Abril Group in Brazil is one of the largest and most influential communication and education organizations in Latin America, with its publishing resources reaching 3.3 million teachers, schoolmasters, and school coordinators daily. When CEO Manoel Amorim was introduced to *The Leader in Me,* he saw it as bringing a needed set of skills for Brazilian students and a perfect fit with the company's mission. So the company acquired the rights to oversee implementation in Brazil, and had more than one hundred schools under way in less than a year.
- *China.* Rainbow Station, a preschool provider, after finding successes with *The Leader in Me* in its U.S. operations, decided to open a network of franchise schools in China. By including leadership principles in its interactive early education program, Rainbow Station creates a rich learning environment that is highly valued by Chinese parents.
- *The Netherlands.* CPS is a leading education consultancy and training company in the Netherlands. "For CPS to get involved with *The Leader in Me* was a natural decision," says CEO Suzan Koning. "We believe that the best teachers are those who support

Students In Taiwan perform for Leadership Day guests.

students in recognizing and developing their talents. Education should enrich the environment of students through social interaction, so that in the end the students are prepared to add value to society. That's exactly what *The Leader in Me* is all about, and why we chose to get involved."

• *Taiwan.* The second Lighthouse School outside of North America is Lih-Jen International, a K–9 school in Taipei. Board directors Ivy Sun and Christina Sun visited A.B. Combs in 2009. Throughout the day they kept looking at each other and thinking, "We've got to do this back home." "Staff and students welcomed *The Leader in Me* like an old friend," they said. "The 7 Habits align well with Chinese values and traditions." Paradigm Education has now been formed to take the process to other parts of Taiwan. Both Paradigm Education and Lih-Jen school have the vision of Lih-Jen being a model for other schools as *The Leader in Me* spreads through Taiwan, China, and other parts of Asia.

- *Japan.* Each year more than twenty thousand students are taught
the 7 Habits in Japanese cram schools, which are after-school
courses designed primarily for secondary students wanting to
get into the best schools. It started in Tokyo, where a company,
FCE, was formed by Mr. Ishikawa and Mr. Suzuki. Their former
company had been training consultants in general business skills.
What they quickly recognized, however, was that what their
consultants needed most were basic life skills: interpersonal skills,
time management skills, conflict management skills, and so forth.
Mr. Ishikawa was an executive board member of the company and
suggested they look into 7 Habits training for their consultants. The
training turned out very successful, but the question Mr. Ishikawa
and his chief training officer, Mr. Suzuki, kept asking was "Why
do we need to train our people in these skills? Why haven't our
consultants been taught these skills earlier in life?" They decided to form a
business so Japanese students could have
the opportunity to be taught the 7 Habits
before entering their upper years of
education and careers.

> We want our children to have Malaysia hearts and global minds.
> —*Dato' Teo Chiang Quan, Chairman, Paramount Corporation, Malaysia*

It is important to note that in each of the above cases the decision
that was first made was not about money. It was about what the habits
could do for the students and for society in general. Only when they
saw that other local alternatives were not available did these individuals and businesses decide to engage.

Indeed, the beauty of these community and business relationships
is that they are about more than a financial relationship. The students
are their children and grandchildren and they are very interested in
their development. They see themselves as making an investment not
only in their community but in their own offspring. And so companies, sponsors, and community leaders are getting involved well be-

yond giving money. In fact, some of their most valuable donations are their talents and leadership knowledge.

In Victorville, California, for example, the local Chamber teamed with the Brentwood Elementary School of Business and Leadership to create a Junior Chamber program. Chamber members participate in breakfasts at the school and visit with students, share leadership tips, and, more important, act as role models. Selected students attend the monthly breakfast of the Chamber, as well as the monthly Rotary lunch. Students help with the business expo, and learn from leaders about various careers and job skills. Students no longer are just talking about growing up to be teachers or firefighters; they are thinking of all kinds of careers they have learned about from their mentors at the Chamber and Rotary. The mayor and police chief are also involved, and as the chief says, "These kids are going to be buying cars, not stealing them."

Brentwood Elementary students share Leadership Notebooks with a Chamber of Commerce guest.

Interacting with leaders from the community—artists, businesspeople, health experts, etc.—opens students' eyes to new vistas. It gets them dreaming. And that is what business and community leaders want. It is what we all want. It is a win-win for everyone.

Personal Reflections

Habit 5: Seek First to Understand, Then to Be Understood encourages people to diagnose a problem before prescribing a solution. Often schools and businesses do not work together simply because they do not understand each other. What steps do you believe both business leaders and educators should take to better understand each other's needs and challenges? What can you do to better seek to understand others before advocating your solutions?

8

Shifting to Secondary and Beyond

Non scholae sed vitae discimus. (Latin, *We learn, not for
school, but for life.*)

—*sign in high school entry*

With the spread of *The Leader in Me* in elementary schools,
it was inevitable that demand would eventually arise at
secondary levels, and it has. What is interesting is how a
sizable portion of that demand has come from students.

At Port Charlotte High School in Florida, for instance, a group of
students approached Principal Steve Dionisio and Assistant District
Superintendent Chuck Bradley with a question. The district had
launched *The Leader in Me* in all ten of its elementary schools, and the
high school students had been hearing their little brothers and sisters
come home from school each day chattering about how they were
decorating hallways, running assemblies, tracking goals, and so forth.
"Why are we not being given those opportunities?" they asked.

A few states away, a student transitioning from elementary to middle school described how he had been told to expect unexpected
things to happen at the new school. What he never expected, however,
was what did not happen. "At my elementary school," he said, "I was
given lots of chances to be a leader. Teachers valued my talents and
opinions. Here at middle school, not once have I been given a chance
to be a leader."

At A.B. Combs, the school has a tradition of inviting graduating high school seniors to speak to graduating fifth-grade students about how to succeed in middle and high school. The speeches are always packed with 7 Habits advice. However, one former student showed up with her speech and was set to go until the time neared for the ceremonies to start. She approached Muriel and said, "I can't do it." Nervous jitters had struck. Muriel offered support: "Of course you can do it. You gave great speeches when you were a student here. You are a talented speaker!" The young woman shook her head and said, "No, Miss Summers, I can't get up in front of these people. I haven't spoken in front of anyone since I left here."

> I work with the science teachers at the middle school that A.B. Combs funnels into. Teachers can tell if a student has been at Combs almost as soon as they meet them, and when the kids get to whatever middle school they go to, they truly miss the leadership theme.
>
> —*Dr. Laura Bottomley, Professor, North Carolina State University*

The Shift to Secondary

Each of the above examples highlights a desire expressed by students for *The Leader in Me* to continue beyond the elementary years. Parents echo the desire. As one parent said, "We have great *Leader in Me* elementary schools; now we need to do something about our middle school."

Shifting from elementary to secondary schools presents a new set of challenges for *The Leader in Me*. Secondary schools are structured differently. Rather than staying with one main teacher all day, as is typical in elementary schools, secondary students shuffle from teacher to teacher, subject to subject, seeing any given teacher for only a few hours each week. Secondary teachers also tend to be teamed more by subject expertise than by grade level, and generally interact less as a full staff. Larger numbers of staff and students also contribute to the structure of secondary schools being different.

Another difference at secondary schools is the nature of the students. Secondary students are smarter and more independent. They can be given more mature responsibilities. They like to deal with real-world issues more. They are more inclined to ask intelligent questions and carry on logical conversations. Indeed, secondary students are wonderful bundles of talents and curiosity and a total joy to teach, except in those times when they are going through romantic upheavals, identity crises, hormonal changes, peer pressures, or those "I'm-going-to-do-it-my-way" stages, which for some students can be much of the time.

Something that often changes for secondary students is their zest for school. Too often it is a downward slope. In a nationwide Gallup poll of 500,000 U.S. students from fifth to twelfth grade, nearly eight in ten elementary students reported being engaged in school. That number dropped to six in ten students by middle school, and four in ten by high school. So only half of the students who were engaged in elementary school remain engaged in high school. Gallup defines "engaged" as those students who feel involved in the learning process and who have positive connections with teachers and the school. "Disengaged" students feel they do not receive much praise or recognition and that their school does not give them a chance to do the things they are best at doing.

So how does the downward slope get reversed? The answer, of course, is multidimensional and includes factors a school has little influence over. But Gallup's Brandon Busteed concludes that students are more likely to stay engaged if they enjoy frequent successes, are given chances "to do what they are best at," and have more positive interactions with adults.

Fortunately, there are talented educators who have a gift for working with secondary students. A number of them have been instrumental in helping us to pioneer practical ways to adapt *The Leader in Me* to the nuances of secondary schools. This chapter highlights some examples.

Research says . . .

A Gallup poll of 500,000 students in fifth through twelfth grades showed the following factors to effect the downward trends in students' engagement levels in school:

Scale 1-5 (5 = strong agreement)	5th	8th	12th
I have a best friend at school	4.68	4.51	4.14
My teachers make me feel my schoolwork is important.	4.56	4.10	3.89
I have at least one teacher who makes me excited about the future.	4.51	4.11	4.09
My school is committed to building the strengths of each student.	4.44	3.88	3.50
I feel safe in this school	4.36	3.97	3.80
At this school, I have the opportunity to do what I do best every day.	4.25	3.83	3.74
In the last seven days, I have received recognition or praise for doing good schoolwork.	4.01	3.42	3.20

Bringing the Habits to Teens

While the full *Leader in Me* process has not been in place in secondary schools for as long as it has in elementary schools, the history of taking the 7 Habits to teens is in reality a much longer one. It began almost as soon as the original 7 Habits book was released in 1989. A parent read the book and gave it to a counselor at Joliet Central High School near Chicago. The counselor was fascinated and passed the book on to another counselor, Tony Contos, exclaiming, "You need to read this!"

At the time, Tony was seriously thinking of abandoning his education career, having tired of the bureaucracy. Yet as he started his reading, each habit seemed to link to a specific decision he was grappling with personally or a challenge a student was facing. He called FranklinCovey to see if student resources existed. FranklinCovey had just hired Chuck Farnsworth, a former superintendent of schools in Indiana, to lead its education division. Though Chuck's initial emphasis was on training adults, he agreed to work with Tony to create a set of student resources. No sooner had Tony begun testing the resources than a mother approached him and asked, "What are you teaching my daughter?" Good things were happening with her troubled daughter and mom was looking for the source.

Before long, numerous secondary schools were teaching the habits. It was not until 1998, however, when Sean Covey authored *The 7 Habits of Highly Effective Teens,* that the effort to bring the habits to teens truly made a leap. The teen version sold a million copies faster than the adult version did and led numerous middle and high schools to bring the habits to their campuses. Hundreds of thousands of teens have since been trained in the 7 Habits, and a number of others

Korean students learning a student-created 7 Habits song with actions.

have also embraced Sean's *The 6 Most Important Decisions You'll Ever Make,* which applies the 7 Habits to pivotal choices teens face, including what to do about school, friends, dating and sex, parents, addictions, and self-worth.

Prior to *The Leader in Me,* the 7 Habits were taught in secondary schools only as a separate topic or curriculum. Schools taught the habits either as part of freshman orientation or within the framework of a single class, such as literature, sociology, or teen living. It was not until *The Leader in Me* arrived in elementary schools that secondary schools started exploring in earnest how to use the 7 Habits to revitalize their school cultures or as a tool to influence academic progress. They found that the same general challenges that elementary schools faced—academics, culture, and life skills (leadership)—were equally present at secondary schools, if not more so. They also found that the same basic *Leader in Me* processes used in elementary schools, if adapted, worked well in secondary schools for:

- Teaching the 7 Habits
- Creating a Culture of Leadership (especially student leadership)
- Setting and Tracking Goals

Teaching the 7 Habits

The first priority for teaching the 7 Habits at secondary levels is to enlist strong role models to do the initial teaching.

For twenty years, Joe Gutmann was a prosecuting attorney for the commonwealth of Kentucky. Much of that time was spent sending teens to prison. While Joe's intentions were to keep communities safe and to protect the rights of individuals, he couldn't shake the nagging sense that he might make an even greater contribution if he was on the proactive side of the fence, preventing teens from getting into trouble. So while giving up a good-paying job and a cushy office was not the easiest thing to do, that is what he did when he signed on to become a teacher.

Gutmann was hired to teach criminal justice at Central High School in urban Louisville. He was a longtime fan of the 7 Habits so he began teaching the habits to his students, many of whom come from volatile home situations. "I teach life," he says. His calm teaching style is not flashy but when Gutmann talks life, students listen. They know what he has given up to be with them. They view him as a friend and advocate, and recognize he has high expectations for them as individuals. They know he tries to live the habits himself. The habits are part of his core.

Joe Gutmann has been teaching the habits for more than a decade, and students current and former will line up in rows to tell how much he influenced their lives. Many have headed to college as a result of his influence, including several who have gone into the field of law and criminal justice. They want to be like Joe. And as Joe says with a humble contentment, "I used to be sending kids to jail. Now I am sending them to law school, to the Peace Corps, and to all types of positive professions in their communities. I couldn't be happier."

As Emma Bullock of Mountainville Academy, a K-8 school in Alpine, Utah, says, "If you're going to be teaching the 7 Habits to secondary students, you've got to be living them. If not, teens will see the hypocrisy, and it will be next to impossible to get them to apply the habits themselves." So, as with elementary schools, the highest form of teaching the habits in secondary schools is modeling, modeling, and modeling.

The ideal is for every teacher and every staff member to be viewed as a role model of the habits, and for every one of them to be capable of teaching the habits. However, it is advantageous to hand-select a few of the students' favorites—the magnetic ones—for teaching the habits on special occasions, such as to kick off the habits during assemblies or school activities.

Second to determining who will teach the habits is the decision of when and how the habits will be taught. At elementary schools, every teacher is expected to teach their students all aspects of the 7 Habits. Doing so in every class at a secondary school might cause students to mutiny: "This is the seventh time today I have had a lesson on Putting First Things First! I can't take it anymore."

The key to teaching the habits at secondary schools is to teach them "somewhere and everywhere." "Somewhere" means to have a specific time when students receive direct lessons on the habits. "Everywhere" refers to all teachers and all staff integrating the habits and leadership language into everyday conversations and lessons, regardless of the subject they teach or the role they have in the school.

The "somewhere" will vary from school to school. However, most schools take one of three general approaches. The first is to designate a specific class and set of teachers to teach the habits. Schools may designate classes like Teen Living, Literature, Sociology, Psychology, or Career Choices as the place where the habits will be taught. West Seneca East High School teaches a monthlong unit on the habits during English 1, a required course for all freshmen. Students read *The 7 Habits of Highly Effective Teens* as part of their nonfiction reading, then discuss the habits as a class. Other schools base the decision on where to teach the habits on who the best teachers are to teach the habits, like criminal justice with Joe Gutmann. Some schools create a separate course, "Leadership 101," and teach the habits during that class. Such classes should provide sufficient time for students to gain solid understanding of the habits.

The second general approach to "somewhere" is to designate an existing time slot when all students are already scheduled to gather outside of normal classes, such as during a homeroom or advisory period, or as part of an alternate schedule. Grain Valley South Middle School in Missouri, for example, wanted all teachers to teach the habits as a way of getting all teachers involved. So the first year they chose to have all teachers teach the habits during their advisory period, which they call "SOAR." They made an outline for the year and distributed a series of 7 Habits activities for all advisory teachers. The activities and associated lessons were highly experiential and students enjoyed them.

Patriot High School in Nokesville, Virginia, takes a similar approach. They designate a combination of advisory and flex periods for teaching the habits. Spanish teacher Janine Byers helps coordinate the schedule and works with staff to coordinate topics and lesson ideas. The first half of the year is mostly spent on covering key concepts, whereas the second half is focused on applications.

The third general approach to "somewhere" is simply a combination approach. Grain Valley South, for example, starting in its second year, began teaching the 7 Habits to all incoming sixth graders as part of a designated Leadership class. In addition to that class, all advisory period teachers do a refresher activity once a week. They have even taken it one step further by creating an elective Leadership class for seventh- and eighth-grade students who want to develop more leadership skills. Students in those classes focus on applying the habits to school projects or to community service. They are also assigned to teach sixth graders leadership skills like public speaking or goal setting. About a third of students sign up for the elective class.

In middle and high schools where students have come from *Leader in Me* schools, staffs find they do not need to spend a lot of time teaching the habits as much as applying the habits. At Rollings Mid-

Students in Leeds, England, engage in learning about Habit 6: Synergize.

dle School of the Arts in Summerville, South Carolina, their students have had the 7 Habits for multiple years at the elementary schools, so most of their discussions of the habits center on teen topics or service applications. The second half of the year, they separate students into thirty-five action teams that design and carry out service projects for the school and community using the leadership principles.

In addition to "somewhere," the 7 Habits and other leadership principles can be integrated into lessons or activities "everywhere." Regardless of the subject they teach, teachers find ways to integrate leadership concepts into everyday lessons. Some subjects, such as literature, sociology, and history, are filled with examples of people who have either exemplified a habit or paid the consequences for not adhering to a certain principle. Other subjects may not be as easily matched to the habits, but the language can still be used in integrated, ubiquitous ways. Any teacher can say things like "our end in mind for today is to . . ." or "let me seek to understand what you are getting at when you say . . ." Hearing the language of the habits in a variety of subject areas reinforces the concepts and allows students to envision ways to apply the habits to a variety of authentic situations.

> If students go through middle school thinking they are a doormat, high school will be real rough. We teach them skills that help them stand up for themselves, but in a proper way.
>
> —*Robin Lady, Teacher, Crestview Middle School, Ellisville, Missouri*

The ideal is for the language of the habits to become a natural part of a teacher's vocabulary to the extent that it comfortably inserts itself into any lesson or activity without much thought. That typically does not happen—especially early on—without some consistent reminders. Clementi Town Secondary School in Singapore, for instance, has designated a few teachers to teach the habits as part of a leadership class. At the beginning of each week, those teachers send out an email to all other teachers and staff regarding what concept will be covered that week. The expectation is that the other teachers will find creative ways to insert that concept into whatever topics they teach that week, and nonclassroom staff can also look for occasions to use the language.

Other ways secondary schools ensure the habits are taught "everywhere" is to embed the language into daily announcements, school assemblies, pep rallies, or other activities. It can be as simple as sharing a leadership quote. Some schools like to launch each year with a fun assembly in which all 7 Habits get introduced, or reintroduced. Posters at high-traffic hallway intersections and in classrooms also reinforce the habits. But perhaps the spirit of "everywhere" is best captured by Henry Duran, seventh-grade English teacher at Buckingham School in Colombia. He says, "I just look for the teachable moments. When students start talking about issues that are heavy on their minds and I can see they are looking for resolution, I find ways to use the habits to help them work through the issues."

As important as "where" and "when" the habits are taught is "how" the habits are taught. When Moss Middle School, led by Principal David Nole in Bowling Green, Kentucky, first launched *The Leader in Me* they chose to have their "somewhere"

> What students need to succeed in the twenty-first century is an education that is both academically rigorous and "real-world" relevant. This objective of rigor and relevance is not just for some students, it is for all students.
> —*Dr. Willard Daggett*

occur during advisory period. Each advisory teacher received a full set of *The 7 Habits for Highly Effective Teens* book to match the number of students in their advisory period. They carefully planned out a schedule of which pages would be read on which day, and began reading with students the assigned portion each day. They did not get far before recognizing the approach was not having the impact they desired. Reading straight out of the book—page by page, day after day—was not grabbing their students' interests. So they made a quick adjustment. They began instead talking with students about challenges teens face on a regular basis. As part of their discussions they would pause and say something like, "Let's read these two paragraphs from the *7 Habits for Teens* book and see what it says about the topic." Overnight, students became far more engaged. Teens like applying the habits to real teen issues. They also like using the habits to try their hand at solving social issues found in newspapers or talk shows. They like doing things other than sitting.

An important instructional strategy often overlooked is to turn the teaching over to students. Many times we have heard students say, "We prefer hearing the habits taught by our peers." Students can create team presentations, teach younger students, write scripts to plays, paint artistic mission statements, design posters, or make up rap songs and share them with other students. South Dade Middle School in South Dade Miami, Florida, is one of many schools that have made 7 Habits videos that are written by, filmed by, edited by, and starred in by students. The point is that as students teach the habits in classes, in assemblies, over the school radio, and so forth, they learn much more than they do by sitting and listening.

Teens in Malaysia teach the habits to their peers.

Maine-Endwell High School in Endwell, New York, has taken the use of students teaching the habits to a peak. Senior students are selected and trained over the summer to be mentors to all freshman students. As part of their training, they come up with a plan for teaching the 7 Habits to incoming freshmen. That teaching takes place during the first few weeks of school. Then throughout the year the mentors stay in touch with their mentees and use the habits as a framework for talking through questions or challenges the freshmen have. It helps the freshmen adjust to the new school and makes the school culture more cohesive.

Creating a Leadership Culture

Grain Valley South Middle School had been teaching the habits for eight years before implementing *The Leader in Me*. But it was not until they started applying the habits to the school culture that things reached a new level. They essentially followed the same process as elementary schools by:

* working on the school environment,
* involving students in leadership roles, and
* holding leadership events.

The School Environment

Like elementary schools, the school environment at secondary schools includes what is seen, heard, and felt.

What Is Seen. A principal in Asia said to us, "In our school, students have three teachers: their parents, our staff, and our physical environment. From what we put on our walls, students will be taught, if only subconsciously."

A visitor to Grain Valley South Middle School noticed a long chain hanging from the ceiling. It stretched the full length of the hallway and was made of construction paper. Each link represented a student. "How long has this been up?" asked the visitor. "Over a month," replied his student guides. The chain was hung low enough that most any student could easily grab it. "And no one has pulled it down?" the surprised visitor asked. The students seemed almost appalled by the guest's question, "Why would someone tear it down? We made this. Each of us has a link and we wrote our strengths on it. It represents that together we are stronger and can accomplish anything."

The impressive thing about the chain was not so much its artistry but rather the amount of ownership the students took for their environment. Indeed, while some impressive wall displays and artwork have surfaced at secondary schools that have been designed by staff or local artists, the ones that students respect most are designed by students. Secondary students like to see their handiwork.

At Vestal High School in Vestal, New York, a courtyard area had become overgrown, run-down, and never used. The student leadership team asked if they could take it over. A student-led Courtyard Committee was assembled and soon they and a host of student volunteers had it cleaned up and looking good. The courtyard is now a favorite place to hang out and eat lunch. A local Boy Scout troop heard about it and built a stage in it that students use from time to time to showcase talents.

Patriot High School was built from the start with the leadership theme in mind. Its mascot is "pioneers," so its general environmental theme is people who have been pioneers in their field. Hallways are named after prominent historical leaders, and quotes from prominent leaders are mounted around the school. Posters displaying its students depicting various character themes also garnish the walls.

Many of the best displays are the combined creations of students and staff. Grain Valley's art teacher, Debbie Ott, led students in decorating the school's walls that previously were nearly empty. She recruited a local graphics company to work with the students to design posters, a cover for the student planner, and banners to hang outside the school. Students were given guidelines such as colors, sizes, and a theme, and then their imaginations were turned loose. A panel of student leaders selected the art pieces that would hang in prominent

Visitors and students at Moss Middle School
know immediately the theme of the school.

places or be used on the planner. Before long, there was a thread of
quality and consistency throughout the building, but more important,
students possessed the feeling that "this place is ours," we created it.

These are but a few examples of what secondary schools are doing
to enhance their school environment in terms of what is seen. In each
case, the walls and facilities proactively communicate the worth and
potential of students. Students hear positive messages every day without anyone saying a word.

What Is Heard. A significant portion of what is heard at *Leader in
Me* secondary schools is adults listening.

Eighth grader Jared had visited with principal Jeff Scalfaro multiple times. His parents were distraught over his lack of direction and
attitude about life. He had no goals and had made unwise choices that
earned him visits with the principal.

One day, Mr. Scalfaro invited Jared to his office. Jared arrived in
a defensive "What did I do?" mode. Mr. Scalfaro assured Jared that
he had done nothing wrong. "I just was thinking about you and won-

dered how things were going," he said. Jared was suspicious at first, but Mr. Scalfaro had always been straight with him before and so within a matter of minutes Jared settled down. Mr. Scalfaro did very little talking. He instead practiced the principles of empathic listening outlined in Habit 5: Seek First to Understand, Then to Be Understood. In his listening, he saw sides of Jared he had not seen before. Trust was built. Jared returned to class feeling heard. Trust was built. We'll return to Jared shortly.

In secondary schools, listening takes precedence to talking. In fact, if adults are not careful, even the language of the 7 Habits can be received by secondary students in negative ways. Some students may even rebel against it if it is overused or used as a tool of criticism. Secondary students are more open to adults using the language talking to them about their worth and potential once they first feel understood.

Caution particularly needs to be taken when first launching the habits. Sometimes the adults are so energetic about using the language

Listening is the key to the language of leadership at secondary schools.

that after a student attends the fifth period of the day they are wondering what happened to their teachers. What's this new language? That is why it is important to use the language naturally. Don't force it. Connect it with hope.

What Is Felt. There are a lot of things secondary students want to feel. For starters, they want to feel the same things elementary students want to feel around the four basic needs. They want to feel safe, to feel they are learning valuable skills, to feel they have friends who accept them for who they are, to be involved in meaningful work, and so forth.

Along with those feelings, secondary students have increased desires to feel ownership and independence, to feel individual worth, and to feel a connection with an adult they respect. They want to feel they have an identity, that they are contributors. Most want to talk about their feelings more than they want to talk about biology or geometry.

When a fight broke out between some new students at one *Leader in Me* secondary school, it was students who jumped in and said, "Hey, we don't act that way at our school. This is our school and we don't want any of that stuff." Those students felt ownership. At another school a group of students came up to the principal after spotting some graffiti on a door and said, "Look what they did to our door!" Again, notice the language, ". . . our door." At another school, an eighth-grade student taking a group on a tour kept saying, "We do this . . . ," "We did that . . . ," "Over here we . . ." Everything was what "we" students had done. Secondary students like the feeling of ownership.

> One of the key cornerstone strategies for effective middle schools is to implement a comprehensive advisory or other time during the week that ensures each student has frequent and meaningful opportunities to meet with an adult to plan and assess the student's academic, personal, and social development.
> —*National Association of Secondary School Principals,* Breaking Ranks in the Middle

Given that many secondary schools have large student populations, the challenge to "develop leaders one student at a time" becomes more difficult with every student. Some teachers are naturals at making every student feel like their favorite student. All they have to do is make eye contact and the student feels appreciated and connected. But for most it is not so easy. That is where it helps to have a process in place.

Patriot High School has nearly three thousand students who could easily get lost in the crowd and graduate with the feeling that no adult staff ever knew or cared about them. To keep that from happening, the staff arranged advisory periods so that students have the same advisory teacher four years straight. The advisory teachers are then committed to getting to know each student, their interests, challenges, and academic progress. Activities are set up to increase the potential of that happening. No one is left unnoticed.

At Crestview Middle School in Ellisville, Missouri, Principal Dr. Nisha Patel instituted "The Power of 10." Each grade-level team identifies ten students who they feel need extra attention. They commit to helping them with academic goals and getting to know them. It is an intentionally designed system for getting to know students, for listening to their ideas, concerns, and aspirations, for improving academics, and for communicating their worth and potential. Then, at the student level, eighth-grade students sign up to be WEB Leaders, an acronym for Where Everybody Belongs. Selected eighth graders are paired and given extensive training over the summer, and are then responsible for mentoring twelve sixth-grade students. They befriend the students and answer questions so no one feels unknown or unwanted.

One last example comes from Heather Thomsen, an English/Language arts teacher at Moss Middle School. She, as well as other teachers, makes it a point to connect with each of her students by greeting them at the door every period. She checks on them to see how their day is going and to compliment them. She says it has changed the whole culture of the classroom, and adds that for as much as it has done for her students, it has even done more for her. "I feel like I am making a difference every day. If I can reach them, I can teach them."

One-on-one connections go a long way to how a student feels at school. Being treated in such a way helps them to feel individual worth and a measure of independence. When that one-on-one connection is with an adult they trust, estimates are that their likelihood of dropping out decreases by up to 50 percent.

Student Leadership

Now back to Jared. One thing Principal Scalfaro discovered when listening to Jared was just how clear of speech Jared was. He articulated things well. So when the idea came up to have students lead the morning announcements, Mr. Scalfaro thought it might be the perfect opportunity for Jared. Jared's eyes lit up when he was offered the role. Morning announcements had always been done by a staff member, so when a student's voice was heard over the intercom system, everyone was surprised. They were even more surprised to learn the voice belonged to Jared. "How come he got to do it?"

> We're growing communicators.
> —*Jeff Scalfaro, Principal,*
> *Grain Valley South*

Jared took the role seriously. But at the end of the two weeks Mr. Scalfaro had heard, "Why does Jared get to do it?" often enough that he felt he needed to give other students a chance. So he asked Jared if he would lead a student communication team. Again, Jared's eyes lit up. Announcements were made twice a day, and a team of about twenty students volunteered to take turns. Jared organized a rotating schedule and thrived in the role. At the end of the year, much to his parents' delight, and as a result of being trusted and given responsibility, Jared went from wanting nothing to do with school and college to doing well in school and actively searching for potential colleges to attend. He had been given a chance to find his voice.

The key to student leadership is more than assigning "jobs"; it is in giving them responsibility and ownership and then empowering them to lead. If you tell them what to do and how to do it, they become

Being given responsibility to oversee announcements
helps students like Jared find their voice.

workers. If you identify a need, give them responsibility, and get out of their way, they become leaders. Students like to be problem solvers.

At Crestview Middle School, teacher Vicki Kemp guides the annual Carnation Flowers fund-raiser at Valentine's Day time. It is a multi-class service project, and students plan it out, handle marketing and sales, choose what organization will receive the donated funds, and how they will celebrate. They do it all. In fact, it is with total smiles on their faces that they complain, "We don't get help up with anything. We ask a question and Ms. Kemp says we need to figure it out ourselves." Their eyes can't hide how much they love it, and they always try to outdo the previous year's class.

Crestview's former principal, Dr. Jill Scheulen, says that as the school was getting under way assigning students leadership roles, she and her staff began looking for authentic, meaningful opportunities for students. They could only come up with a handful of ideas, so they decided to ask students for ideas. The students exploded with ideas. Some had the idea to help the school's popular librarian each morning. Students took ownership for specific shelves and arrived early each day to straighten their shelves. Their names were placed on the shelves. They owned those shelves, and were even asked to suggest potential new books for their particular genre. Before long, more than 100 students were taking part in it, and they always enjoyed staying and chatting until the first bell. The librarian's reward? She was named the school's and the district's teacher of the year.

Students like chances to lead, but mostly when it is their ideas they are pursuing. Another group of students at Crestview chose to collect used sporting equipment for needy children in the St. Louis area. They worked with parents and eventually had to cap that list of volunteers at seventy-five students. They too have marketing teams, sorting teams, a celebration team, and so forth—all run by students during noninstruction times. A set of other students had the idea that seventh- and eighth-grade students should be the sixth-grade camp leaders instead of high school students doing it as had always been done. It would give them a chance to lead and would create a bond with younger students. The first year the staff was amazed at the leadership demonstrated by the students, particularly when the camp was hit by a tornado and the student leaders calmed everyone down and did exactly the right things.

Classroom teachers have also caught on to student leadership. It starts with teachers asking students, "What am I doing that you as students would like to be doing?" Math teacher Stephanie Miller at Moss Middle School asked her class that question and was surprised by their response. Her routine was to start each day having students solve a math problem as a warm-up activity. Afterward, she would lead a discussion of who solved it correctly, what worked, what were common mistakes, and so forth. The students said, "We can lead that discussion." So Ms. Miller gave them the stage. She created a sign-up sheet for students to volunteer for a day and in no time the sheet was filled. After leading the day's kickoff discussion, the "math leaders" get to sit at a special parlor table in the back of the room—an area that formerly was reserved for students with discipline issues.

Math teacher Tracey Gamble at Grain Valley South uses more than fifty volunteer student "Learning Leaders" to tutor students during advisory period. It gives them a chance to contribute and feel of worth. Meanwhile, a teacher down the hall was asked by a visitor in between classes about the Leadership Roles chart she had on her wall. Instead of explaining how it worked, she said, "Just stay here and watch." As students arrived, one started collecting homework, one started passing out the previous day's homework, another cleared the whiteboard from the previous class, another recognized the birthday of the week, and so forth. It was flawless. The teacher never said a word. The students felt ownership, appreciated.

Teacher Mary Ann Hall has been teaching the habits for years and knows the value of student empowerment and turning questions into leadership opportunities. A student complained one day that he wanted honey mustard dressing in the cafeteria. She turned it right back to him and asked how he could apply his leadership skills to make it happen. The next thing she knew, he had designed a survey, collected student feedback, kindly approached the cafeteria staff, and honey mustard dressing was on its way. The student learned, felt heard, and the cafeteria staff was viewed as friends. It turned out to be a win-win.

These are but a few samples of the ways secondary schools are giving students leadership opportunities. As one teacher concluded, "We were totally nervous at first about turning over the reins to students. Now, all we can say is, why didn't we do this fifteen years ago?" Secondary students like choice and voice. And for students like Jared, it can be a life changer.

Leadership Events

Leadership events in secondary schools provide additional opportunities for students to be leaders and to teach leadership principles. But their biggest value is to build a sense of community and vision.

Vestal High School had a tradition of holding pep assemblies on the first Friday of each month to whoop it up for the sports teams. But when the reins were turned over to the student leaders to guide the agenda, they said that instead of pep rallies they wanted Leadership Assemblies. They felt that non-sports-related students deserved equal honor for their talents, and they didn't want to wait for the end-of-year awards assembly. At one of the first assemblies, Nate, a sophomore member of the Student Lighthouse Team, suggested using "WAO" as a theme, an acronym for "We Are One." Within seconds of the announcement, students were using it on Twitter and closing text messages with it. It was a hit.

A series of popular leadership events at Vestal is their community service projects. One year, the city was severely flooded, causing much damage and postponing the start of school by a week. But students didn't want to sit idle. They organized cleanup teams and spent the days helping the community. They even turned their Homecoming Dance into a fund-raiser to help flood victims. That spirit of community service continues every week as students assemble and deliver backpacks of food for students with needy families.

> Giving a student a chance to dance may be enough to keep them in school.
> —*Helen Arudsson, Rektor, Sweden*

Secondary students at PSKD Mandiri in Indonesia perform a traditional Saman dance from Aceh to welcome Leadership Day guests from eleven nations.

The same spirit of building community can go into classroom. Language arts teacher Ericka Harris recognized that after weekends her students needed some time to regroup, and to download what happened over the weekend. So on Mondays she would take a little time to listen and let the students talk. It was a standard Monday "event." But at one point the students said, "Why don't you let us lead those discussions?" So every Monday, student "Leaders of Highs and Lows" take turns leading the discussion. It builds relationships among the students and teacher.

These same types of events—pep rallies, service projects, talent shows, and class activities—are held at many schools. But the key at leadership schools is that the events are student led and designed to build community and create vision.

Achieving School Goals

Goal setting is an area that needs to be tailored to individual schools at the secondary level. Crestview Middle School has an outstanding staff that values goal setting but also understands how some middle school students resist it. So Dr. Patel suggested that the way they go about it was to first ask the teachers to model goal setting. Each teacher was to write a personal mission statement, one personal goal and one professional goal, to post them in their rooms in a visible place, and to discuss them with their advisory students. Some even invited classes to be their accountability partners and to encourage them along. When it came time to talk to students about setting goals, students already understood the process and saw the value.

Buckingham School's secondary program in Colombia is one that has found success in having students set Wildly Important Goals (WIGs) in core classes and to track them. Each Monday morning, students are given time in homeroom to reflect on their goals and decide action steps for the week. At Moss Middle School and Grain Valley South, students keep a simple one-page scoreboard for core classes and can see how they are progressing.

At a school level, Crestview Middle School decided to set one school goal, which they chose to focus on literacy. All students are asked to set a literacy goal, along with clear action steps. Accountability chats with their advisory teacher on a weekly basis help everyone to rethink their goals and to be self-accountable. The process is kept simple, yet it gets students learning about goal setting and thinking about how they might improve their literacy.

An important aspect of goal setting in secondary schools is having students write personal mission statements. For many students the writing of a personal mission statement and defining a vision and plan for their lives can have significant impact. One high school student, for example, was filled with a venomous desire for revenge after his older brother was fatally stabbed during a fight and was ready to put his own blood on the line to get that revenge. But then he was touched by a passage out of *The 7 Habits of Highly Effective Teens* that he read as part of a freshman class. He went home and wrote a three-page sonnet and called it his mission statement. In place of exacting revenge and possibly going to prison or worse, he committed to devoting his life to "doing good" in honor of his brother.

A student wrote a personal mission statement as part of an English class that taught the habits. It consisted of three words: "Never give up." Every word meant something to her. She came from a family where no one had gone to college. Yet she wanted to go to college. Years later, after completing her university studies, she reported that it was her high school mission statement and the feelings she had when writing it that propelled her to overcoming many obstacles to earn her four-year degree.

A Chinese secondary student in Singapore struggled to keep up in school. He lacked focus. After reading *The 7 Habits for Teens* as part of one of his classes he began viewing himself differently. One of the first things he did was to create a mission statement and career plan. His grades spiked upward. He became a leader at his school. He gained direction. The change came when he grasped the vision that he could be the leader of his life.

For a number of years, Vestal High has focused students on setting goals that have to do with their life beyond high school. They then complete projects throughout their high school years that move them toward their life goals. Furthermore, instead of maintaining Leadership Notebooks to track academic progress, they develop digital Leadership Portfolios beginning their freshman year. In their portfolios, students store and track all their information for applying to college, resumes, leadership participation records, goals, and best works. "We continually ask students," says Assistant District Superintendent Mary Surdey, " 'What's your legacy going to be?' They take goal setting seriously." Her sentiments are echoed by the middle school coordinator at Buckingham School, Elena Rokhas, who notes that "goal setting with secondary students goes well beyond setting academic goals, it is a way of unlocking dreams."

Writing a mission statement and setting goals can also be impactful for the school as a whole. New Hope High School is located in New Hope, Alabama, a rural town with a population less than three thousand. It is a friendly place, yet bad economic times have led some to call it the town of No Hope. The school has 350 students, 46 percent from low socioeconomic settings. When Principal Lavell Everett heard of *The Leader in Me,* he knew the process was mostly being implemented in elementary schools, but everything he read connected with what he felt his students needed. So he took a few staff members and visited a few *Leader in Me* elementary schools. What they saw impressed them. "We just have older students. They'll like this!" they determined.

They secured funds through a drop-out prevention grant, and off they went. The staff volunteered days for trainings over the summer. Principal Everett says that it was a soul-searching opportunity for staff members to apply the principles to their personal lives and families. They wrote personal mission statements and set their sights on developing a new mission statement for the school. Everyone had input. The more they worked on the mission statement, the shorter it became: "New Pride. New Passion. New Hope."

What surprised everyone was how quickly the new mission statement took life. Teachers wanted to fix up the school and give it a new look that matched the mission. They painted a new mural. In their excitement, they almost had to keep reminding themselves that the new mission was also meant for the students. Fortunately, when the students arrived, they too felt the vision, drew energy from the adults, and painted a string of murals of their own. Parents and others in the community caught on and got involved. Local churches put the mission statement up on their marquees. The mission and vision spread through the town. When it came time for students to write their mission statements and set goals, the process was already embedded in their minds; they had just seen it modeled. Only a year into the process, the school has seen a tremendous turnaround.

Secondary students like to dream. They want vision.

Students took ownership of capturing and spreading the new vision at New Hope High.

Colleges and Universities

Some ask if anything has been done to take the 7 Habits to college or university levels. The question comes at a time when a third or more of college students drop out within the first year.

The answer to the question is Yes. For more than two decades the 7 Habits have been a mainstay on college campuses as part of freshman orientation or specific programs such as MBA or nursing programs. The greatest swell of most recent interest has been in relation to first-year student retention and other related "college success" matters. An unsettling proportion of college students are arriving on campus unprepared. Of course, there are those who show up without the proper academic foundations, such as adequate reading, writing, or math skills. But more often than not, their challenges have roots in "life skills." They have never had to keep their own schedule, deal with unfamiliar roommates, balance priorities, select food on their own, make all-new friends, exercise without being told, balance a budget, and so forth. When all this is heaped atop what their professors are demanding, it amounts to more than they can absorb. They crumble.

Contrary to what some students may think, college and universities really do want to retain them. They are not deviously trying to weed them out. Most are doing all they can within professional reason to help students survive the first year, including providing training in remedial academic skills and basic life skills. A number have turned to the 7 Habits for help, seeing them as a robust set of skills and principles that cover a range of needs.

A sample of what career schools and universities are doing includes:

Utah Valley University (UVU), Orem, Utah. The Department of Student Leadership and Success Studies at UVU has offered a full-semester course on *The 7 Habits of Highly Effective People* for more than fifteen years. It is an elective offering with up to twenty-five sections each year. Lead Instructor Denise Richards says, "The department has enjoyed extraordinary success with the overwhelming majority of students who complete the class. Outcomes-assessment results show that most students make comments such as, 'this was a life-changing experience,' or "this class had a huge, positive impact on my outlook, decisions, and life,' or 'this is the one class that got me through the first year.' " The department is currently working to leverage the personal leadership aspects of the course by partnering with their on-campus leadership center in tandem with FranklinCovey's collegiate leadership initiatives.

Alamo Colleges District (Five Community Colleges), San Antonio, Texas. More than 60,000 traditional students and 30,000 continuing-education students throng the five campuses of the Alamo College system, headed by Chancellor Bruce H. Leslie. Years ago, while at a different college, Dr. Leslie had been invited to greet each graduating student at the commencement exercises. What surprised him was the number of students who did not know how to look him in the eye or firmly shake his hand. "That was after four years of college," he grimaced. He realized that it was only the tip of an iceberg—many of the students "lacked the real foundation of success, the skills to stand up with confidence, to make critical decisions and solve problems, to think for themselves."

In pursuing the 7 Habits at Alamo, Dr. Leslie says, "My interest in the 7 Habits is not just to teach our students soft skills like listening or speaking up or shaking hands, although those things are important. My real interest is teaching them to think critically. The 7 Habits teach how to analyze and evaluate our own paradigms, to think more effectively. I see it as a higher order of learning." And that is a big part of why since 2001 the Alamo Colleges Student Leadership Institute (SLI) has provided leadership education that includes the 7 Habits for select students, and why Alamo is seeking to expand the offering to more students across its campus.

CHN University, Leeuwarden, the Netherlands. CHN explicitly labels itself a "Leadership University," combining career preparation with scholarship and service. With eleven thousand students in the Netherlands and campuses in South Africa, Thailand, and China, CHN defines leaders as people "who act according to universal principles, take responsibility, value differences in people, synergize, and develop themselves." Dr. Robert Veenstra, chairman of the board, says, "I want a leadership-focused university. Leadership is for me the way to bring out the best in people."

Dr. Veenstra pioneered the use of the 7 Habits in the "Value Driven Leadership" program of the university. More than seven hundred students participated in the first program, with a 75 percent excellent rating. Many students over the years report that the program has helped them change their perspectives and become successful.

Niagara County Community College (NCCC), Sanborn, New York. NCCC has formed a Leadership Initiative Team made up of faculty, staff, students, and administration from across the campus. The mission of the team is to "model the core principles and behaviors of the 7 *Habits of Highly Effective People,* in order to build a community at NCCC that empowers all to achieve their full academic potential and to become leaders for life." They are conducting 7 Habits workshops not only for college staff and students but also for the community, including veterans and high school students.

Longwood University, Farmville, Virginia. The College of Business and Economics houses the SNVC Leadership Institute based on the principles of the 7 Habits. The institute offers the 7 Habits to faculty and staff each semester. The institute's mission also includes outreach to high schools. The 7 Habits of Highly Effective College Students is also offered to students in the college.

Wrapping Up

For sure, secondary schools (and certainly colleges and universities) are different than elementary schools. Secondary schools must examine their unique staffs, students, structures, and goals and determine the best ways to implement *The Leader in Me.* As they do, they see benefits to the school, to the students, and to the staff.

One such staff benefit was described by Yamberli Cruz, who was the lead teacher and point person in supporting Principal Brian Hamilton in bringing *The Leader in Me* to South Dade Middle School. Not long ago, she and her husband found themselves in an uncomfortable situation. It was night and they had just parked in a dark area outside a restaurant where they planned to enjoy a meal. They noticed they were being approached by a clan of teen boys. They kept the doors locked and began thinking of alternatives in case something bad happened. Then, in a sliver of light, Mrs. Cruz recognized one boy as one of her students. As her eyes focused, she realized that all of the boys were from her school. They had spotted her car and went out of their way to come talk with her. What had looked like a threatening situation turned out to be a very rewarding experience as Mrs. Cruz and her husband visited with the boys, laughed, and exchanged memories.

Teens that have those kinds of relationships with adults are far less likely to drop out of school or make poor choices. Teachers who have those kinds of experiences are more likely to stay engaged and feel the value of their work. So while to date *The Leader in Me* process is less formalized in secondary schools and colleges than in elementary schools, many schools are seeing positive outcomes. If keeping students engaged in school means listening to them, providing opportunities for them to have meaningful connections with adults, and offering opportunities for them to do what they do best, then we are in favor of doing what we can to make it happen.

Personal Reflections

Habit 6: Synergize is about seeking out the strengths of individuals and combining them so that the whole is greater than the sum of the parts. Adults are sometimes quick to point out the problems of secondary students when a more effective approach is to identify their strengths and then to leverage those strengths in ways that contribute to the good of a school or family. Thinking of teens you know, what strengths do they have? How can those strengths be harnessed to improve a school culture? If you have teens at home, how can their strengths be used to strengthen the home? What goals do they have?

9

Keeping It Alive

Transformation is everyone's job.

—*W. Edwards Deming,* Out of the Crisis

The first school in Canada to embark on *The Leader in Me* was Crestwood Elementary in Medicine Hat, Alberta. Principal David George is a certified 7 Habits facilitator for his district and was in the process of training his staff when he learned of *The Leader in Me.* Soon he and two teachers were on a plane to attend a Leadership Day at A.B. Combs. They returned inspired and holding fast to two pieces of advice from Muriel. First, "Do not water down the *7 Habits.* Trust that students will understand the language." Second, "Do not boil someone else's water. Do it your way, make it your own."

Crestwood's "way" started out slow. Emphasis in year one was on the staff applying the 7 Habits to their personal lives and with each other. They regularly reviewed the habits in staff meetings and applied the habits to school challenges. They introduced students to one habit per month, and each teacher submitted two lesson plans at the end of the month to be posted on a file share for all to access. At year's end, the 7 Habits were becoming part of the everyday language.

Year two, the habits took on less of a monthly focus and more of a ubiquitous approach. All 7 Habits were integrated in lessons through-out the year, and leadership language was used in morning announcements. Quotes went up on walls, and student-crafted bulletin boards appeared in high traffic locations. Students also began taking on leadership roles, and students caught exemplifying a habit were honored as "7 Habits Heroes" during assemblies. At the end of the year, eighty parents (up from thirty the year prior) responded to the annual parent survey, and 100 parents gave the 7 Habits a "very favorable" rating.

As year three approached, the school was set to lose fifty students due to natural attrition. Two teachers would lose their jobs. Yet as the summer unfolded, Mr. George began getting knocks on his door from parents outside the school's boundaries. They had heard the school was teaching the 7 Habits and wanted their children enrolled. It happened enough that when the new year arrived there was a full allotment of students and all teachers were retained. To ensure the consistency of the habits being taught evenly across the school, 7 Habits units were developed and taught to fifth-grade students as part of their "Health and Life Skills" requirements. It was one of a few new ideas for the year.

That is how it has gone at Crestwood for nine years and counting. Each year, the staff decides what to *keep* doing, *stop* doing, and *start* doing. Something new is always added to keep things fresh and progressing. And it must be having some impact, as 60 percent of the school's 520 students now come from outside the school's boundaries, primarily because of parents talking to parents.

A Sense of Permanency

Getting *The Leader in Me* going and keeping it alive is akin to launching a satellite. The initial thrust takes careful planning and two or three solid booster rockets to get it off the ground. Once it reaches a certain altitude, however, it should settle into a nice orbit, needing only occasional adjustments to the trajectory and pace. And for schools like A.B. Combs, Crestwood, and others, that is exactly how it has evolved. After the initial thrust, each year they have made a few tweaks and inserted a few new ideas to keep things fresh and continuously improving. Meanwhile, some schools have struggled to get off the ground or to make it beyond year one.

So what is the difference between the schools that soar into orbit and those that sputter at launch? This chapter identifies a few of the strategic lessons that have been learned over the process of getting two thousand schools launched. It describes what it takes to get off to a good start and to keep the process alive. The most strategic lessons involve:

- Gaining and Sustaining Commitment
- Establishing Purpose, Path, and Pace
- Aligning Systems
- Storytelling
- Engaging the District
- Working on Paradigms
- Doing it Again

Gaining and Sustaining Commitment

In the third century BCE, the great mathematician Archimedes declared, "Give me a lever long enough, and a fulcrum on which to place it, and I shall move the world." With all due respect, though we have some amazing educators, no one educator is so big as to single-handedly launch and sustain a school transformation of lasting quality, let alone move the world. It is not a solo task.

The best implementations we have seen at schools that have successfully launched and sustained *The Leader in Me* have combined the synergistic efforts of a highly effective principal, an engaged Lighthouse Team, a fully collaborating staff, an involved family and community base, and spirited students—don't forget the students.

A Highly Effective Principal. At the helm of every strong *Leader in*

Me school is a strong principal. No single individual has more influence to ignite or stall a school transformation effort than the principal, especially in the beginning. Yet if the principal is the only one pulling on *The Leader in Me* lever, little will happen. It takes more than one person. Once *The Leader in Me* is in motion, however, the principal can greatly help sustain progress by consistently using the language, walking the talk, respecting everyone as leaders, clearing the path, and keeping the *why*—the constancy of purpose—alive. The more they focus on teaching the principles of the 7 Habits, the more the school becomes principle-centered, not principal-centered.

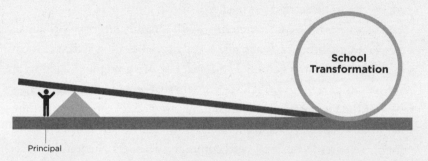

It takes more than the pull of a strong principal to transform a school.

Engaged Lighthouse Team. One of the first tasks for getting *The Leader in Me* under way is to assemble a Lighthouse Team. A Lighthouse Team consists of seven to ten staff members and perhaps a parent. The Lighthouse Team sets the proper path and pace for implementing *The Leader in Me* at the school level. The team sustains *The Leader in Me* by spreading the workload to all staff and students so that everyone feels ownership and no one carries the entire load. They ensure ongoing staff and new staff training in the 7 Habits and *The Leader in Me,* and fill mentoring and modeling roles. The freshness of the team is kept alive by rotating in a few new members on an annual basis. Strong Lighthouse Teams enable *The Leader in Me* to continue even with the arrival of a new principal, should that occur.

Fully Collaborating Staff. The Leader in Me is not something to be forced upon a staff. Nor does it require 100 percent buy-in to get started. Nevertheless, the more people are engaged early on and collaborating, the better. Book studies of *The Leader in Me,* visiting a model school, or hearing parent and community support may be enough to sway some people to engage. For others it may not be until they go through the 7 Habits training or spend time with the process that they embrace. Once they are engaged, it is important that they are reengaged each year. This happens as they share best practices, celebrate positive results, and experience improvements to their own effectiveness and job satisfaction. *The Leader in Me* is a collaborative process not to be carried out in silos.

Involved Family and Community. With a highly effective principal, an engaged Lighthouse Team, and a fully collaborating staff, the most vital stakeholders for getting *The Leader in Me* going and keeping it alive are in place. Nevertheless, schools that implement *The Leader in Me* at the highest levels are those that are not content with limiting their adult resources to staff members only. They enlist the talents and support of parents, business, and community leaders. Such individuals can greatly contribute to the effectiveness of *The Leader in Me* and lighten the load for teachers.

Students. If there is a resounding theme throughout this book, it is that involving students provides tremendous leverage to getting the process launched and keeping it alive. This includes involving them in teaching the habits, in improving the physical environment, in filling leadership roles, in making decisions, and in setting and tracking goals—involve, involve, involve. Once *The Leader in Me* gets going, students can provide some of the most enthusiastic and sustaining leverage.

The more staff, students, parents, and community members are informed and are involved in the process, the more committed they will become. The more stakeholders are involved and committed, the more the fulcrum will shift closer to the target and create greater leverage. Remember, no involvement, no commitment.

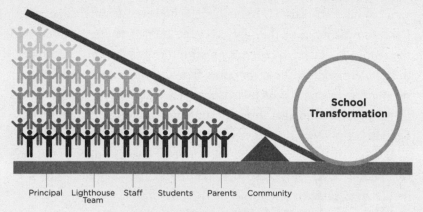

Principal   Lighthouse   Staff   Students   Parents   Community
Team

With each added stakeholder, the fulcrum shifts,
and the more leverage is added.

Establishing Purpose, Path, and Pace

A second strategic lesson learned is the value of establishing a balanced purpose, path, and pace—each year.

In Port Charlotte, Florida, the Charlotte County Public Schools district invited all ten of its elementary schools to participate in *The Leader in Me*. All ten responded favorably. Four schools wanted to start immediately, while the other six wanted to take a year or so to study it out, establish buy-in, and implement at a slower pace. Of the four schools that started immediately, two progressed faster than the other two due to factors unique to their students and staff. Within two years the other six schools had implemented, and to date all ten schools are progressing. Three have been named Lighthouse Schools, and all are collaborating to share best practices.

In California, when Janson Elementary was approached by its district to see if it had interest in adopting *The Leader in Me*, Principal Gabriel Cardenas wondered how his staff would respond to the idea. They were already stressed by large class sizes, low budgets, other initiatives, and a high percentage of students who spoke English as a second language. And indeed, Mr. Cardenas was not surprised when some of his staff resisted. Enough staff, however, wanted to give *The Leader in Me* a try, so they got everyone trained in the 7 Habits and then moved gently. No one was pressured to implement. Fortunately, things went well in the classrooms that did implement that by year two most everyone was on board. From there, the pace was quickened to the point that in year three the staff was honored as a Lighthouse School.

In each of the above cases, the schools took the time to become clear about their purposes, their path, and the pace at which they would go given their unique needs and circumstances.

Purposes: Why is it that *The Leader in Me* is important to our school? What objectives are we trying to achieve? Such purposes need to be clear and at the forefront of all involved. Without a clear *why*, it will be a challenge to get staff to embrace any *how*. A.B. Combs spends time prior to the start of each year reinspiring each other, setting goals, and reestablishing their why. Teachers make a new commitment to a personal goal they want to achieve that year

A.B. Combs staff members post an annual commitment for all to see.

and post it on a commitment board. For *The Leader in Me* to be properly launched and sustained, there needs to be ongoing constancy of purpose.

Path: How are we going to achieve our purposes? Who will do what, and when? Having a yearlong plan to launch the first year or to start each additional new year creates balance, saves time, allocates resources, reduces stress, and increases the likelihood of success. How else will staff know if they are on the right path if no path has been designated? A path should take into account the needs and talents of staff members, but if it starts to focus more on staff than students, it may not be leading to the desired destinations.

Pace: The story is told of a hospital patient who in one day received a gall bladder removal, a tonsillectomy, and a knee replacement. All three operations were performed to perfection, but the patient died of shock.

Embedded in *The Leader in Me* are strategic steps for improving academics, culture, and leadership—all three. Each is doable and designed to make things more effective. But if undertaken all at once, or if one area is focused on exclusively at the expense of the others, both staff and students will feel the shock.

There are far, far more ideas in this book than should ever be attempted in a single year. A school will want to choose the ideas that match its needs and interests, come up with some of their own ideas, and then spread them out over a period of years. Most school transformations take three years to truly gain staying power. A.B. Combs has been adding ideas for fifteen years. Sometimes fast is slow, and slow is fast. It is not a race.

By establishing a realistic pace prior to the start of each year, schools take a balanced approach and greatly reduce the likelihood of doing too much or too little during any period (see "Why Change Efforts Fail"), or of getting to the end of the year and recognizing they have forgotten key events or initiatives.

Purpose, path, pace—and patience—all go together.

Why Change Efforts Fail

Many factors go into determining the proper path and pace for school transformation. It is often a matter of finding the right balance between too little or too much.

Too Little	Too Much
No compelling purpose for change	Purpose not hitched to reality
People unwilling to change	People change too often, careen from fad to fad
Lack of a strong principal	Too dependent upon a strong principal
Not enough time spent getting buy-in	Excessive time trying to gain total consensus
Lack of strategy	Strategy too detailed—people not empowered
Not enough preparation, planning	Always planning but never implementing
Move too slow—people lose enthusiasm	Move too fast—people feel overwhelmed
Not enough teamwork—individuals do own thing	Too much team focus—individual effort stifled
Successes not recognized or rewarded	Successes declared too soon or over praised
No accountability or feedback	Too much checking up—micromanaging
Not enough district support	District imposes the change
Give up too soon	Keep doing same things when they don't work
Students are not involved	Students are over involved
Not enough doing	Lots of talking

Aligning Systems

A third strategic lesson learned for sustaining *The Leader in Me* long term is the value of aligning systems. In fact, when we asked principals who have sustained *The Leader in Me* for more than three years what they did to keep it alive, almost every one offered, "We built it into our systems."

Principal Rose Kerr at the Staten Island School of Civic Leadership is one whose immediate reply was "It's in all our systems." Mrs. Kerr is a veteran principal in New York City's public schools and has seen about everything there is to see in a school. When the chancellor offered her the opportunity to open a new school and gave her leeway to design it the way she wanted, she jumped on it. The school was literally in the process of being built and hiring staff when the planning team came across *The Leader in Me*. They determined to make "Leadership" one of three pillars that would serve as the basis for the school's philosophy, the other two pillars being "Academics" and "Civic Responsibility." As a staff they identified nonnegotiables that would lead them to achieve all three pillars, and then built those nonnegotiables into their systems. So it was no accident when three years later the school was pronounced the top academically performing school in all of New York City public schools, and for three years onward it was in the top 10 percent of New York state schools, the 98th percentile of New York City schools, and the top public school in the borough of Staten Island.

Common systems found in most schools that can help sustain *The Leader in Me* include:

- Hiring and Selection
- Learning
- Communication
- Collaboration
- Evaluation
- Rewards

- Calendaring
- Organizational Structure

Below are a few examples of how schools have used these systems to their advantage in sustaining *The Leader in Me.* It is not intended that a school will do all these things; they are merely provided as samples.

Hiring and Selection Systems. Great schools come from hiring and retaining great people. There is no greater factor. So the more schools hire and retain people whose competencies and character already fit a highly effective school culture, the better.

One principal related how she hired a particular teacher based on her outstanding teaching credentials. And indeed, students and parents loved her. Yet she turned out to be very *independent* and not very *interdependent*. She closed her door and worked in isolation. She wanted nothing to do with her grade-level team. She refused to share best practices, fearing that if colleagues "stole" her secrets then parents might not request her. She loved *The Leader in Me* but had to do it better than everyone else. As good as she was in the classroom, everyone sighed in relief when she chose to go elsewhere.

Hiring people with 7 Habits qualities is not always easy, but is easier than hiring people with the opposite qualities and then dealing with the adverse consequences. It is what leadership guru Jim Collins calls "getting the right people on the bus." It begins with building good questions into the interview process that will help detect if the individual is a good fit for a 7 Habits culture.

Learning Systems. Something that Crestwood Elementary has done extremely well is to ensure proper training in the 7 Habits and *The Leader in Me* for all new and ongoing staff. New hires receive 7 Habits training from the district soon after their arrival, while Mr. George personally takes lead on getting them versed in *The Leader in Me,* including his vision for how he would like it implemented at the school.

For ongoing staff development, staff meetings are held the first Monday of each month and thirty minutes are reserved on the agenda for discussing a habit. Generally, a Lighthouse Team member shows a 7 Habits video and the staff discusses two questions: 1) How can we better apply this principle in our school? 2) What can I [meaning each staff member] do to better apply the principle? Mr. George says he generally ends up cutting off the discussion as the staff is ready to continue sharing ideas. He adds that it does not require a lot of preparation, and, in fact, makes the preparation for meetings easier.

A common format in other schools is "7 Minutes for 7 Habits," where a staff member is given seven minutes to highlight a best practice or key learning about one of the 7 Habits during a staff meeting. They make it a standard part of the agenda. Horizon Primary in Singapore every Tuesday during staff meeting reads a small portion from *The Leader in Me* and discusses it. They say they are in no hurry to get through the book.

Some schools find it helpful to build in systems for teaching the habits to students. Previously mentioned examples include building LEAD time into the first ten minutes of the day. Crestwood Elementary built standard lessons into their Health and Life Skills modules.

The chance to speak in public at Leadership Day
is a built-in learning system for students at A.B. Combs.

Chua Chu Kang Primary built lessons into the first thirty minutes each Monday, with each lesson containing: 1) concept overview, 2) school application, 3) home application, and 4) review of content. These are simple systems these schools use to make teaching and learning leadership principles more consistent.

· *Communication Systems.* All schools have systems for communicating with students, parents, and staff. Common systems include morning announcements, newsletters, assemblies, take-home packets, phone calls, emails, parent-teacher conferences, bulletin boards, and websites. The language of leadership can be embedded into all of these systems.

One of A.B. Combs's favorite systems for communicating leadership principles is its daily morning news that is transmitted to every classroom via television. Shortly after the bell rings, the "news" begins. After leading the announcements and flag ceremony, student leaders share a brief insight on one of the habits and recognize Leaders of the Week. Adults who participate use affirmative language, "I saw a student exhibit one of the habits, yesterday, and . . ." It is kept short and simple, and starts the day off well.

Some schools have used their phone system to communicate how it values students. When one calls after hours, a prerecorded student voice answers, "Hi, this is [name]. I am a leader at [name] Elementary. It is now after hours. Please call back between eight a.m. and four p.m., and make it a great day." Students live for the chance to be "voice of the week," and work hard to practice their diction and public speaking skills so they can do it right.

Collaboration Systems. The thirty-four-nation Organisation for Economic Co-operation and Development (OECD) reports that teachers in high-achieving countries provide 15–25 hours a week of teacher collaboration time, which is significantly more time than is found in other countries, including the United States, which averages 3–5 hours per week. Collaboration time includes time for observing colleagues teaching, analyzing student learning, and engaging in lesson study and action research.

It is not enough to merely tell staff, "Everyone find time to talk and share." Systems must be put in place for collaboration. That is why, in addition to regular grade-level meetings, A.B. Combs has a daily collaboration system called "hallway huddles." Prior to school starting each day, music (selected by teachers) sounds over the intercom to let grade-level teams know it is time to gather in the hall outside their rooms. They spend a few minutes conversing about important things they are working on that day, discussing students who need special attention, coordinating schedules, and the like. It lasts only minutes but ensures collaboration.

A collaboration system that Crestwood Elementary has established is an annual staff field trip. Where do they go? They go from classroom to classroom, office to office within the school. They observe what other teachers and staff members are doing with lesson plans, bulletin boards, counseling sessions, and so forth. It is a potpourri of ideas and a way for teachers to be acknowledged. No bus is needed, but everyone enjoys the trip and learns from each other. William Yates Elementary in Independence, Missouri, does something similar as a couple of times each year they "Go Fishing," meaning they visit each other's rooms to share ideas and applaud creativity.

> Teaching has been described as the second most private act in which adults engage. In fact, schools have been characterized by some critics of public education as little more than independent kingdoms (classrooms) ruled by autonomous feudal lords (teachers) who are united only by a common parking lot.
> —*Richard DuFour and Robert Eaker,*
> Professional Learning
> Communities at Work

A broader system for collaboration is *TheLeaderinMeOnline*. It has an entire Community section dedicated to educators from around the world sharing ideas. Furthermore, regional symposiums are held throughout the United States, where thousands of educators share best practices, visit model schools, listen to well-known thought leaders, and network.

Evaluation Systems. The old adage is "What gets measured gets done." Misaligned evaluation systems drive misaligned behaviors.

Evaluation systems include systems for grading students, evaluating staff, monitoring discipline, evaluating culture, and so forth. Something Crestwood did to align its evaluation system for students was to add a section on report cards that provides feedback on how students are doing relative to each of the 7 Habits. It is a friendly system intended to catch students doing things right, and to encourage good citizenship and personal effectiveness. Parents seeing it are also reminded of the habits.

At the staff level, Principal Mike Fritz in Red Deer, Alberta, includes having a 7 Habits goal as a standard part of each teacher's annual progress evaluation. It lets teachers know that modeling the habits is an important part of their job. At Charlotte County Public Schools, a portion of principals' and other district leaders' annual evaluation is a 360-degree assessment of how leaders' interactions with people align with the 7 Habits.

Evaluating staff performance is always a sensitive topic and is often governed by strict legal or union guidelines. Not long ago a team of teachers were found in tears. They had been told their school could not do *The Leader in Me* because their state's teacher and principal evaluations were based solely on academics, and their principal did not want to do anything that was not solely focused on academics. This totally frustrated the teachers. The good news for them is that several of the more prominent teacher evaluation rubrics have begun in recent years to favor approaches like *The Leader in Me*. They take into account a teacher's ability to help learners engage in critical thinking, problem solving in authentic situations, and taking responsibility for their growth. They evaluate a teacher's ability to collaborate with families, establish a culture for learning, manage student behavior, utilize physical space, help students set and track goals, communicate with students, and use assessment in instruction. All of these factors align well with *The Leader in Me*.

Reward Systems. Closely tied to evaluation systems are reward systems. They are intended to motivate and celebrate students and staff. All schools and classrooms have reward systems of one form or another. In fact, reward systems are so plentiful that if educators fail in any way at rewarding students, it is in over-rewarding them, particularly with extrinsic rewards. Whereas extrinsic rewards are shorter-lived and can even be viewed as manipulative or controlling, intrinsic rewards have longer staying power. If used, extrinsic rewards should be paired with intrinsic rewards.

Some teachers cleverly use additional opportunities for learning as rewards. In North Carolina, for example, a state standard requires students to learn social etiquette. Instead of telling students to sit down, be quiet, and listen to a lesson on etiquette, teachers at A.B. Combs turn the requirement into a fun goal with a reward attached. Early in the year, they inform students that if they demonstrate good performance in specific areas, their class will be rewarded with a special Silver Tray Luncheon featuring some of "the best food the cafeteria has ever served." Students salivate as they take it upon themselves to make sure that everyone lives up to the requirements. When the time comes for the fancy event, students cannot fathom what "all those forks" are for. Scarcely do they know that all their hard work over the year is being rewarded with another opportunity for learning.

Then there is the teacher who had an old pair of socks hanging from her door. When asked, "Why the socks?" she responded, "My students knocked my socks off today with their performance and I wanted to let them know it." It is not hard to imagine her students trotting off with an extra skip in their step, not because they got a big treat or party, but because they knew their teacher had caught them doing something good.

Indeed, the most impactful reward systems seldom cost a penny. As Muriel relates, "You will hear us compliment students all the time. You will hear us thank them. We tell them how much we appreciate them. We have nine hundred students and it is important to us that we connect with each of them every day. We let children know we believe in them. It is part of our core value system."

Calendaring Systems. When plans are made and schedules are fixed at the beginning of the year, the biggest priorities deserve to be calen-

WANTED!

PROACTIVE FIFTH GRADERS

I am being proactive at school when I show up on time. When I help others, I am being proactive at school. At home, I am being proactive by helping my mom with some chores. Walking the dogs is another way I am proactive at home.

REWARD

BEING BETTER PREPARED FOR LIFE

Effective reward systems help students feel intrinsic worth and progress.

dared from the get-go. When will new-hire training in *The Leader in Me* be completed? When will student-led conferences be held? When will Lighthouse Team meetings occur? When will favorite traditions be celebrated? When will Leadership Days or other important events take place? When will milestones toward Wildly Important Goals be reached? Scheduling strategic events before the year starts significantly increases the chances they will happen, keeps the calendar balanced, and ensures that WIGs are not subordinated to PIGs. Regularly calendared events become traditions.

Organizational Structures. A school's organizational structure designates who does what in the school. While some of the best outcomes at schools happen unexpectedly, sustainable school transformation requires someone other than "serendipity" to be in charge.

A little story has appeared in various forms over the years. Our version goes like this. There were five very talented people on the

Lighthouse Team. Their names were Everybody, Somebody, Anybody, Nobody, and Busybody. One year there was a Wildly Important Goal to pursue. Everybody was asked to take the lead on it. Yet Everybody felt strongly that Anybody had much more talent to do it, and was certain that Somebody would volunteer. So Everybody got busy working on some Pretty Important Goals. In the end, Nobody wound up working on the Wildly Important Goal, and that gave Busybody plenty to gossip about for days.

Some leaders end up doing an overabundance of work because they fail to delegate or assign clear responsibilities. Having clear assignments with clear and meaningful expectations divides work into manageable actions and engages people in the process. It also helps sustain the process. Again, no involvement, no commitment.

So there are a few examples of how schools have built *The Leader in Me* into their systems. Systems that are aligned with the mission of the school and with stakeholder needs relieve stress and strain and reduce needing to "reinvent the wheel" over the years. The more *The Leader in Me* is embedded into existing school systems, the more likely it is that it will be sustained over time.

Storytelling

A fourth strategic lesson learned in launching and sustaining *The Leader in Me* is the value of storytelling. Telling and retelling stories reinvites commitment, grows the culture, and helps keep the efforts alive.

A.B. Combs has a collection of stories that have hung around for years. One day music director Jacquie Isadore was inadvertently delayed. She arrived late to find fourth grader Aneesa standing in front of the choir directing warm-ups. She had been given no direction to do it. "Someone needed to step up and be the leader," she said, "So I did it." Her story has been told and retold to give students a vision of what a leader does.

Summerville Road Elementary in Decatur, Alabama, dedicates an entire wall to telling and retelling stories. The long wall that students pass by every day is turned into a giant timeline. On it are placed numerous photos of events and accomplishments from the year that reinforce the school's mission and communicate students' worth and potential. The story builds every week and keeps the memories and vision alive.

Dana Elementary is only three years into *The Leader in Me* yet has already been asked to tell and retell its story many times. Located in rural Hendersonville, North Carolina, its staff was looking for something that would prepare its 500 students for life. Its student enrollment is 44 percent minority, 33 percent less than English proficient, and 80 percent free or reduced lunch. "Having those demographics has never stopped us from wanting to have high expectations for our students and raising the bar," says Principal Kelly Schofield. "We always try to think of what is in our Circle of Influence, what we can do instead of what we can't do." Finding *The Leader in Me* on a library shelf set them on a new path.

Since embarking, Dana Elementary has received several state and national awards. The National Title I Association named Dana a "Distinguished School" for its sustained student achievement. It was one of six schools in the United States to win the National School Change Award. It was also a finalist for the national Intel award for gains in math proficiency, and won recognition as a North Carolina rewards school. Each time it receives an award, the Dana staff has an opportunity to tell and retell its story. Each time it strengthens the staff's resolve to keep doing what they are doing.

Many of the awards that Dana has received have been for academic gains. In the last four years, Dana's Hispanic students rose from 20 to 80 percent proficiency in reading, while its "less than English proficient" students improved from 15 to 75 percent proficiency, its Caucasian students moved from 61 to 85 percent, and its needy students shifted from 47 to 80 percent. Incredible! Mrs. Schofield says that the goal-setting and data-tracking processes have had "huge effects" on

John Hopkins University Report

The Leader in Me encourages schools to track and celebrate progress in leadership skills, school culture, and student achievement. It helps tell their story. Examples of such progress in all three areas can be gleaned in a Johns Hopkins University case study of two *The Leader in Me* (TLIM) schools. The report revealed that:

"Without question, the strongest consensus was that TLIM positively improved school climate. For the teachers and principals, the main contributors to climate changes were improved student behavior and the establishment of a culture, guided by the 7 Habits. Students translated the climate effects into feelings of increased order and security. Several noted explicitly that bullying was decreased because of classmates' exposure to the 7 Habits. . . .

"A second clear impact of TLIM was developing students' self-confidence and motivation. Practicing the habits provides a sense of direction and responsibility, which are motivating and reinforcing. . . . There is less fear than in a typical school environment of being embarrassed or ridiculed in the wake of failure.

"A third type of impact was getting along better with others and resolving conflicts. Teachers, principals, and parents reported that there were fewer arguments, fights, disciplinary actions, and suspensions than in the past. Students reported feeling better equipped to respond in a positive way to conflicts. . . .

"A fourth impact was making teaching easier and more enjoyable. This effect seems directly attributable to students behaving better and accepting responsibility for their actions, the overall school climate improving, and a school culture and order developing around the 7 Habits. . . . Teacher focus groups noted the benefits of TLIM for increasing students' self-motivation, organization, and personal accountability for completing homework and class assignments."

students taking responsibility for their rise in academics. It is always a big part of their story.

Such storytelling helps keep the energy alive and helps to sustain *The Leader in Me.* Therefore, *Leader in Me* schools are strongly encouraged to keep records of their successes, including gathering any data that helps them know how they are progressing in making improvements to academics, culture, or leadership skills.

Engaging the District

Another strategic learning is the value of district involvement. The more a district supports *The Leader in Me* process, the greater the probability that the process will be sustained over time. Below are two examples, one from Florida and one from Texas.

Port Charlotte, Florida. Charlotte County Public Schools has been advocating the 7 Habits since 2003. That is when the former superintendent, Dr. Dave Gayler, Assistant Superintendent for Learning Chuck Bradley, and the district board decided to make the 7 Habits a central part of the district's culture. That decision has continued under the current superintendent, Dr. Doug Whittaker.

More than five hundred of the district's employees have been trained in the 7 Habits. Many have also participated in other Franklin-Covey offerings such as *Great Leaders, 5 Choices,* and *The Speed of Trust*—all are part of the suite of trainings provided for the district's aspiring leaders program. Dr. Whittaker and Chuck Bradley are themselves certified 7 Habits facilitators and help guide various courses.

Upon hearing of *The Leader in Me,* the district administration was immediately interested. They saw it as a way to empower students to be the next generation of leaders and citizens, and to gain the habits that would best help them in their future careers and personal lives. They also felt it had potential for making an impact on the community.

Chuck Bradley indicates that one benefit of having the district involved is the cost savings that come from having district personnel lead portions of the training. Another benefit is the collaboration that goes on between schools. When principals get together for monthly meetings, time is provided for them to swap ideas. The district's involvement is a big reason all ten elementary schools are engaged, and they are now looking into taking it to middle schools.

San Antonio, Texas. North East Independent School District (NEISD) has thirty-eight schools started in *The Leader in Me* process. It too was no stranger to the 7 Habits and other FranklinCovey content when *The Leader in Me* emerged. Pat Sanford, leadership development specialist for the district, has been a certified 7 Habits trainer for years. She, along with former and current superintendents Dr. Richard Middleton and Dr. Brian Gottardy, have led most of the district's leaders through the *7 Habits* (631 administrators), *Great Leaders* (288 administrators), and *Four Disciplines of Execution* (three divisions).

NEISD's vision and philosophy supports a whole child philosophy, or what they call a 360-degree education. In addition to strong academics, they want students to be well-rounded, empathic listeners, to make good decisions, and to be able to chart their own course. *The Leader in Me* fit that philosophy, so when it became available, NEISD was geared to go. But they wanted to roll it out in a strategic, responsible way. So they started with five schools. District staff led most of the 7 Habits trainings and brought in FranklinCovey consultants for other portions. Those five schools became models for the next cohort of eight schools. Those schools became models and mentors for the next cohort, which each year has involved eight or nine schools.

In all, more than 2,000 staff and 30,000 students in the district have been trained in the 7 Habits. Members of the district PTA council have also been trained. One of the biggest benefits the district has seen is the number of students and staff who are speaking the same common leadership language. There is alignment between the district staff, the school staffs, and the students. Pat Sanford says that by bringing the habits to all students, "We have closed the gap between those students who are taught life skills at home and those who are not." She added that the biggest benefit to the district has been the tremendous improvement in the cultures of the various schools as "students' voices are being heard."

Charlotte County and NEISD are but two examples of districts engaged in *The Leader in Me*. Three important lessons are gleaned from district-wide implementations: 1) If a staff is not interested or ready to engage, don't force it. The staff needs to own it. 2) Someone at the district level needs to champion the process. Chuck and Pat are two great champions. 3) Economies of scale, efficiencies, and collaboration come as a district synergizes about the best ways to implement.

Working on Paradigms

The remaining strategic lesson for sustaining *The Leader in Me* over time is to continually work on paradigms. Ultimately, it is people who choose whether or not to participate in the process. People establish the purpose, path, and pace. People design the systems. People do the storytelling. And what drives those people's behaviors are their paradigms.

For some people, applying *The Leader in Me* requires very little shift in paradigms. They have been thinking along the lines of *The Leader in Me* their entire career. For others, some of the paradigms represent enormous shifts.

What are those paradigms? Several have been identified throughout the book. Each of the 7 Habits represents key paradigms. Other paradigms that are pivotal to launching and sustaining *The Leader in Me* include:

- *Working from the Inside Out.* Lasting change in a school comes from lasting change in individuals. If a person is reactive and suffering from chronic "victimitis"—always blaming others and circumstances for problems—they may need to be gently but regularly reminded that change starts within. For teachers trying to improve a student's or a parent's behavior, they may need to be reminded that the place to start is within themselves, with examining their own paradigms of that student or parent. Lasting change works from the inside out.

- *Every Person a Leader.* Some teachers struggle to see students as "real leaders" whose opinions and gifts are to be honored and implemented. It is an enormous paradigm shift for them. They may need recurring encouragement to actively seek out student opinions and to help students find their voice. Some may even struggle to see themselves as leaders.

- *Release Versus Control.* For some educators it is a real shift to view themselves as a "guide on the side" rather than the "sage on the stage," the one who is always in control versus the one who lets others lead out. Shifting to a paradigm of releasing people's potential, not controlling it; looking for strengths, not trying to "fix" them, is really difficult for some. It shows up in the way they teach lessons, resolve discipline issues, or plan events.

> Many of the ideas in organizations never get put into practice. One reason is that new insights and initiatives often conflict with established mental models.
> —*Lee G. Bohman and Terrence E. Deal,* Reframing Organizations

- *The Whole Child.* This is a paradigm that most educators start their career with. They want to address the whole child—body, mind, heart, and spirit— and that is why they join the field of education. The challenge is that with all the pressures and rewards systems that focus on teaching to a test, some educators come to view students as test scores. They need to feel supported in reexpanding their view.

We could highlight more paradigms, but here is the point. Paradigms (how we *see* things) drive our behaviors (what we *do,* our habits), and what we do drives the results we *get.* If you want to make temporary, quick-fix improvements, work on changing behaviors. If you want to make lasting, quantum leaps in schoolwide transformation, work on people's paradigms.

Some people argue there is nothing that can be done about changing people's paradigms. Not so. Stanford professor Dr. Carol Dweck

The 7 Habits are based on timeless principles that are being
made child-friendly across the world, like in Australia.

has concluded, "For twenty years, my research has shown that *the
view you adopt for yourself* profoundly affects the way you lead your
life. It can determine whether you become the person you want to be
and whether you accomplish the things you value." She goes on to say,
"You have a choice. Mindsets [or paradigms] are just beliefs. They're
powerful beliefs, but they're just something in your mind, and you can
change your mind."

The best way to work on paradigms is to teach principles. Principles are timeless and universal; practices are situational. That is why
A.B. Combs places the 7 Habits, which are based on principles, at the
foundation of their schoolhouse model, along with the Baldrige quality principles (see illustration, the A.B. Combs Schoolhouse model).
The windows in the model represent leading practices that the staff
feels will help them reach their goal of creating twenty-first-century
citizens—students who are prepared to meet the new reality. Muriel

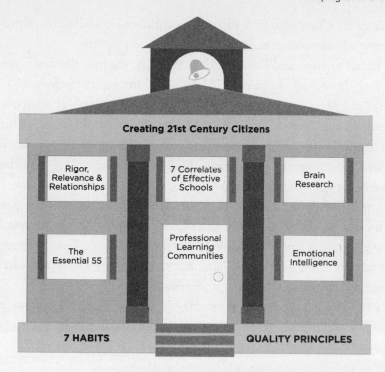

The A.B. Combs Schoolhouse model.

says, "We incorporate a lot of programs and practices (windows), and those will change as things change in our district, in our state, and in the field of education. But what will not change is the foundation of our schoolhouse, which is the 7 Habits and Baldrige principles, and the constancy of our purpose." Principles will provide a lasting foundation for change wherever a student chooses to go in life.

Excellence Is a Journey

Excellence is a journey, not a final destination. Excellence does not happen overnight.

Teaching the 7 Habits, creating a leadership culture, and achieving school goals take time, sometimes years. Yet that hard work can disappear almost overnight if not nurtured. And so the actions described in this chapter are not one-time events, they are ongoing processes.

The intent is that with time they will become easier and will need only simple adjustments to maintain their orbit and trajectory.

David George and Crestwood Elementary are into the ninth year of their *Leader in Me* journey. When asked the secret to the school's longevity, Mr. George goes right back to the two pieces of advice he gleaned from Muriel. First, "Don't water down the 7 Habits." Trust the students that they can learn the habits and apply them. Second, "Don't boil someone else's water. Make it your own." He says that "the beauty of *The Leader in Me* is that it is not a canned program. It is a principle-based process and philosophy that enhances any program sent to the school from the district or province." Whenever a new program is sent to the school from the district, Mr. George simply presents it to the staff in the language of the habits and it gets easily absorbed into what the school is already doing.

Mr. George concludes, "The day we say we have done it, we're done. So the real key that keeps it alive is never losing sight of the end in mind."

Personal Reflection

Habit 7: Sharpen the Saw is the habit of renewal and continuous improvement. For a school to keep The Leader in Me alive and doing well, individuals need to keep their personal effectiveness sharp. Thinking of your body, mind, heart, and spirit, what one thing would most improve your personal effectiveness? What can you do this week to improve that area of your life?

10

Ending with the Beginning in Mind

With the first word I used intelligently, I learned to live, to think, to hope.

—*Helen Keller,* My Key of Life

As we approach these final pages, we look back at a few main points made in the opening chapters. It is our way of ending with the beginning in mind. As with each of the previous chapters, we begin with a story.

Riley was diagnosed on the autism spectrum at age four. His parents, Rick and Roselien, had no idea where his paths would lead him. He might struggle through life, or he might do okay. "But he is still our awesome little guy," they felt, "and we are going to do the best we can."

Riley would cry when sunlight hit his skin or when the fan in the car was turned on. Flushing toilets frightened him, and he couldn't handle a shirt being put on over his head. So when the day came for Riley to enter Joseph Welsh Elementary in Red Deer, Alberta, Roselien couldn't help but feel nervous. "How will he do? How will he be treated?"

At the front of the school to greet them was Principal Mike Fritz. Roselien remembers it well. Mr. Fritz shook her hand and said, "You have come to the right place, and I am so glad you are here." During a welcome assembly, the first words from Mr. Fritz were "We thank you for the privilege of educating your child, and we thank you for trusting us to do so." Roselien looked around and observed closely the teachers and students. "The love I saw each teacher and staff member extend to each child overwhelmed me," she said. "I could feel it, see it, and hear it. I cried the whole way through."

Over the ensuing months, Rick and Roselien visited the school many times. They heard regular conversations around the 7 Habits and became familiar with the habits themselves. They said they would hear comments in meetings and in hallways like "Does that fit into our mission?" or "That can be a leadership role for a student!" The language was always positive and walking the talk. Riley was consistently hearing "You are important" or "We believe in you" or "You can do it. Here you go . . . lead."

But before things start to sound "too good to be true," not everything went so well for Riley. The more he was around other students, the more he picked up cues that he was not "the same" as them. He did not like reading. His teachers struggled to find what might perk his interests. This went on not just for a day or for a few weeks but for the first few years. At one point, Riley described himself as a "horrible person." Nevertheless, teachers, aides, counselors, Mr. Fritz, and the rest of the staff persisted in trying to discover what inspired Riley.

The breakthrough came in third grade. The school was asked to make a presentation to the school board. The typical template was for adults to do most of the talking while a few students tagged along to briefly showcase some artwork or explain a project. Since the school was a *Leader in Me* school, the staff decided to empower students to do the entire presentation. When they asked for student volunteers, they were surprised to see Riley's hand shoot up.

With the help of his education assistant, Riley put together a presentation on how his brain works. He made a drawing of his brain that showed black, blue, and red spots. When his big moment came, he explained to the audience of suits, ties, and dresses that the colors represented his various moods. He spoke with total confidence and earned a rousing applause. He smiled big.

The next day, Riley showed up to school wearing a collared shirt and tie. "I am important, and important people wear ties," he explained. For the next few days, which stretched into weeks, people noticed how proudly and tall he was walking. Ties became a daily part of who he was. But more important, from that point on, Riley became an avid reader. All aspects of his academics improved significantly. He was given multiple leadership roles and viewed each one as important. He didn't even flinch when later asked to speak in front of four hundred adults, and he grinned as wide as his tie when he got a standing ovation. He learned that everyone does not have to be "the same" to be a leader. And Riley blossomed.

Riley has since moved on to middle school and still struggles with certain aspects. But what has come to the forefront is his compassion for others and his desire to be a leader. "When he sees a needy child, he wants to adopt them," says Roselien. "He cannot pass a homeless person without insisting that we need to be leaders, to help him." She says that as a result of the steady, collaborative effort of the staff over the period of years, Riley went from feeling "I am a horrible person" to being a very social boy who firmly believes he is a leader. "He has found his voice," she says.

"Modern-Day Miracle Workers"

Riley's story captures the essence of *The Leader in Me*. It is reminiscent of a statement we made in the opening chapter, which was that many of today's educators are "modern-day miracle workers."

"Miracle worker" is the title used to describe Anne Sullivan, the woman who mentored Helen Keller. Those familiar with the story know that Helen was born with full sight and hearing, but by age three was left blind and deaf through disease. Her physical losses led to her developing wild, animal-like behaviors. Nothing, not even the best advice from doctors, could calm her wildness—not until the day in 1887 when Anne entered her life. Helen called it her soul's birthday.

That day never would have happened had it not been for some caring teachers in Anne's life. Anne's mother died when Anne was about eight years old. Afterward, her alcoholic father abandoned her and her younger brother, Jimmie. Relatives refused to take them in, so they were sent to an almshouse, a place where the diseased and unwanted souls of the day were housed. There Jimmie died of tuberculosis, and disease stole much of Anne's eyesight.

The one thing that never abandoned Anne was her spirit, which included a thirst for learning. One day, when she was fourteen, a government inspector visited the almshouse. Anne waited for the right moment before lunging at him and clinging to his leg, begging desperately for an opportunity to go to school. Unable to read and lacking social skills, she was sent to the Perkins Institute for the Blind, where she quickly became known for her rebellious nature and temper tantrums. Classmates mocked her. Some teachers were even less kind.

There were, however, a few teachers at the institute who had eyes to see, ears to hear, and hearts to feel what others could not. They spotted potential in Anne and nourished her ambitions. One went so far as to help her gain access to a series of surgeries that restored much of her eyesight. Teacher Laura Bridgman taught her how to communicate using a manual alphabet. So it was not one singular event or one incredible teacher that fed Anne's spirit, but a steady array of kind nudges from several well-doers. And Anne blossomed.

At age twenty, Anne was named valedictorian of her class. With an aura of new confidence she stood before her peers on graduation day and declared:

> And now we are going out into the busy world, to take our share in life's burdens, and do our little to make that world better, wiser and happier. . . . The advancement of society always has its commencement in the individual soul. . . . Let us go cheerfully, hopefully, and earnestly, and set ourselves to find our especial part.

At the time, Anne had no idea what her "especial part"—her *voice*—might be. She had no employment prospects, and no family to

turn to. But destiny heard her plea and soon a call came for a govern-
ess to work with a seven-year-old girl named Helen.

Helen's initial reaction to Anne was no different than her reaction
to all the others who had attempted to work with her. She was violent
and obstinate. Yet there was something about Anne that brought new-
ness to Helen. Perhaps it was a feeling of being understood.

Helen's breakthrough came a week after Anne's arrival. It happened at the water well. Anne placed one of Helen's hands into the
flowing water, while into her other hand she signed the word *water*.
For the first time, Helen caught the connection between her teacher's
touch and its relation to the outside world. With that one word came
new light, new hope. Anne wrote in her journal:

> The wild creature of two weeks ago has been transformed into a gentle
> child. She is sitting by me as I write, her face serene and happy. . . . It
> now remains my pleasant task to direct and mold the beautiful intelli-
> gence that is beginning to stir in the child-soul.

Anne's approach was to enter Helen's world, to follow Helen's
interests, and to then add vocabulary to those activities and interests.
And Helen blossomed.

Helen went on to become a renowned speaker, writer, and advocate for the blind and disabled. She was the frequent guest of kings,
queens, and dignitaries. In her later years, she summarized her days
with Anne by saying:

> A person who is severely impaired never knows his hidden sources of
> strength until he is treated like a normal human being and encouraged
> to try to shape his own life.

"A New Level of Thinking?"

Anne and Helen's story happened more than a hundred years ago. So what does it have to do with *The Leader in Me*?

In every school we visit across the world we find Annes, Helens, and Rileys. Some have physical challenges. Some have been blinded by circumstances regarding their worth and potential. Some have spirits that have been deafened by the sound of criticism. They feel alone and occasionally act out in wild-like behaviors.

Fortunately, alongside such students we have also met noble teachers and caring staff members who have eyes to see, ears to hear, and hearts to feel what others cannot. We find them seeing it as their "pleasant task to direct and mold the beautiful intelligence" of students. We observe them helping students find their "hidden sources of strength," treating them "like a normal human being," and encouraging them "to shape his [or her] own life." They are modern-day "miracle workers."

In most cases, it is not a single teacher who makes the difference in a student's life, but a series of individuals—teachers, staff members, parents, and community members—who have collaborated to help students find their voices. Seldom are their efforts a singular event, but rather a series of steady, small events that have been gently woven in and out of the student's life over an extended period.

In the opening chapter, we referred to Dr. Martin Seligman taking counsel from his five-year-old daughter, Nikki, and how it led him to a new level of thinking. He concluded that for the better part of a century the field of psychology was focused on "fixing" people, identifying what was wrong with them and relieving suffering rather than focusing on what makes people happy and effective. Ultimately he determined, "raising children . . . was far more than just fixing what was wrong with them. It was about identifying and amplifying their strengths and virtues, and helping them find the niche where they can live these positive traits to the fullest."

In hindsight, Seligman's conclusion sounds a lot like the approach

Anne took with Helen a hundred years ago. She didn't try to "fix" Helen; she didn't fixate on her GAPs. Her approach was "to enter Helen's world, to follow Helen's interests, and to then add vocabulary to those activities and interests." In contrast to the others who had attempted to work with Helen, Anne encouraged her to "shape her own life" and search out her "hidden sources of strength." Only then was Helen's potential released.

We believe that in many ways, *The Leader in Me* represents a new level of thinking. We know of no other process quite like it that approaches all three challenges—academics, culture, and leadership—in the same fashion. The 7 Habits alone bring a unique combination of powerful principles together that for many people offer new ideas and a new level of thinking. Even some of the most effective leaders we know have told us how the 7 Habits have raised their level of thinking and living.

Yet at the same time, *The Leader in Me* represents an old level of thinking. The 7 Habits are based on principles that have been around for centuries, and will be around for centuries to come. They are timeless. So for as much as *The Leader in Me* represents new levels of thinking, it also represents a call for a return to timeless principles.

This is why for some educators, *The Leader in Me* feels like an old comfortable pair of shoes that they have worn and relished for years. It is the way they have been teaching and doing things for as long as they have been working with young people. And yet for others, it may feel uncomfortable at first. Perhaps it is because they have grown accustomed to "fixing" students, after having been driven for years by high-stakes pressures to raise tests scores. Some may feel a need to be in control, having never learned how to manage things and lead people. Again, there is nothing wrong with "fixing"; it is an important part of life. But if that is all a school or teacher is focused on, therein may lie the need for a new level of thinking, or at least a return to an old, principle-centered level of thinking.

"Not One More Thing"

In the tale of *Alice in Wonderland,* a worn-out, beleaguered Alice comes upon the Queen of Hearts, who tells her, "Now here, you see, it takes all the running you can do, to keep in the same place. . . . If you want to get somewhere else, you must run at least twice as fast as that."

The last thing educators want to hear is that to improve things they must run twice as fast as they already are. Most are running faster than they have strength. Some have lost vision of why they entered the field of education. "One more thing" might do them in.

There are two general reasons why we have emphasized throughout the book that *The Leader in Me* is to be viewed as "not one more thing." The first is that we agree with more and more parents, business leaders, educators, and thought leaders who are seeing the mindsets and skill sets embedded in the 7 Habits as not one more thing but as a "main thing." The skills are not just another nice topic to cover if time happens to allow. They are a vital part of any student's chances of doing well in today's new reality.

The second general reason *The Leader in Me* is described as "not one more thing" is due to the number of educators who have told us it is instead "a better way of doing what we are already doing." There are at least five reasons we have identified in the book as to why this is so:

#1: The Leader in Me is a mindset and a process, not a program. It is a way of thinking, a philosophy. Like an operating system on a computer or mobile phone, it influences actions and decisions of all kinds. Once in place, it is intended to make things run smoother. In fact, numerous schools that have other initiatives already in place, such as Professional Learning Communities or International Baccalaureate (IB) schools, have reported to us that *The Leader in Me* has helped them to significantly strengthen those initiatives.

#2: The Leader in Me uses a ubiquitous, integrated approach. Instead of seeing academics, leadership skills, and culture as three separate

activities, *The Leader in Me* sees them as interdependent activities. It is a holistic approach. By improving one of the three areas, the other areas also reap benefits.

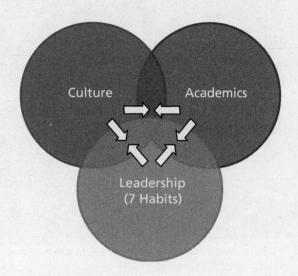

#3: The Leader in Me helps educators remove items from their current plate and replace them with other more valuable, more relevant items. By identifying Wildly Important Goals (WIGs), a school can focus on its highest priorities and say no to tasks, topics, or events that do not contribute to meeting their stakeholders' primary needs. By saying no to unimportant things—including nonvaluable content—they find more time for the important things.

#4: The Leader in Me enables teachers to spend less time dealing with culture-related problems. One of the benefits we commonly hear is that by spending ten minutes or so a day working on the habits and the culture of the classroom and school, teachers save an equal, if not greater, amount of time by not having to deal with discipline matters. Less time disciplining equates to more time for academics and teaching leadership skills.

#5: The Leader in Me improves teacher effectiveness and efficiency. As staff members apply the habits to their personal and professional lives, they become more effective and efficient in what they do. This

Today's world dictates what "First Things" are to be teaching students.

results in more time for things like relationship building, planning, and leadership. Some of that efficiency comes as teachers share leadership responsibilities with students. Remember the teacher who used to spend twenty to thirty minutes closing down her classroom at the end of each day, turning off computers, closing blinds, etc.? Now her students do it in two minutes. Sharing responsibilities frees up time for higher priorities.

The more *The Leader in Me* is viewed as "not one more thing" and as "a better way of doing what we are already doing," the easier and longer lasting will be the implementation.

"One Child at a Time"

Helen Keller was the only student Anne Sullivan ever had—not the typical class size. Far more often, literally hundreds of students arrive in near unison each morning like a wave pouncing upon the shore, and then depart in mass at the end of the day like the tide rolling out.

So it can be difficult to view every child as a unique individual, or to seek out and nurture every Riley.

Nonetheless, how else can we expect a child's talents and unique potential to be fully understood or nurtured without some adult making time to in some way enter the individual world of that child? Many young people—particularly secondary students—find themselves without compass, searching for direction, searching for identity. Their life is not easy. Many counterfeit and misguided pressures threaten to steal away their unique identities. In that reality is a challenge for adults to step forward, to get involved, and to meet today's young people in one-on-one ways at their critical crossroads. Sometimes all that is needed is to be given an opportunity to lead, or to be given the right compliment.

No, today's young people may not be ready to run a multinational corporation upon graduation. No, they may not become their country's leader someday. And no, they may not be able to get the highest test score. But those are not the ultimate ends in mind. The ultimate end in mind is to enable them: 1) to effectively lead their lives, 2) to work well with others, and 3) to make positive contributions in the world around them. For many students, those outcomes may never

Every "one" is an important one.

happen unless someone meets them at their crossroad and gives them a chance to shine. *The Leader in Me* is designed to help adults give students that chance.

The Leader in Me—The Ends in Mind

Primary Purposes
To help students to effectively . . .

- Lead their lives. To be confident and independent.
- Work well with others. To succeed at being interdependent.
- Make meaningful contributions to their workplaces, homes, and communities in a balanced manner.

Secondary Purposes
- To enable school staff to be more effective and efficient in their professional and personal lives.
- To bring greater effectiveness and efficiencies into homes.
- To create a better future workforce and a friendlier, safer community

---

As this book was going to press, two exciting things happened. One, A.B. Combs was again recognized as the #1 Magnet School in the United States. They are the first school to receive the award twice. That is an enormous credit to the entire staff and students, along with the parents and community.

But as exciting and deserving as that award is, the A.B. Combs staff will insist that the most exciting outcomes are what happened at the individual level. Which brings us to the second exciting thing that happened.

Shawn Maggiolo, fifth-grade teacher at A.B. Combs, has been one of the teachers to make the entire journey with Muriel from the beginning. Yet still she did not anticipate what occurred just prior to this book going to press. She was teaching a group of fifteen students about timelines. Each was to make his or her own timeline and to place on it eight events from their young lives that they felt were most important. She made no suggestions as to what they should choose, and there was no discussion as the students went about their assignments. When the timelines were completed, Shawn asked the students to identify the one event they saw as most impactful. When all was done—and again with no discussion or prompting—eight of the students had chosen attending A.B. Combs as their top life event. Shawn was stunned.

Shawn asked the students *why*—why did they choose A.B. Combs as their top life event? In essence, they said they loved the environment. They loved being viewed as leaders. For some it was the first time someone believed in them; they felt valued. Their expressions were deeply sincere. They had each felt the individual attention, their personal worth. Shawn said she wanted to cry. Then one of the students described how he had moved to A.B. Combs from another school. "My other school was all about reading, writing, and math. Here it is about so much more. It's about how you treat people, and what you do with your life." He went on about the difference it had meant for him. At that point, Shawn grabbed a tissue and faked a sneeze; her emotions were tender. She felt that over the years she had contributed a small part to what these children were saying. She felt validated as a teacher. She and the other teachers at A.B. Combs were indeed making a difference in these students' lives, one child at a time.

"Live Life in Crescendo"

In closing, we refer back to Dr. Covey's motto, mentioned in the opening tribute: "Live life in crescendo." He always liked to live and work as if his greatest contribution was yet ahead. When he graduated from Harvard's MBA program, his brother John asked him what he wanted to do in life. Stephen responded with three words, "Release Human Potential." And that he did. Millions of people the world over acknowledge him for having helped them to better their lives. At the conclusion of his speeches, Stephen often quoted the words of George Bernard Shaw:

> This is the true joy in life. That being used for a purpose recognized by yourself as a mighty one. That being a force of nature instead of a feverish, selfish little clod of ailments and grievances complaining that the world will not devote itself to making you happy. . . . I want to be thoroughly used up when I die. For the harder I work the more I live. . . . Life is no brief candle to me. It's a splendid torch which I've got to hold up for the moment and I want to make it burn as brightly as possible before handing it on to future generations.

We believe that for you and for each of us the best is yet ahead. We hope this book has been an opportunity for you to pause from your busy schedule to reevaluate your thinking around how to best prepare young people for life. We hope you have been able to arrive at your own conclusions as to whether you think the ideas in this book sound "too good to be true" or if you feel they match today's new reality.

More important, we hope you have come to see how this book applies to you. We hope it has given you a window to think about your own "voice," or what Anne Sullivan called her "especial part." What is unique about you? What are your passions? How might you bring the ideas and concepts contained in these pages to your professional life, your community, and your home? How might you inspire others to find their voice? What contributions will be part of your crescendo?

Too many leaders lie at anchor, resigned to the status quo and confined by what worked in the past. They assume that the words *change* and *leadership* are meant for someone else. They are spectators. We hope you view yourself as a proactive leader. School change starts with individual change. It is an inside-out process. By changing ourselves we change our surroundings.

In today's global economy, we simply cannot afford to continue waiting until young people receive their first promotion into corporate leadership before we teach them how to get along with others, to set goals, to think ahead. We cannot idly wait for them to become school-teachers, doctors, firefighters, engineers, or parents before we teach them how to organize their lives, to take initiative, or to work in teams. We cannot afford to relax and hope they detect their worth and potential on their own. They deserve better. They deserve hope.

Personal Reflections

Habit 8 is Find Your Voice, Then Inspire Others to Find Theirs. What is your voice? Who is someone you can inspire to find their voice in a one-on-one way? Is there a child or school nearby that can benefit from what you have to offer? How will you go about applying the principles in this book to your own life, starting today? How will you live your life in crescendo?

Notes and References

In Tribute

The following FranklinCovey books were referenced in the opening tribute and are also referred to occasionally throughout the book:

Stephen R. Covey. *The 7 Habits of Highly Effective People: Powerful Lessons in Personal Change.* New York: Simon & Schuster, 1989.

Stephen R. Covey. *The Leader in Me: How Schools and Parents Around the World are Inspiring Greatness, One Child at a Time.* New York: Free Press, 2008.

Sean Covey. *The 7 Habits of Highly Effective Teens: The Ultimate Teenage Success Guide.* New York: Simon & Schuster, 1998.

Sean Covey. *The 6 Most Important Decisions You Will Ever Make: A Guide for Teens.* New York: Fireside, 2006.

Sean Covey. *The 7 Habits of Happy Kids.* New York: Simon & Schuster, 2008.

Chapter 1: Too Good to Be True?

4 *According to Daniel Pink . . . The last few decades:* Daniel Pink, *A Whole New Mind: Why Right-Brainers Will Rule the Future.* (New York: The Berkley Publishing Group, 2006), pp. 1, 3.

7 *more than 30 percent of students are dropping out of college in the first year:* M. Lee Upcraft, John N. Gardner, and Betsy O. Barefoot, *Challenging and Supporting the First-Year Student* (San Francisco: John Wiley & Sons, 2004) p. 29. (Drop-out rates range from 17–47 percent, depending on the type of school.)

7 *According to the legendary Howard Gardner:* Howard Gardner, *Five Minds for the Future* (Boston: Harvard Business School Press, 2007), p. 17.

7 *Similarly, in* How Children Succeed, *Paul Tough:* Paul Tough, *How Children Succeed: Grit, Curiosity, and the Hidden Power of Character* (Boston: Houghton Mifflin Harcourt, 2012), p. xv.

9 *For years, Dr. Martin Seligman has been one*: Martin Seligman, *Authentic Happiness: Using the New Positive Psychology to Realize Your Potential for Lasting Fulfilment* (New York: Free Press, 2002), pp. 27–29.

Chapter 2: How It Started—and Why

22 *One parent even shared a list from:* The list of *Top 10 Qualities & Skills Employers Seek* that was given to Muriel was credited to The National Association of Colleges and Employers.

23 *In the early 1990s, University of Michigan sociologist Duane Alwin:* For more on Duane Alwin's research on changing parent attitudes, see Anne Remley, "From Obedience to Independence," *Psychology Today* (October, 1988), which refers to "Middletown" research, started in 1924 by sociologists Helen and Robert Lynd and replicated fifty-four years later by sociologists Theodore Caplow of the University of Virginia and Howard Bahr and Bruce Chadwick of Brigham Young University.

24 *Toward the close of the 1990s, the United Nations Education: Learning, the Treasure Within: Report to UNESCO of the International Commission on Education for the Twenty-First Century* (Paris: UNESCO), 1996. This report, though published in the 1990s, remains currently a source of guidance in many parts of the world.

25 *Many educators were being influenced by Daniel Goleman's research:* Daniel Goleman, "A Great Idea in Education: Emotional Literacy," *Great Ideas in Education: A Unique Book Review and Resource Catalog*, no. 2 (Spring, 1994), pp. 33–34. For more on research that describes how emotional intelligence impacts leadership in the workplace, see Daniel Goleman, Annie E. McKee, and Richard E. Boyatzis, *Primal Leadership: Realizing the Power of Emotional Intelligence* (Cambridge, MA: Harvard Business School Press, 2002), p. 39.

25 *"for success at the highest levels":* Daniel Goleman, *Working With Emotional Intelligence* (New York: Bantam Books, 1998).

26 *in 2007, the Partnership for 21st Century Skills:* Public Opinion Strategies and Peter D. Hart Research Associates, *Survey of American Adult Attitudes Toward Education.* The national survey involved 800 registered voters from September 10–12, 2007. For a description of the Framework for The Partnership for 21st Century Skills, see www.21stcenturyskills .org.

27 *surveyed two thousand employers from twenty-four countries:* Edexcel, *Effective Education for Employment: A Global Perspective,* see http://www .eee-edexcel.com/xstandard/docs/effective_education_for_employment _web_version.pdf.

27 *In 2010, Tony Wagner launched his book:* Tony Wagner, *The Global Achievement Gap: Why Even Our Best Schools Don't Teach the New Survival Skills Our Children Need—and What We Can Do About It* (New York: Basic Books, 2008).

28 *a 2013 nationwide Gallup poll of U.S. adults:* quoted in Shane Lopez and Valerie J. Calderon, "Americans Say U.S. Schools Should Teach 'Soft' Skills," August 21, 2013, see http://www.gallup.com/poll/164060/ameri cans-say-schools-teach-soft-skills.aspx.

37 *Daniel Goleman and the:* CASEL (Collaborative for Academic, Social, and Emotional Learning), "CASEL Brief: How Evidence-Based SEL Programs Work to Produce Greater Student Success in School and Life," 2011, see http://casel.org/wp-content/uploads/2011/04/academic brief.pdf. Cited inside the brief were two other research reports that have been singled out in the summary.

37 *When students are attached to school and to prosocial:* J. D. Hawkins, J. W. Graham, E. Maguin, R. D. Abbott, and R. F Catalano RF, "Exploring the Effects of Age of Alcohol Use Initiation and Psychosocial Risk Factors on Subsequent Alcohol Misuse," *Journal of Studies on Alcohol,* 58, no. 3 (1997): pp. 280–90.

37 *Providing students with opportunities for participation:* Reed W. Larson and Mihaly Csikszentmihalyi, "The Significance of Time Alone in Adolescent Development," *Journal of Current Adolescent Medicine,* 2 (1980), pp. 33–40.

Chapter 3: Teaching the 7 Habits

47 *Some teachers, for example, use Alexander's:* Judith Viorst, *Alexander and the Terrible, Horrible, No Good, Very Bad Day* (New York: Atheneum Books for Young Readers, 2009).

50 *Many* Leader in Me *schools adhere to:* Harry Wong, *The First Days of School: How to Be an Effective Teacher,* 4th ed. (Mountain View, CA: Harry K. Wong Publications, 2009).

53 *The well documented book* Teaching Practices: Joseph Johnson, Cynthia Uline, and Lynne Perez. *Teaching Practices from America's Best Urban Schools* (Larchmont, NY: Eye on Education, 2013).

57 *One time, they used the book* The Pout-Pout Fish: Deborah Diesen, *The Pout-Pout Fish* (New York: Farrar Straus Giroux, 2008).

Chapter 4: Creating a Leadership Culture

63 *"The fact is that given the challenges":* Ken Robinson, *The Element: How Finding Your Passion Changes Everything* (New York: Viking, 2009).

75 *In the high-trust classroom:* Lonnie Moore, *The High-Trust Classroom: Raising Achievement from the Inside Out* (Larchmont, NY: Eye on Education, 2009).

77 *A six-year study funded by the Wallace Foundation:* Karen Seashore Louis, Kenneth Leithwood, Kyla L. Wahlstrom, and Stephen E. Anderson, *Investigating the Links to Improved Student Learning: Final Report of Research Findings* (commissioned by The Wallace Foundation, research carried out by the University of Minnesota and the University of Toronto, July 2010).

80 *Empathy is the one skill:* Gary McGuey, *The Mentor: Leadership Trumps Bullying* (self-published, 2012).

94 *74 percent of school-level administrators now recognize:* Based on 2013 "Quality Counts" report published by *Education Week*, cited in Celia Baker, "Improving School Character: Climate Change That Helps," *Deseret News* (February 7, 2013), see http://www.deseretnews.com/article /865572600/Improving-school-character-climate-change-that-helps.html ?pg=all#1TkLPtsBXwklK87k.99.

Chapter 5: Achieving School Goals

96 *Every enterprise requires commitment to common goals:* Peter F. Drucker, *The Essential Drucker: The Best of Sixty Years of Peter Drucker's Essential Writings on Management* (New York: HarpersCollins, 2001).

98 *Far and away the biggest mistake [leaders]:* James C. Collins and Jerry I. Porras, *Built to Last: Successful Habits of Visionary Companies* (New York: HarperCollins, 1994).

100 *four-step process:* Chris McChesney, Sean Covey, and Jim Huling, *The 4 Disciplines of Execution: Achieving Your Wildly Important Goals* (New York: Free Press, 2012).

103 *According to Harvard's Tal Ben-Shahar:* Tal Ben-Shahar, *Happier: Learn the Secrets to Daily Joy and Lasting Fulfillment* (New York: McGraw-Hill, 2007), p. viii.

105 *When success in the classroom is defined in terms of competitive status:* Robert J. Marzano, *What Works in Schools: Translating Research into Action* Alexandria, VA: Association for Supervision and Curriculum Development, 2003), p. 149.

107 *Autonomy must be balanced by accountability:* Richard DuFour and Michael Fullan, *Cultures Built to Last: Systemic PLCs at Work* (Bloomington, IL: Solution Tree Press, 2013).

114 *In* Visible Learning: John Hattie, *Visible Learning: A Synthesis of Over 800 Meta-Analyses Relating to Achievement,* pp. 163–67, 173–78. Also cited with the research are:

114 *Goals should be challenging:* L. S. Fuchs and D. Fuchs, "Curriculum-Based Assessment of Progress Toward Long-Term and Short-Term Goals." *Journal of Special Education.* 20, no. 1 (1986), pp. 69–82.

114 *Goal achievement is highest when:* M. K. Burns, "Comprehensive System of Assessment to Intervention Using Curriculum-Based Assessments." *Intervention in School and Clinic,* 38, no. 1 (2002), pp. 8–13.

114 *Trying to beat "personal bests":* A. J. Martin, "Personal Bests (PBs): A Proposed Multidimensional Model and Empirical Analysis." *British Journal of Educational Psychology,* 76 (2006), p. 816.

115 *Regular, timely feedback helps students:* E. A. Locke and G. P. Latham, *A Theory of Goal Setting and Task Performance* (Englewood Cliffs, NJ: Prentice Hall, 1990), p. 23.

115 *Many teachers claim they provide:* G. A. Nuthall, "The Cultural Myths and Realities of Classroom Teaching and Learning: A Personal Journey." *Teachers College Record,* 107, no. 5 (2005), pp. 895–934.

115 *Extrinsic rewards (stickers, awards, etc.) often undermine:* E. I. Deci, R. Koestner, and R. M. Ryan, "A Meta-analytic Review of Experiments Examining the Effects of Extrinsic Rewards on Intrinsic Motivation." *Psychological Bulletin,* 125, no. 6 (1999), p. 659.

118 *A partial answer to the question is revealed:* sent via email, December 13, 2012.

121 *One resource that was used throughout the year was Accelerated Reader (AR) books:* The books are published by Renaissance Learning, see http://www.renlearn.com/ar/.

121 *Don't be afraid to give up the good to go for the great:* Jim Collins, *Good to Great: Why Some Companies Make the Leap . . . and Others Don't* (New York: HarperCollins, 2001).

Chapter 6: Bringing It Home

130 *Karen L. Mapp of Harvard University's Graduate School of Education reports that:* Reported in Christina A. Cassidy, "Schools Learn to Roll Out Red Carpet for Parents," Associated Press (September 8, 2013).

133 Stephen R. Covey, *The 7 Habits of Highly Effective Families: Building a Beautiful Family Culture in a Turbulent World* (New York: Golden Books, 1997).

134 *Where a school cannot change the income:* Robert J. Marzano, *What Works in Schools: Translating Research into Action* (Alexandria, VA: Association for Supervision and Curriculum Development, VA, 2003), p. 128.

Chapter 7: Engaging the Community

156 *The research is abundantly clear:* Michael Fullan, "Broadening the Concept of Teacher Leadership," in S. Caldwell, ed., *Professional Development in Learning-Centered Schools* (Oxford, OH: National Staff Development Council, 1997).

159 *The reasons why are reflected in: Leaders and Laggards: A State-by-State Report Card on Educational Effectiveness* (Washington, D.C.: U.S. Chamber of Commerce, 2007).

Chapter 8: Shifting to Secondary and Beyond

180 *In a nation-wide Gallup poll of 500,000:* The nation-wide Gallup poll data and Brandon Busteed quote is reported in Ceelia R. Baker, "Teacher, I'm Bored," *Deseret News*, National Edition (December 2, 2013).

188 *What students need to succeed:* Willard R. Daggett, quote was provided by the International Center for Leadership in Education. For more on Dr. Daggett's work on Rigor and Relevance see www.leadered.com.

194 *One of the key cornerstone strategies for effective middle schools is: Breaking Ranks in the Middle: Strategies for Leading Middle Level Reform* (Reston, VA: National Association of Secondary School Principals, 2006).

196 *their likelihood of dropping out decreases by up to 50 percent:* See, for example, R. G. Croninger, and V. E. Lee, (2001). "Social Capital and

Dropping Out of High School: Benefits to At-Risk Students of Teachers' Support and Guidance." *Teachers College Record*, 103 (2001), pp. 548–81.

Chapter 9: Keeping It Alive

209 *Transformation is everyone's job:* W. Edwards Deming, *Out of the Crisis* (Cambridge, MA: Massachusetts Institute of Technology, 1982).

219 *"getting the right people on the bus":* Jim Collins, *Good to Great: Why Some Companies Make the Leap . . . and Others Don't* (New York: HarperCollins, 2001).

221 *The thirty-four nation Organisation for Economic Co-operation and Development (OECD) reports that:* Richard DuFour, "Why Educators Should be Given Time to Collaborate," *Education Week*, 30, No. 9 (October 27, 2010), p. 15.

222 *Teaching has been described as the second most private act:* Richard DuFour, and Robert Eaker, *Professional Learning Communities at Work: Best Practices for Enhancing Student Achievement* (National Educational Service, Bloomington, IN: 1998), p. 115.

228 *Johns Hopkins University Report:* Steven Ross, and Laurenzano, *Implementation Quality and Outcomes of The Leader In Me (TLIM) Program: Case Studies at Two Diverse Elementary Schools,* Center for Research and Reform in Education (CRRE), Johns Hopkins University, 2012.

232 *Many of the ideas in organizations never get put into practice:* Lee Bolman and Terrence Deal, *Reframing Organizations: Artistry, Choice, and Leadership* (San Francisco: Jossey-Bass, 2013).

234 *Stanford professor Dr. Carol Dweck has concluded:* Carol Dweck, *Mindset: The New Psychology of Success* (New York: Ballantine Books, 2008), pp 6, 16.

Chapter 10: Ending with the Beginning in Mind

237 *With the first word:* Hellen Keller, *My Key of Life: Optimism: An Essay* (London: Isbister and Co., 1904).

237 *Riley was diagnosed:* Story of Riley is excerpts from a presentation made by Riley's mom at *The Leader In Me* Symposium, Edmonton, Alberta, April 30, 2013.

240 *And now we are going out into the busy world:* Anne Sullivan's entire valedictory address can be found at www.perkins.org/culture/helen keller/sullivanvaledictory.html. For the other Anne Sullivan Macy and Helen Keller quotations, see Joseph P. Lash, *Helen and Teacher: The Story of Helen Keller and Anne Sullivan Macy* (New York: Merloyd Lawrence, 1980).

244 *In the tale of* Alice in Wonderland: Lewis Carroll, *Through the Looking Glass,* in *Logical Nonsense: The Works of Lewis Carroll,* Philip C. Blackburn and Lionel White, ed. (New York: G. P. Putnam's Sons, 1934), p. 177. *Through the Looking Glass* was first published in 1872.

252 *This is the true joy in life:* George Bernard Shaw, *Man and Superman,* first published in 1903.

About the Authors

Dr. Stephen R. Covey

Stephen R. Covey was an internationally acclaimed leadership authority, consultant, and teacher. He was author of several renowned books, including the international bestseller *The 7 Habits of Highly Effective People*, which was named the #1 Most Influential Business Book of the Twentieth Century, selling more than 25 million copies in thirty-eight languages. Other bestsellers include *The 8th Habit: From Effectiveness to Greatness, First Things First, Principle-Centered Leadership, The 7 Habits of Highly Effective Families, The Third Alternative*, and *Everyday Greatness*.

Dr. Covey received the National Speakers Association Speaker of the Year recognition, the Fatherhood Award from the National Fatherhood Initiative, the Thomas More College Medallion for continuing service to humanity, the Toastmasters Golden Gavel Award, the Sikhs' International Man of Peace Award, the International Entrepreneur of the Year Award. Dr. Covey was also recognized as one of *Time* magazine's 25 Most Influential Americans and received eight honorary doctorate degrees. He was cofounder and former vice chairman of FranklinCovey Company. He passed away during preparations for this 2nd edition of *The Leader in Me* and is dearly missed, though his legacy carries on.

Sean Covey

Sean is Executive Vice President of FranklinCovey and leads its Education Division. He is devoted to transforming education around the globe through bringing leadership principles and skills to as many students, educators, and schools as possible. He is a *New York Times* bestselling author of *The 6 Most Important Decisions You'll Ever Make*, *The 7 Habits of Happy Kids*, and *The 7 Habits of Highly Effective Teens*, which has been translated into twenty languages and sold over 4 million copies worldwide.

Sean is a frequent national conference keynote speaker. He graduated from Brigham Young University with a bachelor's degree in English and earned his MBA from Harvard Business School. As the quarterback for BYU, he led his team to two bowl games and was twice selected as the ESPN Most Valuable Player of the Game.

Born in Belfast, Ireland, Sean's favorite activities include going to movies, working out, hanging out with his kids, riding his dirt bike, and writing poor poetry. Sean and his wife, Rebecca, live with their children in the Rocky Mountains.

Muriel Summers

Muriel Summers has been the principal of A.B. Combs in Raleigh, North Carolina, since 1998. She holds a BA degree from UNC–Chapel Hill, a master's in elementary education from UNC–Charlotte, a master's in school administration from the University of Maryland, and an honorary doctorate from California University. It was Ms. Summers's vision to create the first leadership-based elementary school in the United States. Her school, A.B. Combs Elementary, has received many national awards under her guidance, including The National Blue Ribbon, The National School of Character, The National Magnet School of America, the National Title 1 Distinguished School, and the National Elementary School of the Year, as well as being designated as the inaugural Lighthouse School by FranklinCovey Education. She is the very proud mother of two children, Banks and Colin. Her passion is collaborating with fellow educators in making a difference for children around the globe.

Dr. David K. Hatch

Dr. David K. Hatch is Global Director of Strategic Initiatives for Franklin Covey Education. David's consulting career has taken him across the world to more than thirty-five countries. His individual and organizational leadership assessments have been utilized by millions of leaders worldwide. He is coauthor of *Everyday Greatness* with Dr. Stephen R. Covey and was the lead researcher for the 1st and 2nd editions of *The Leader in Me*. He has consulted in corporate, government, and education sectors, with the past decade being devoted to innovating and applying practical tools for school and individual transformation. He resides in Lindon, Utah, with his wife, Mary Ann, and their children, and is dedicated to making the world a little better for them and others wherever he travels.

Acknowledgments

No project of this scope is possible without the synergistic contributions of many individuals. We recognize the literally hundreds of educators at Leader in Me schools around the world who have offered content expertise, quotations, photos, stories, and creative artistry. In particular we express thanks to FranklinCovey Education's Board, represented by Chuck Bradley, Jan McCartan, Matt Miller, Eileen Cronin, Kim Cummins, and John Peck.

Significant contributions were made by the dynamic headquarters and international teams, led by Sarah Noble, Aaron Ashby, Joshua Covey, Zac Cheney, Angie Witzel, Judy Yauch, Meg Thompson, Landon Shewmake, Gloria Mellios, Gwen Cochran, Scott Osbourn, William McIntyre, Eduado Amorim, Ella Bjornsdottir, Deb Lund, and Annie Oswald.

Careful input was also provided by our professional team of consultants and coaches, including Dr. Nancy Moore, Jonathan Catherman, Chuck Farnsworth, Dr. Jane Knight, Tom Hewlett, Lonnie Moore, Gary McGuey, Charles Fonbuena, Jennifer Williams, William Blackford, Mike Suto, John Flokstra, Eric Stenlake, Robin Seay, Jennibelle Williams, Connley Skeen, Lynne Fox, Dr. Paul Pitchford, Shelly Hollis, Kathy Leeser, Dr. Jill Scheulen, Janita Anderson, Mike Webb, Lynn Kosinski, and Dana Penick, along with our outstanding client partners and business partners in the United States and across the globe.

Our highest gratitude is also expressed to our friends at Simon & Schuster, Ben Loehnen, Brit Hvide, Phil Metcalf, Aline Pace, and Beth Maglione, who have been relentless in their pursuit of excellence on this project, and to Jan Miller and Shannon Marven at Dupree-Miller Associates, who faithfully believe in and champion our causes.

Furthermore, we extend our heartfelt appreciation to our families, whose consistent support throughout the project has sustained our energies. And, finally, we express gratitude for the thousands of students for whom this work is dedicated. They give us hope, teach us about joy, and provide the inspiration to pursue this work.

About Us

For nearly three decades, FranklinCovey Education, a division of FranklinCovey, has been one of the world's most prominent and trusted providers of educational leadership programs and transformational processes. FranklinCovey's programs, books, and content have been utilized by thousands of public and private primary, secondary, and post-secondary schools and institutions, including educational service centers and vocational schools in all 50 states within the United States and in over 150 countries.

Our Mission

We enable greatness in schools, educators, and students everywhere.

Our Vision

Our vision is to profoundly impact education across the globe by enabling millions of educators and students to achieve their great purposes and potential.

Our Commitment

We are committed to empowering every school with whom we partner to achieve transformational results. The services and products we offer are best in class. We continuously invest significant resources into our training, coaching, and materials and we partner with educators to develop and improve these offerings. To increase our ability to impact the lives of millions of students, we significantly discount our educational offerings by 40 to 60 percent.

Our People

The FranklinCovey Education team is primarily composed of outstanding former teachers and administrators from various education levels and entities. Our people are our greatest competitive advantage and are passionately committed to making a positive difference in education.

The Leader in Me

YOU CAN

LEAVE A LEGACY

To get started...

1. Conduct a book study with key stakeholders.

Download a *Leader in Me* book study guide or purchase hard copies from TheLeaderinMe.org.

2. Schedule a *Leader in Me* overview.

Contact a FranklinCovey representative to schedule an overview of *The Leader in Me* process with your school staff and other key stakeholders.

3. Conduct a staff-commitment survey.

Gauge staff buy-in and collect feedback with our staff commitment survey tool, available through your FranklinCovey representative.

4. Attend a *Leader in Me* event.

Attend a school Leadership Day or a Symposium event to see *The Leader in Me* in action. Find events at TheLeaderinMe.org.

For additional information, contact your FranklinCovey representative.

www.TheLeaderinMe.org
1-800-272-6839

FranklinCovey | EDUCATION

You can be the difference by...

1. Sponsoring a school.

Private funding has enabled hundreds of schools to implement *The Leader in Me*. We are committed to maximizing your investment to provide the necessary process and tools to as many schools and students possible. Our funding department can help you identify a need that aligns with your philanthropic objectives.

2. Sharing *The Leader in Me.*

If you like what we are doing, share a copy of *The Leader in Me* book with educators and key stakeholders in your community. Take the initiative to start the discussion of developing your future leaders. Please contact us for resources and support in this effort. You can find additional resources and videos to share at TheLeaderinMe.org.

Get involved! Contact FranklinCovey Education to discuss opportunities.

www.TheLeaderinMe.org
1-800-272-6839

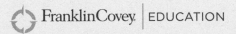

Index

Page numbers in *italics* refer to illustrations.

A.B. Combs Elementary, 1–2, *2*, *3*, 12, 16–23, 28, 31–35, 40, 127, 157
  aligning results for, 97–98
  Baldrige principles and, 34, 232, 233, *233*
  business leaders and, 21–23, 31, 40, 155, 159
  collaboration system, 221
  discipline at, 1–2, 21, 33, 92–93
  diversity at, 2, 19, 21, *21*, 34, 70
  enrollment, 21, 34
  leadership events, 88–89
  leadership principles at, 1–3, 12–23, 31–32, *32*, 33–34, 45, 48–49, 55, 69–70, 82–83, 88–89, 97–98, *98*, 155, 157, 160–61, 173, 177–78, 208, 214, *214*, 215, 219–20, *220*, 223, 232, 246–47
  as magnet school, 17, 18–20, 22, 28, 31–32, *32*, 33, 34
  mission statement of, 33, 69, 71, 98
  parents at, 19, 21–24, 31, 40
  physical environment, 69–74
  7 Habits and, 2, 16, 17–18, 31–34, 45, 48–49, 52, 55, 70, 71, 83, 155, 157, 160–61, 178, 208, 209, 232
  storytelling, 225
  student opinions, 82–83
  teachers at, 21–23, 31, 33–34, 40
  test scores at, 21, 33, 34
  transformation and, 214–15
  vision statement of, 33, 69, 98
  what students want, 28–29
Aaldijk, Sheila, 47
Abril Group, 172
abstract thought, 24
academics, 6, 7, 36, *36*, 37, 39, *61*, 66, *94*, 100, 101, *125*, 215, 241, *243*
  goals, 102–23, *125*, *125*
  secondary schools, 182–89
Accelerated Reader (AR) books, 121
accountability, establishing, 101, 107–8, 109, 110, 112, 115, 122, 200, 201
achievement, *26*, 82, 91, 94
  celebrating, 112–13, *113*, 114–16
  of family goals at home, 150–52
  goal, 96–127, 200–203
action steps, translating goals into, 101, 103–4, *104*, 108, 109, 114
action team, 67, 77
Adams County Schools, 169

adaptability, 26, 27
addictions, 5, 10, 165, 169, 182
Adequate Yearly Progress (AYP), 61
advisory periods, 184, 185, 194
affinity diagrams, 117
Africa, 35, 36
Alamo Colleges Student Leadership
    Institute (SLI), 205
Alberta Project Promoting active
    Living & healthy Eating
    (APPLE), 162
*Alexander and the Terrible, Horrible,
    No Good, Very Bad Day*, 46–47
Alice in Wonderland, 242
alignment, 97–101, *101*
    for results, 97–101, *101*
    systems, 210, 219–25, *225*, 225
Almond, Pam, 85–86
Alwin, Duane, 23–24
American Chamber of Commerce
    Executives (ACCE), 157
American Psychological Association
    (APA), 9
Amorim, Manoel, 172
analytical skills, 23
anger, 142, 144
An-Nisaa', 164
Archimedes, 210
art, 48–49, *49*, 52, 69, 74, 85, 138, 140,
    190–91, *191*, 203, *203*
Arth, Julie, 123
Arudsson, Helen, 198
Asia, 35, 173, 174, 189, 244
assemblies, 86–87, 113, 187, 198–99,
    209, 219
attachment, 37
attendance, 37, 91, 168, 170
    goals, 123–24, *124*
Australia, 35
Authentic Happiness (Seligman), 9
autism, 59–60, 80, 235–37
award ceremonies, 86

back-to-school night, 135
Baldrige principles, 34, 232, 233, *233*
Bandag, 163
Barker, Mary Jo, 122
Barth, Roland S., 54
basic needs, 29–30, 76
Bassett, Martha, 48–49, 99
Beaumont Elementary, 51, 96–113,
    117
    aligning for results, 97, 99–101
    goals at, 100–111, *111*, 112,
        118–20, 125–26, 127
    mission statement, 100, 119
    7 Habits and, 100, 111, 112–13,
        119, 120
    "Success Room," *111*
bedtime stories, 140
Begin with the End of the Mind, 19,
    43, *45*, 48, 95, 242
    conflict resolution and, 142
    effective school culture and, *68*
    personal reflection, 95
behavioral problems, 10, 73, 92, 128
"below-average" students, 105, 106
Ben-Shahar, Tal, 103
Be Proactive. *See* Proactivity
Berrian Elementary, 133
Berry, Rita, 167
Berthelot, Sarah, 169, 170
Bessie Nichols Elementary, 47
Beyond the Three Rs, 26
Blessed Sacrament, 71
Bohman, Lee G., 230
Bottomley, Dr. Laura, 178
Bowmar Avenue Elementary, 168
Brachmann, Kathy, 64, 74, 75, 94–95
Bradley, Chuck, 177, 226, 228, 229
Bradley, David, 167
Brady, Dr. Deirdre, 84, 171, 172
Brazil, 35, 172
Brentwood Elementary School, 175,
    175

Bressner, Glen, 162–63
Bridgman, Laura, 238
Brinson, Melissa, 96–97, 102, 103, 104, 107, 108, 109, 113, 126
bubble maps, 117
Buckingham School, 187, 200, 202
building bonds, *26*
Built to Last (Collins and Porras), 98
bulletin boards, 70, 219
Bullock, Emma, 183
bullying, 3, 6, 51, 55, 67, 76, 80, 81
Bunch, Ron, 166
bus behavior, 123
bus drivers, 12, 76
business leaders, 7, 18, 19, 28, 43, 44, 45, *45*, 54, 91, 118–19, 139, 155–57, 242
   A.B. Combs and, 21–23, 31, 40, 155, 159
   Chambers of Commerce and, 166–68
   education and, 7, 18, 19, 21–23, 31, 40, 155–76
   foundations, 163–64
   independent contributors, 160–63
   investment in our future and, 172–76
Busteed, Brandon, 179
Butterfield, Nigel, 74
Byers, Janine, 185

cafeteria, 198
calendaring systems, 218, 224, *225*
Canada, 35, 47, 80, 128, 129, 162, 164, 208, 235
Canadian Natural Resources Limited, 162
Cardenas, Gabriel, 213
Carver, Marty, 163
Carver, Ruth, 163
Carver Foundation, 163
caterpillar scoreboard, 121–22, *122*

CBE Group, 166
celebrations, 112–13, *113*, 114–16
Cenizal, Robyn, 140
Central High School, 183
Cerritos Elementary, 46
certified skills, 24, *25*
challenges, evolving, 6–7, *7*
Chambers of Commerce, 157, 158, 165, 166–68, 175, *175*, 176
   executives convention, 166–68
   Junior program, 175–76
change, 208–13
   creating, *26*
   why change efforts fail, *216*
   See also transformation
character, 13, 19, 44–46
   traits, 44–45, *45*
Charlotte County Public Schools, 213, 222, 226–28
Cherng, Andrew, 160–61, *161*, 162
Cherng, Peggy, 160–61, *161*, 162
Chestnut Grove Elementary, 155–57
   7 Habits and, 155–57
Chile, 35
China, 35, 172, 173, 201, 205
CHN University, 205–6
chores, 140, 147, 148
Chua Chu Kang Primary School, 51–52, 219
circle time, 87
classes, parent, 137
class meetings, 86, 87
classroom goals, 108–9, 110
classroom management, 91
cleanliness, 112
clearing the path, 108
Clementi Town Secondary School, 187
Code of Cooperation, 82
collaboration, 24, 26, *26*, 28, 100, 111, 228
   systems, 217, 220–21, *225*

Collaborative for Academic, Social, and Emotional Learning (CASEL), 37
College of Staten Island, 163
colleges and universities, 4, 6, 7, 127, 131, 201, 203–6
7 Habits and, 203–6
Collins, Jim, 98, 121, 218
Colombia, 35, 164, 187, 200
Columbine High School, 23
commitment, gaining and sustaining, 210–13, 214, *214*
common language, 72–74
communication, 5, 22, 27, 28, 44, 195
secondary school, 195–96, *196*, 197–98
skills, 22, 24, *26*, 28
systems, 217, 219–20, *225*
community, 15, 39, 60, 70, 87, 127, 155–76, 186, 221, 240
bringing schools together with, 158–60
business leaders and education, 21–23, 31, 40, 155–76
Chambers of Commerce and, 166–68, 175, *175*, 176
efforts, 165–76
engaging the district, 226–29
foundations, 163–64
globalization and, 172–74
independent contributors, 160–63
investment in our future and, 172–74
school transformation and, 210, *211*, 212, *212*, 213
secondary schools and, 198–200
Sweden and, 170–71
United Way and, 168–70
competence, 24, 44, *45*
personal, 24, 25, *25*, 26
social, 24, 25, *25*, 26, 37
complementary systems, 90, *90*

complementary teams, 90, *90*
compliments, 112
computers, 14, *26*
concentration, 24
concerts, 137, 138
conferences, student-led, 116–17, 136–37
conflict management skills, 24, *25, 26*, 44, *45*, 56
conflict resolution, key actions to, 141–44
context, 36
Contos, Tony, 180–81
contribution, *45*
control versus release, 230–31
conversations, one-on-one, 149–50
cooperation, 82
core subjects, *25*, 28
counselors, 12, 55–56, 72, 76
Covey, Jane, 147, 149, 150
Covey, Dr. John, 147, 149, 150
Covey, Sandra, 140
Covey, Sean, 140, 167, 181, 182
Covey, Stephen R., 17, 18, 39, 43, 140, 149, 157, 248–49
CPS, 172
Craig, Boyd, 162
creating change, *26*
creativity, 4–5, 6, 22, 23, 26, *26*, 27, 28, 29, 38, 44, 82, 140
Crestview Middle School, 55, 186, 194, 196–97, 200–201
Crestwood Elementary, 208–9, 218–19, 221, 222, 233
crime, 165
critical thinking, 6, *26*, 27, 28
Cruz, Yamberli, 206–7
cultural DNA, 31
cultural sensitivity, 27
culture, 6, 7, 36, *36*, 37, 39, 50, *61*, 63–94, *94*, 95, 125, *125*, 215, 241, *243*, 244

common language, 72–74
creating leadership, 63–95, 189–200
effectiveness of, *68–69*
emotional environment, 74–76
environment, 68, 69–70, *70*, 71–76,
    189–95
goals, 111–12
habitats and habits, 66–67, *67*,
    68–69
leadership events, 68, 86–89, *89*
of leadership at home, 140, 144–50
leadership paradigm, 89–90, *90*,
    91–93
management, 90–93
physical environment, 69–72
secondary schools, 182, 189–200
shared leadership, 68, 76–77, *77*,
    78–81, *81*, 82–86
Cultures Built to Last (DuFour and
    Fullan), 107
Cummins, Kim, 123
Cunningham Elementary, 57, *135*,
    136
curiosity, 28
custodians, 12, 76, 77, 112

Dads and Donuts, *135*, 136,
Daggett, Dr. Willard, 187
Dana Elementary, 225–27
dating, 182
daydreams, 102
deadlines, 90
Deal, Terrence E., 230
Decatur City Schools, 45, 156
Deming, W. Edwards, 208
depression, 10
desire to learn, *45*
*Developing Leaders One Child at a
    Time*, 98
developing others, *26*
Dewey Elementary, 168–69
Dharma Bermakna Foundation, 164

Dibble, Lori, 167
Dickens, Christie, 168
DiCosmo, Darcy, 46
direct lessons, 46, 50–53, 140–41
    at home, 140–45
discipline, 6, 10, 43, 55, 82, 85, 91–92,
    123, 168, 245
    at A.B. Combs, 1–2, 21, 33, 92–93
    lack of, 2, 91
    management approach to, 92–93
"disease model," 11
displays, wall, 70, 71, 72, 74, 190–91,
    191, 203, *203*, 219
district, engaging the, 210, 226–29
diversity, 5, 22, 24, 44, *45*
    at A.B. Combs, 2, 19, 21, *21*, 34, 70
divorce, 130
doing it again, 210
Douglas, Al, 162–63
drama, 85, 86
Drucker, Peter, 96
drugs, 5, 10, 165, 169, 182
Dubovsky, Betsy, 163
DuFour, Richard, 107, 221, 244
Dunamis Foundation, 164
Duran, Henry, 187
Dweck, Dr. Carol, 28, 232

Eaker, Robert, 221, 244
École Edwards, 80
economy, 102, 120
    global, 159, 249
Edexcel, 27
education, 10, 16
    adult attitudes on, 23–24, 26, *26–27*
    business community and, 7, 18, 19,
        21–23, 31, 40, 155–76
    evolving challenges, 6–7
    globalization, 5, 24–25
    in information age, 4
    new level of thinking, 8–11, 240–42
    new reality, 4–8, *8*

education (*cont.*)
  1990s "back-to-the-basics" decade
    of, 23
  parents and, 21–28, 31
  shift to secondary schools,
    177–202
  themes to look for, 11–14
  today's voices on, 23–28
  UNESCO's four pillars of, 24–25,
    25
  what students want in, 28–31
Education Week, 94
effective habitats, 66–69, *67–69*
effectiveness, 89, *90*, 244
efficiency, 89, *90*, 244
8th Habit, 63–65, *65*, 66, 242
  personal reflection, 249
Einstein, Albert, 8–9, 12, 48
Element, The (Robinson), 63
elementary schools, 15, 177–78
  shift to secondary, 177–80
  See also specific schools
Emotional Bank Account, 143
emotional environment, 74–76
Emotional Intelligence (EQ), 25–26
emotional needs, 29–30, 31, 37, 44,
    76, 147
  of secondary students, 193–95
emotional stability, *45*
empathy, 6, 24, *26*, 27, *45*
employable skills, 22–23
end-of-year scores, 107
Enersolv Corporation, 155–57
English as a second language, 213
English Estates Elementary, 48, 52
enrollment, 21, 34
entrepreneurialism, 27
environment, 68, 69–70, *70*, 71–76,
    189–95
  common language, 72–74
  emotional, 74–76
  home, 144–46, *146*, 147

physical, 69–72
  secondary schools, 189–95
ethics, 26, *26, 45*
Europe, 35, 172, 205, 244
evaluation systems, 217, 222, *225*
events, leadership, 68, 86–89, *89*,
    135–38, *135–39*
  at home, 144, 149–50
  in secondary schools, 189, 198–99,
    199, 200
Everett, Lavell, 202
Everett, Paul, 52
excellence, 82
  as a journey, 233–34
exercise, 29, 49, 143, 153
extrinsic rewards, 112–16, 223

family, 57, 127, 128–55
  creating leadership culture, 140,
    144–50
  engaged at school, 131, *134*,
    135–36, *135, 136*, 137, 138, *139*
  goals, 140, 150–52
  The Leader in Me and, 133, 139–40,
    154
  mealtime, 149, 153
  mission statement, 150–52
  nights, 86, 129, 135, *136*, 137, 149
  one-on-one conversations, 149–50
  school transformation and, 210,
    211, 212, *212*, 213
  7 Habits for, 128–38, 140–45
  See also home
Family Time, 57
Farnsworth, Chuck, 181
father, *5*, 128–29, *134*, *136*, 150
  absent, 5
  single, 129
  See also parents
FCE, 174
feedback, 107–8, 115, 143, 222
Feigley, Charlotte, 157

field trips, 86, 138, 221
Find Your Voice, and Inspire Others
    to Find Theirs, 63–66, 242
    personal reflection, 249
First Things First, 19, 43, *45*, 127, 129,
    184, 242, *244*
    conflict resolution and, 142
    effective school culture and, *68*
    for family, 129
    personal reflection, 127
fishbone diagrams, 117
fitness goals, 123
5 Choices, 228
Five Minds for the Future (Gardner), 7
Fleming, Mick, 157
focus, 43
food, 29, 52, 143, 198, 223
    mealtime, 149, 153
force-field analysis, 117, *118*
Ford Motor Company, 164
forgiveness, 143
"formative" measures, 107
foundations, 163–64
Four Disciplines of Execution, 228
Fox, Terry, 47
FranklinCovey Co., 144, 150, 157, 181,
    205, 228, 229
friendship, 29, 182
Fritz, Mike, 222, 235, 236
front offices, 55–56, *56*, 76–77
Fullan, Michael, 107, 155
fun, *45*, 52, 109, 153
future, 48, *49*

Gamble, Tracey, 198
games, 52, *53*, 87, 105
gangs, 24, 54
Gantt charts, 117
GAPs, 125–26
Gardner, Frances, 59
Gardner, Howard, 7, 28
GarudaFood Group, 164

Gayler, Dr. Dave, 226
George, David, 208, 209, 233–34
giftedness, 12
Giles Junior School, 84
Global Achievement Gap, The
    (Wagner), 27
global awareness, 26, *27*
globalization, 5, 24–25, 27, 35–38, 71,
    159, 172–74, 249
    community and, 172–74
goals, 24, 28, 39, 43, *45*, 48, 49, 82, 87,
    90, *90*, 96–127, 186, 214, *225*
    accountability and, 101, 107–8,
        109, 110, 112, 115, 122
    achieving, 96–127, 200–203
    action steps and, 101, 103–4, *104*,
        108, 109, 114
    aligning for results, 97–101, *101*
    attendance, 123–24, *124*
    at Beaumont Elementary, 100–111,
        111, 112, 118–20, 125–26, 127
    celebrations, 112–13, *113*, 114–16
    classroom, 108–9, 110
    culture, 111–12
    family, 140, 150–52
    health and fitness, 123
    Leadership Notebooks and, 116,
        117, *117*, 119, 121, 123, 124
    paradigms and, 125–26
    quality tools and, 117–18, *118*
    research on, 114–15
    results and, 118–20
    rewards and, 112–16
    schoolwide, 110–11, *111*, 112
    scoreboards, 101, 105–6, *106*, 107,
        108, 109, *110*, 112, 114, 121–22,
        122
    secondary schools, 182, 200–203
    speech, 124
    at Stanton Elementary, 120–23, 125
    student-led conferences and,
        116–17

goals (*cont.*)
    tools, 116–18
    Wildly Important, 101–3, *104*,
        108–12, 114, 121, 200, 244
Goethe, Johann Wolfgang von, 72
Goleman, Daniel, 25, 37
Gonzalez, Gayle, 91–92
Good to Great (Collins), 121
Gottardy, Dr. Brian, 228
government, 91
GPA, 11
graduation rates, 37
Grain Valley South Middle School,
    184–85, 189, 190, 195, 200
grandparents, 158
    day, 136, 137
Gray, Dayle, 56
Great Leaders, 228
greatness, 13, *13*, 15, 69, *146*
Gregory, Joyce, 55
ground rules, 50
Gruzeski, Shannon, 123
guns, 5, 23
Gutmann, Joe, 182–83, 184

habitats, 66–67, *67*, 68–69
Hall, Mary Ann, 198
hallway huddles, 221
Hamilton, Brian, 206
Harris, Ericka, 200
Harrison, Dean, 128
Harvard University, Graduate School
    of Education, 130
Hattie, John, 114
health, 28, 29, *45*, 176
    goals, 123
Heinigen, Pat, 169
Heritage Elementary, 83–84, 171–72
high schools, 127, 131, 159,
    177–203
    goals, 182, 200–203
    leadership culture, 182, 189–200

7 Habits and, 133, 140, 153,
    177–203, 206–7
    shift to, 177–203
    student leadership, 188–89,
        195–96, *196*, 197–99, *199*, 200
    teaching the 7 Habits, 182–89
    See also secondary schools; *specific
        high schools*
High-Trust Classroom, The (Moore),
    75
hiring and selection systems, 217, 218,
    225
history, 43, 47, 48, 186
hobbies, 141
home, 39, 54, 127, 128–55
    creating leadership culture at, 140,
        144–50
    direct lessons at, 140–41
    engaging parents at school, 131,
        134, 135–36, *135, 136*, 137, 138,
        139
    environment, 144–46, *146*, 147
    goals, 140, 150–52
    integrated approaches at, 140–41
    The Leader in Me at, 131, 133,
        139–40, 154
    leadership events at, 144, 149–50
    letters, 133
    mealtime, 149, 153
    mission statement, 150–52
    modeling at, 141–44
    school relationship and, 130–32,
        132, 133, 134–39, *135–39*
    shared leadership at, 144, 147–49
    7 Habits for, 128–38, 140–44
    See also family
homework, 51, 91, 198
Honda Foundation, 164
honesty, 22, *45*
hope, 3–4, 10, 11, 31
Horizon Primary School, 51–52, 138,
    219

How Children Succeed (Tough), 7
Huffman, Dr. Jason, 170
humility, 143
hygiene, 29, 112

I Am A Leader Foundation, 162, 170
imagination, 13–14, 28
improving practices, 90, *90*
independence, 43–44, 45, *45*, 60, 193, 218
independent contributors, 160–63
India, 35
Indonesia, 35, 47, 164, *199*
influence, 27
information age, 4
information management, 28
initiative, 22, 24, *26*, 27, *45*
innovation, 24, 27, 52, 90, *90*
inside-out approach, 53–55, 230
inspirational leadership, *26*, 38, 90, *90*
integrated approaches, at home, 140–41
integrated instruction, 46–50, 243
integrity, 22, *45*
Intel award, 226
intelligence, 24, 25, 29
interdependence, 24, 44, 45, *45*, 60, 218, 243
interior design, 74
International Baccalaureate (IB) schools, 243
Internet, 32, 50, 133, 159
intrinsic rewards, 112, 115, 223
IQ, 25
Isadore, Jacquie, 48, 225

James, William, 76
Jämjö church school, 170
Jändel school, 170
Janson Elementary, 79, 213
Japan, 174

job fairs, 138
John C. Fremont Elementary, 57
John Deere Foundation, 163–64
Johns Hopkins University report on TLIM schools, 227
Johnson, Brady, 167
Johnson, Eric, 91–92
Joliet Central High School, 180–81
Jones, Marvin, 167
Joseph Welsh Elementary, 235–37
Junction Elementary, 137
Justis, Bob, 166
juvenile rehabilitation, 165

Kai, Arlene, 41–62
Keller, Helen, 235, 237–38, 239, 240, 241, 245
Kelley, Ed, 48
Kelley, Nancy, 167, 168
Kemp, Vicki, 196
Kerr, Rose, 217
key actions to conflict resolution, 141–44
Kilroy, Christi, 168
kindness, 29, 84, 85
Knight, Dr. Jane, 157
knowledge, 22, 24, 57
   skills, 24, *25*
knowledge worker, 4–6
Koehler, Joann, 16–17
Koning, Suzan, 172
Korea, 35, *181*

Lady, Robin, 186
lagging indicators, 107
Lane, Donnie, 155–56, *156*, 157, 160
language, 145, 186–87, 208
   common, 72–74
   home environment, 145–47
   secondary school, 191–93
LEAD, 82
Leader-Go-Rounds, 57

Leader in Me, The (Covey), 1, 35, 37,
    39, 46, 50, 54, 59, 60, 67, 72, 74,
    78, 87, 95, 99, 102, 107, 112,
    120, 126–27, 153, 162, 208,
    230
  business community and, 155–76
  ending with the beginning in mind,
    235–49
  at home, 131, 133, 139–40, 154
  Johns Hopkins University report
    on, 227
  not one more thing, 242–45
  shift to secondary schools,
    177–203
  strategies, 208–34
  Student Journals, 50, 51
  website, 50, 133, 221
Leaders and Laggards, 158–59
leadership and leadership principles, 2,
    14, 24, 26, *26, 30*, 36, *36*, 38–39,
    61, 94, 125, 215, 241, *243*
  at A.B. Combs, 1–3, 12–23, 31–32,
    32, 33–34, 45, 48–49, 55, 69–70,
    82–83, 88–89, 97–98, *98*, 155,
    157, 160–61, 172, 177–78, 208,
    214, *214*, 215, 219–20, *220*, 223,
    232, 246–47
  achieving school goals and,
    96–127
  alignment and, 97–101, *101*
  business community and, 155–76
  colleges and universities, 203–6
  creating culture, 63–95, 189–200
  culture at home, 140, 144–50
  ending with the beginning in mind,
    235–49
  homes and families, 128–55
  of others, 38–39
  paradigm, 89–90, *90*, 91–93
  rewards, *113*
  secondary schools, 177–203
  of self, 38

  shared with students, 68, 76–77, *77*,
    78–81, *81*, 82–86, 140, 147–49,
    177, 189, 195–96, *196*, 197–98,
    212–13, 230, 235–37
  strategy and, 208–34
  teaching the 7 Habits, 41–62
  transformation and, 208–34
  ubiquitous strategy, 46–55, 243
  whole school, 11–12
  *See also specific principles and
    schools*
Leadership Camp, 50
Leadership Day, 63–66, 88–89, *89*,
    92, 118, 137, *139*, 170–71, *173,
    199, 220*
leadership events, 68, 86–89, *89*,
    135–38, *135–39*
Leadership Notebooks, 116, 117, *117*,
    119, 121, 123, 124, *139, 175*,
    202
Leadership Portfolios, 202
Leadiators, 81
leading indicators, 107
LEAD time, 51
Learning: The Treasure Within
    (UNESCO report), 24–25, *25*
learning specialists, 77
learning systems, 217, 218–19, *225*
Learning to Be, 25, *25*
Learning to Do, 24, *25*
Learning to Know, 24, *25*
Learning to Live Together, 24, *25*
Lee Ridge Elementary, 74
Leslie, Bruce H., 205
letters home, 133
librarians, 11, 56, 76, 138, 197
life skills, 6–7, 19, 24, *25*, 36, *36*, 37,
    44, 51, 182
Lighthouse Award, 164, 173, 199, 213,
    214
Lighthouse Team, 210, 211, *211*, 212,
    212, 219, 225

Lih-Jen International, 173
listening, 44, *45*, 51, 75, 85, 143
  in secondary schools, 191–92, *192*,
    193, 198
literature, 47, 52, 184, 186
  "success," 43
Little Red Hen, The, 47
live life in crescendo, 247–49
loneliness, 81
Longwood University, 206
lotus diagrams, 117
loyalty, 82

Maggiolo, Shawn, 246–47
MAGIC, 82–83
Maine-Endwell High School, 189
Malaysia, 35, 174, *188*
management, 90, *90*, 91
  culture, 90–93
  paradigm, 89–90, *90*
manners, 23, 27, *45*
Mapp, Karen L., 130
Markin, Allan, 162
Martin Petitjean Elementary, 123–24,
    124, 169–70
Marzano, Robert J., 105, 134, 244
mathematics, 12, 23, 26, *26*, 28, 34, 48,
    85, 169, 197–98, 204, 245
  goals, 111
Matthews, Tonya, 166
MBA, 204
McCabe, Cheryl, 124
McCartan, Jan, 51, 99, 113, 119
McCarty, Dr. Paul, 57
McDorman, Eva, 50
McGee, Rochelle, 118–20
McGuey, Gary, 80
McLees Academy of Leadership, 81
mealtime, 149, 153
meaning, *45*, 76
media, 31, 56
media literacy, *27*

memorization, 24
mental health, 10
mental needs, 29, 30, 31, 44, *45*, 76,
    147, 151
mental skills, *45*
*Mentor: Leadership Trumps Bullying,
    The* (McGuey), 80
mentors, peer, 80–81, *81*, 122, 188,
    188, 189
Mexico, 35
Meyer, Dr. George, 168
Michener, James A., 47
middle schools, 127, 177–203
  goals, 182, 200–203
  leadership culture, 182, 189–200
  7 Habits and, 133, 140, 153,
    177–203, 206–7
  shift to, 177–203
  student leadership, 188–89,
    195–96, *196*, 197–199, *199*, 200
  teaching the 7 Habits, 182–89
  See also secondary schools; *specific
    middle schools*
Middleton, Dr. Richard, 228
military, 29
Miller, Matt, 120, 121, 125
Miller, Stephanie, 197
mission and mission statements, 50,
    87, 100, 101, *101*, 102, 119, 137,
    150, 188, 200, 201, *225*
  at A.B. Combs, *33*, 69, 71, 98
  at Beaumont Elementary, 100, 119
  family, 150–52
  secondary school, 201–3
modeling, 46, 53–55, 56, 82, 88, 222
  at home, 141–44
  secondary schools, 182–84
modern-day miracle workers, 237–39,
    240, 245
Moms and Muffins, 136
Moore, Lonnie, 75
Moore, Dr. Nancy, 33, 34

morning announcements, 195, *196*,
208, 219
Moss Middle School, 187, *191*,
194–95, 197–98, 200
mother, 5, 108, 136, 150
single, 5, 145
See also parents
Mountainville Academy, 183
Mukilteo Elementary, 75, *139*
multitasking, 27
Mundt, Bob, 167
music, 48, 52, 85, 138, 140, *181, 199*,
221
My Key to Life (Keller), 235

National Association of Secondary
School Principals, 193
National School Change Award, 226
Nation at Risk, A, 159
Netherlands, 35, 172–73, 205–6
networks, 27
New Hope High School, 202–3, *203*
newsletters, 133
New York City public schools, 217
Niagara County Community College,
206
no, saying, 143, 152–53
Nolan, Julie, 59
Nole, David, 187
nonclassroom teachers, 55–56
North East Independent School
District (NEISD), 228–29
not one more thing, 242–45
Nuckolls, Heather, 99
nurses, 12, 76, 204

obedience, 23
office staff, 12, 55–56, *56*, 76–77
one child at a time, 245, *245*, 246–47
one-on-one conversations, 149–50,
193–95
openness, *45*

operating system, 14
opinions, student, 82–84, 147–49
optimism, 9–11, *26*, 31
optimization, 90, *90*
oral communications, *26*, 27
orderliness, 78, 79
Organisation for Economic Cooperation and Development
(OECD), 220
organizational/team leadership, 39
organizational skills, 3, *26*, 43, *45*
organizational structures, 218, 224–25,
225
Osterstrom, Justin, 92
others, leadership of, 38–39
Ott, Debbie, 190
Out of the Crisis (Deming), 208
ownership, 193–95, *196*

pace, 213–16, *216*
Panda Charitable Foundation, 161–62
Panda Express, 160, 161
Paradigm Education, 173
paradigms, 40, 125–26, 132, 229–33
goals and, 125–26
leadership, 89–90, *90*, 91–93
management, 89–90, *90*
shift, 46, 230, 231
strategy, 210, 229–32, 233, *233*
Paramount Corporation, 174
Parent Lighthouse Team, 138
parents, 1–3, 5, 7, 15, 18, 21–28, 35,
44, 45, *45*, 59, 60, 77, 93, 108,
123, 157, 172, 182, 209, 241,
243
at A.B. Combs, 19, 21–24, 31, 40
classes, 137
creating leadership culture at home,
140, 144–50
engaged at school, 131, *134*,
135–36, *135, 136*, 137, 138,
139

nights, 86, 129, 135, *136*, 137
school relationship and, 130–32, *132*, *133*, 134–39, *135–39*
school transformation and, 210, *211*, 212, *212*, 213
7 Habits at home and, 128–38, 140–45
7 Habits taught by, 56
single, 5, 129, 144
teacher conferences, 117, 219
volunteers, 138
See also family; father; home; mother
Parent Teacher Association (PTA), 119, 171, 229
Partnership for 21st Century Skills, 26
Patel, Dr. Rig, 1–3
Patel, Dr. Sejjal, 1–3, 194, 200
path, 213–16, *216*
Patriot High School, 185, 191, 194
Payne, Jeanne, 45
peace of mind, 29
peers, 31, 37
mentors, 80–81, *81*, 122, 188, *188*, 189
sharing leadership with, 78–82
Penaluna, Tom, 166
people skills, 6, 22
pep rallies, 199, 200
Perkins Institute for the Blind, 238
permanency, 209–10
person, whole, 12–13, 25, *25*
personal best, 114
personal competence, 24, 25, *25*, 26
personal leadership, 43
personal reflections, 40, 62, 95, 127, 154, 176, 207, 234, 249
photos, family, 145
physical education, 48, 49, 70–71, 123
physical environment, 69–72
physical needs, 29, 31, 44, 45, 76, 147, 151

Pink, Daniel, 4, 5–6, 28
planning skills, 23, 39, 43, 44, *45*, 152
plus-delta charts, 117
Porras, Jerry I., 98
Port Charlotte High School, 177
positive affirmations, 146
positive psychology, 9–11
positive thinking, 9–11, 27, 72–73, 74, 87
Pout-Pout Fish, The, 57, *58*
poverty, 169, 225
Powell, Debbie, 48
Power of 10, 194
prejudice, 24
Pretty Important Goals (PIGs), 102, 111, 225
principals, 1, 17, 55, 61, 77, 83, 84, 91, 94, 155, 171, 217, 222, 228
school transformation and, 210, *211*, *211*, 212, *212*
Private Victory, 43, 44
Proactivity, 19, 43, *45*, 47, 52, 57, 58, 62, 67, 84, 130, 134, 135, 146, 242
conflict resolution and, 142
effective school culture and, *68*
personal reflection, 62
problem solving, 6, 8, 22, 24, 26, *26*, 27, 44, *45*, 79, 88, 118, 222
Professional Learning Communities at Work (DuFour and Eaker), 221
Professional Learning Community, 77, 120, 243
PSKD Mandiri, 47, 164, *199*
psychology, 9–10, 144, 184, 241
Public Victory, 44
purpose, 213–16, *216*
Put First Things First. *See* First Things First

quality tools, 117–18, *118*
Quan, Dato' Teo Chiang, 174

Quincy Public School District, 168–69
Quincy University, 168

Rainbow Station, 174
Rasyid, Ny. Rosfia, 164
reading, 12, 23, 26, *26*, 28, 34, 102,
    141, 169, 187–88, 201, 204
    goals, 102–12, 121–22, *122*
reality, 4, 15
    new, 4–8, *8*
real-life projects, 138
Reframing Organizations (Bohman and
    Deal), 230
Reilly, Leslie, 1
relationships, 29–30, 37, *90*, 91
release versus control, 230–31
research, 24, 37, 77, 114–15, 179, 180
respect, 23, 29, *45*, 75, 82, 84, 94
responsibility, 22, 23–24, 25, 26, *26*,
    27, 35, 43, *45*, 82, 92–93, 147,
    222, 225
    sharing leadership with students,
    76–81, *81*, 82, 195–96, *196*, 197
rewards, 112–13, *113*, 114–16, 231
    extrinsic, 112–16, 223
    intrinsic, 112, 115, 223
    systems, 217, 222–23, *224, 225*
Richards, Denise, 204
risk, 24, 37
Robinson, Sir Ken, 28, 63
Rokhas, Elena, 202
role models, 182–84
Rollings Middle School, 186
Rotary Club, 171, 175
Ruhkala Elementary, 45, 55

safety, 22, 23, 29, 76, 80
sameness, 12
Sanford, Pat, 228, 229
Satit Bangna, 35
Saw, Sharpening of, 20, 44, *45*, 141,
    175, 244

conflict resolution and, 143–44
effective school culture and, *69*
personal reflection, 234
Scalfaro, Jeff, 191–92, 195
schedules, 89, *90*
Scheulen, Dr. Jill, 196
Schofield, Kelly, 225, 226
schoolwide goals, 110–11, *111*, 112
science, *27*, 41, 42, 85
Scioto Ridge Elementary School
    (SRES), 59
scoreboards, keeping, 101, 105–6, *106*,
    107, 108, 109, *110*, 112, 114,
    121–22, *122*, 200
secondary schools, 15, 127, 177–203,
    245
    culture, 182, 189–200
    downward trend in student
    engagement, 179, *180*
    environment, 189–95
    goals, 182, 200–203
    leadership events, 189, 198–99,
    199, 200
    role models, 182–84
    7 Habits and, 133, 140, 153,
    177–203, 206–7
    shift to, 177–203
    structure of, 178–80
    student leadership, 188–89,
    195–96, *196*, 197–199, *199*,
    200
    teaching the 7 Habits, 182–89
    See also high schools; middle
    schools
Seek First to Understand, Then to Be
    Understood. *See* Understanding
self-assessment, *26*
self-awareness, 22, 23, *26*, 153, 232
self-confidence, *26*, 33, 58, 74, 76, 94,
    114, 144, 147, 161, 171 182, 193
self-control, *26*
self-direction, 26, *26*

self-evaluation, 114
self-leadership, 38
self-motivation, 22
Seligman, Dr. Martin, 9–11, 28, 94,
    132, 153, 240–41
Seminole County Public Schools, 1
service, 26
7 Habits Heroes, 209
7 Habits of Happy Kids, The (Covey),
    50, 133, 140–41
7 Habits of Highly Effective Families,
    The (Covey), 133, 140
7 Habits of Highly Effective People,
    The (Covey), 2, 16–18, 31–33,
    35, 43, *61*, 87, 88, 89, *94*, 100,
    102, 126, 128, 129–30, 133, 168,
    204, 228, 230, *232, 233*, 241
  at A.B. Combs, 2, 16, 17–18, 31–34,
    45, 48–49, 52, 55, 70, 71, 83,
    155, 157, 160–61, 178, 208,
    232
  at Beaumont Elementary, 100, 111,
    112–13, 119, 120
  business community and, 155–76
  case for, 42–46
  at Chestnut Grove, 155–57
  colleges and, 203–6
  common language, 72–74
  culture and, 63–95
  direct lessons and, 46, 50–53
  ending with the beginning in mind,
    235–49
  go easy, 152–53
  at home, 128–38, 140–45
  integrated instruction and, 46–50
  key actions to conflict resolution,
    141–44
  modeling and, 46, 53–55
  overuse of, 52–53
  shift to secondary schools, 177–207
  strategy and, 208–34
  teaching, 41–62, 218–19
  training, 218–19
  ubiquitous method of teaching,
    46–55
  universal nature of, 43–44, *44*
  workshop, 137
  for young people, 19–20
  See also specific habits
7 Habits of Highly Effective Teens, The
    (Covey), 133, 140, 153, 181,
    184, 187–88, 201
Seymour, John, 157
shared leadership, 68, 76–77, *77*,
    78–86, 147
  at home, 144, 147–49
Sharpening the Saw. *See* Saw,
    Sharpening of
Shaw, George Bernard, 248
siblings, 133, 138
simplicity, 153
Singapore, 35, 51, 138, 187, 201, 219
6 Most Important Decisions You'll Ever
    Make (Covey), 140, 181
skills, 22–28, 37, 39, 43–44, *45*
sleep, 143
Smith, Rachel, 83
Snow White and the Seven Dwarfs, 52
SOAR, 184–85
social competence, 24, 25, *25*, 26, 37
social-emotional learning (SEL),
    25–26, 37
social-emotional needs, 29–30, 31, 37,
    44, 76, 147, 151
social responsibility, 22, 23–24, 26,
    26, 37
social skills, 24, *25*, 37, 45
social workers, 72
sociology, 184, 186
South Africa, 205
South America, 35, 172
South Dade Middle School, 189,
    206–7
South Whidbey Elementary, 56

speaking skills, *45*, 63–66, 85, 87, 95, 178, 186, 195, 220, *220*
special needs, 12, *59*, 63, 72, 80, 114, 124, 128, 235–37
speech goals, 124
Speed of Trust, The, 228
spelling, 115–16
spiritual needs, 29, 30, *30*, 31, 44, 76, 147, 151
sports, 49, *52*, 71, 86, 105, 115, 141, 199
staff, 12, *55*–56, 76–77, 244
    evaluations, 222
    nonclassroom teachers, 55–56
    school transformation and, 210, 211, *211*, 212, *212*, 213
    sharing leadership with, 76–78
    whole school, 11–12
Stanton Elementary, 58, 120–23, 125
    goals at, 120–23, 125
Staten Island Foundation, 163
Staten Island School of Civic Leadership, 217
Stehlin, Trish, 58
storytelling, 210, 225–27
strategy, 108, 150, 208–34
    alignment, 210, 217–25, *225*
    commitment, 210–13, 214, *214*
    doing it again, 210
    engaging the district, 210, 226–29
    paradigms, 210, 229–32, 233, *233*
    purpose, path, and pace, 210, 213–16, *216*
    storytelling, 210, 225–27
    ubiquitous, 46–55, 243
stress, 143
stretch zone, 103
strong work ethic, 22
student-led conferences, 116–17, 136–37
students, 28–31, 37, 39, 57–60, 77, 93

downward trend in engagement levels, 179, *180*
dropping off at school, *134*
finding their voice, 85–86, *86*
goal setting and, 96–127
home and school relationship, 130–32, *132, 133*, 134–39, *135–39*
Junior Chamber program, 175–76
as mentors, 80–81, *81*, 122
new, 92, 133
opinions, 82–84, 147–49
rewarding, 222–23, *224*
school transformation and, 210, 211, 212, *212*, 213
secondary school, 177–203
seeking and valuing opinions of, 82–84
7 Habits at home and, 128–38, 140–45
sharing leadership with, 68, 76–77, *77*, 78–81, *81*, 82–86, 140, 147–49, 177, 189, 195–96, *196*, 197–98, 212–13, 230, 235–37
as teachers, 57–59, 76–86, 116–17, 133–34, 136–37, 177, 182, 188–89
success, celebrating, 112–13, *113*, 114–16
Sullivan, Anne, 237–40, 241, 245, 248
"summative" measures, 107
Summers, Muriel, 12, 16–23, 28–29, 31–33, 73, 82–83, 97–98, 157, 159, 178, 208, 223, 233, 246
Summerville Elementary, 167, 225
Sun, Christina, 173
Sun, Ivy, 173
Surdey, Mary, 202
Sweden, *35*, 83, 165, 170–71, 198
Swift, George, 167
Synergy, 20, 42, 44, *45*, 46, 51, 57, 75, *185, 232*, 242

at A.B. Combs, 45, 71
conflict resolution and, 143
effective school culture and, *69*
personal reflection, 207
systems, 217–25
  aligning, 217–25, *225*
  calendaring, 218, 224, *225*
  collaboration, 217, 220–21, *225*
  communication, 217, 219–20, *225*
  evaluation, 217, 222, *225*
  hiring and selecting, 217, 218, *225*
  learning, 217, 218–19, *22*
  organizational, 218, 224–25, *225*
  reward, 217, 222–23, *224, 225*

Tahija, Laurel, 164
Taiwan, 35, *117*, 173, *173*
talent, 148–49, 199, 200
talent/thought leadership, 38
tardiness, 168
teachers, 3, 12, 16, 30, 35, 37, 39, 44, 45, *45*, 76, 77, 83, 85, 90–91, 197, 209, 244
  at A.B. Combs, 21–23, 31, 33–34, 40
  accountability and, 107–8
  collaboration systems, 220–21
  contract negotiations, 99
  evaluations, 222
  hiring, 218
  home and, 131, 140
  modern-day miracle workers, 237–40
  new, 58, 83
  nonclassroom, 55–56
  performance, 11
  school transformation and, 210, 211, *211*, 212, *212*, 213
  secondary schools, 182–89
  setting goals and, 100–127
  7 Habits and, 41–62, 218–19

students as, 57–59, 76–86, 116–17, 133–34, 136–37, 177, 182, 188–89
turnover, 172
ubiquitous strategy, 46–55
Teaching Practices from America's Best Urban Schools, 53
teaching principles, 90, *90*
Teach to Learn, 58
Teague, Lauretta, 155–56
teamwork, 6, 22, 24, *26*, 27, 35, 39, 44, *45*, 87, 109, 111, 125
  complementary, 90, *90*
  rewards, *113*
  skills, 22
technology, 5, 23, 48, 76, 79, 85
  skills, 22, *26*
  student leaders, 79
teenagers, 133, 140, 145, 153
  pregnancies, 170
  7 Habits and, 133, 140, 153, 177–207
television, 152, 219–20
Terpel Foundation, 164, *164*
test scores, 1, 3, 13, 29, 96, 100, 169, 231
  at A.B. Combs, 21, 33, 34
  goal setting and, 100–112, 120, 121
Thailand, 35, 205
TheLeaderinMeOnline, 50, 221
thinking, new level of, 8–11, 240–42
Think Win-Win. *See* Win-Win
Thomsen, Heather, 194–95
Thoreau, Henry David, 16, 85
Thorson, Melody, 45–46
timelines, 246
Time magazine, 48, *49*
time management skills, 22, 24, 43, *45*
Titan Hill Intermediate School, 167
tolerance, 22, 24

tools:
  for goal-setting purposes, 116–18
  quality, 117–18, *118*
Tornham school, 170
Tough, Paul, 7, 28
transformation, 208–34
  alignment systems, 210, 217–25,
    225
  commitment and, 210–11, *211*, 212,
    212, 213, 214
  engaging the district, 210, 226–29
  paradigms, 210, 229–32, 233, *233*
  purpose, path, and pace, 210,
    213–16, *216*
  why change efforts fail, *216*
transparency, *26*
trust, 75, 76, 87, 100
twenty-first-century citizens, creating,
    232, 233, *233*
Twitter, 199

ubiquitous strategy, 46–55, 243
Understanding, 20, 44, *45*, 192, 242
  conflict resolution and, 143
  effective school culture and, *68*
  personal reflection, 176
uniqueness, 12, 13, 29
United Kingdom, 27, 84, *185*
United Nations Educational, Scientific
    and Cultural Organization
    (UNESCO), 24–25
United Way, 165, 168–70
unity, 57
universal nature, 43
  of 7 Habits, 43–44, *44*
urban schools, 53, 61
Utah Valley University, 204–5

vacations, 140, 141, 147–48
Valentine's Day, 196
Veenstra, Dr. Robert, 205–6
Venn diagrams, 117

Vestal High School, 190–91, 198–99,
    201–2
Vicksburg Warren County School
    District, 168
video games, 5, 105, 152
Vincent, Carrie, 137
violence, 3, 5, 23, 73, 201
Visible Learning (Hattie), 114
vision and vision statements, *45*, 76,
    87, 99, 102, 201
  at A.B. Combs, 33, 69, 98
vocational schools, 24
voice, finding, 85–86, *86*, 95
volunteers, parent, 138

Wagner, Tony, 27
Waitley, Denis, 140
Wallace Foundation, 77
wall displays, 70, 71, 72, 74, 190–91,
    191, 203, *203*, 219
WAO theme, 199
Washington, Booker T., 93
Waterman, Cheryl, 169
Wayne Avenue Elementary, 77
Weber, Rick, 52
WEB Leaders, 194
website, 50, 133, 219, 221
Welcome Packet, 133, 138
Wentworth, Shelley, 55
Wenzell, Brian, 51
West Seneca East High School, 184
What Works in Schools (Marzano),
    105, 134
Whittaker, Dr. Doug, 228
wholeness, 11–14, 25, *25*, 29, 44, 228,
    231
  basic needs and, 29–30
  continuous improvement, 44, 45,
    45
  imagination, 13–14
  person, 12–13, 231
  school, 11–12

Whole New Mind, A (Pink), 5
Wilderness Oak Elementary, 135
Wildly Important Goals (WIGs),
    101–3, *104*, 108–12, 114, 121,
    200, 225, 244
  classroom, 108–9, 110
  research on, 114
  schoolwide, 110–11, *111*, 112
William A. Butler Elementary, 138
William Yates Elementary, 221
Winchester Elementary, 63–66, 74–75,
    85, *86*

Win-Win, 20, 44, *45*, 47, 48, 84, 154,
    242
  conflict resolution and, 142–43
  effective school culture and, *68*
  personal reflection, 154
Wong, Henry, 50
word accuracy, 104
work ethic, 22
writing, 12, 23, 26, *26*, 27, 34, 42, 47,
    52, 85, 102, 204
  goals, 111, 120